MIMBRES DURING
THE TWELFTH CENTURY

MIMBRES DURING

ABANDONMENT, CONTINUITY, AND REORGANIZATION

THE TWELFTH CENTURY

Margaret C. Nelson

The University of Arizona Press   Tucson

The University of Arizona Press
©1999 The Arizona Board of Regents
First printing
Manufactured in the United States of America
04 03 02 01 00 99   6 5 4 3 2 1

Library of Congress Cataloging-in-Publication Data

Nelson, Margaret Cecile, 1951–
Mimbres during the twelfth century: abandonment, continuity, and reorganization / Margaret C. Nelson.
p. cm.
Includes bibliographical references and index.
ISBN 0–8165–1868–8 (cloth: alk. paper)
    1. Mimbres culture.   2. Indians of North America–New Mexico–Migra-
tions.   3. Indians of North America–Land tenure–New Mexico.   4. Land
settlement patterns–New Mexico.   5. Archaeological surveying–New
Mexico.   6. New Mexico–Antiquities.   I. Title.
E99.M76 N45 1999   98–40197
978.9–dc21   CIP

British Library Cataloguing-in-Publication Data
A catalogue record for this book is available from the British Library.

Publication of this book is made possible in part by the proceeds of a
permanent endowment created with the assistance of a Challenge Grant from
the National Endowment for the Humanities, a federal agency.

Title page illustration: From a Classic Mimbres bowl found in Room 2 on
Ronnie Pueblo, Palomas Creek drainage, Eastern Mimbres area. (Drawing by
Dulce Aldama)

CONTENTS

FIGURES

TABLES

ACKNOWLEDGMENTS

Research for this book has been a collaboration among many colleagues. Michelle Hegmon (Arizona State University) and I have been collaborating since 1993. The excavation data from Phelps Pueblo, Lizard Terrace Pueblo, Mountain Lion Hamlet, and Las Animas Village are the result of our work together. She has spent countless hours discussing and reading through this text with me. Stephen Lekson (University of Colorado at Boulder) and I conducted most of the survey along Palomas Creek drainage, although I also collaborated with Ben Nelson (Arizona State University) on a portion of the Lower Palomas survey and with Robert Kelly (University of Louisville) and Barbara Mills (University of Arizona) on portions of the mountain survey. Keith Kintigh and George Cowgill commented on the dating analysis, and Jeffrey Dean discussed with me the sampling design for the dating program. Michael Diehl (Desert Archaeology, Tucson) and I have collaborated and consulted with Paul Minnis on the ethnobotanical analysis.

Excavation of the Palomas sites has been funded by Arizona State University and University of New Mexico field schools, the State University of New York at Buffalo through its archaeological field school and a faculty research development grant, United University Professions' Research Development grant (Grant No. 067103-07), the U.S. Department of Education (FIPSE Grant Number G00873059889), the Biomedical Research Support Grant Program, Division of Research Resources, National Institutes of Health (BRSG Grant Number S07 RR 07066), the National Geographic Society (Grant No. 4551-91, 5213-94), and the Turner Foundation. The National Geographic Society and the Turner

Foundation also funded most of the analysis of datable samples and much of the ethnobotanical and faunal analyses. The Mimbres Foundation, through Steven LeBlanc, has supported excavation through contribution of equipment.

The survey of Palomas drainage has been supported by the University of New Mexico, State University of New York at Buffalo, the New Mexico State Historic Preservation Office, the New Mexico Bureau of Reclamation, and the Phelps Anderson family. The Rio Grande survey was funded by the New Mexico Bureau of Reclamation and New Mexico State Historic Preservation Office; data were provided by Stephen Lekson. Facilities for both surveys were provided by Caballo Lake State Park; the USDA Forest Service provided facilities for the mountain portion of the survey. Survey data, unpublished reports, and publications with limited distribution were provided by Rosemary Talley and Steve Townsend at the Laboratory of Anthropology, Museum of New Mexico, Neil Ackerly at New Mexico State University, Karl Laumbach at Human Systems Research, Jeanne Schutt at the Office of Contract Archaeology of the University of New Mexico, Stephen Lekson of the University of Colorado at Boulder, Katherine Trinkaus (then) of the Maxwell Museum at the University of New Mexico, Darrell Creel of the Texas Archaeological Research Laboratory at the University of Texas at Austin, and LaVerne Herrington.

None of the fieldwork would have been possible without the cooperation of landowners in Truth or Consequences, New Mexico, and surrounding towns and villages, and the hard work of many graduate and undergraduate students. I am especially grateful for the hospitality of the owners, managers, and employees of the Ladder Ranch, the many owners of Las Palomas Land and Cattle Company, the owners of Big A-Burger, and employees of the United States Forest Service, Gila National Forest. The people of this area have a strong commitment to archaeological research and to preservation of cultural resources. Students from Arizona State University, State University of New York at Buffalo, University of New Mexico, and New Mexico State University have contributed to fieldwork and analyses through field schools as well as graduate and undergraduate programs. My children, Anna and David, have participated in all aspects of this research with patience and sometimes interest.

The American Association of University Women through their post-doctoral fellowship program provided support for writing. Comments on portions of this manuscript have been provided by Roger Anyon, George Cowgill, Darrell Creel, Patricia Gilman, Michelle Hegmon, LaVerne Herrington, Stephen Lekson, Paul Minnis, Ben Nelson, Harry Shafer, and many graduate students at Arizona State University, New Mexico State University, and State University of New York at Buffalo. Wes Bernardini, Linda Countryman, Victoria Vargas, Diane Stoffel, and Chris Hughes worked on the illustrations. Judy Voelker provided editorial comments on portions of the text. I would like to acknowledge, as well, the enormous effort and patience of Tiffany Clark and Jennifer Brady in helping to bring this book to its final form. Ben Nelson, as always, provided the greatest support and encouragement. I am grateful to all funding agents, landowners, co-workers, colleagues, and participants for their contributions.

MIMBRES DURING
THE TWELFTH CENTURY

ABANDONMENT IS
NO MYSTERY

Prehistoric abandonments—of structures, sites, and regions—have been viewed as final events in the histories of people. Yet modern Pueblo people remind archaeologists that they do not use and view land in the same way as do non-Native Americans. Movement is part of the life of Pueblo people (Naranjo 1995). Recently, archaeologists working in the North American Southwest have returned to an interest in migrations, evaluating not only the causes for leaving a settlement or region but also the processes of migrating and resettling. These studies, linking push-and-pull factors and examining social scales of decision making, improve our understanding of the ways in which movement is integral to arid landscape use. Site abandonment and migration, however, may never have resulted in discontinued use and residence in any area of the prehistoric Southwest. A new direction in archaeological research examines the processes of regional reorganization that accompany the depopulation of village centers. While we once assumed that the abandonment of large centers signaled "collapse" and regional abandonment, marking the end of a "culture," we are beginning to view abandonment of centers as a strategy of land use that is suited to arid landscapes, as an aspect of the mobility of human groups. Continuity and change, rather than closure, are the processes of emerging interest in research on abandonment. This book is a case study of movement and reorganization within the Mimbres region in southwestern New Mexico; land-use patterns and social arrangements were transformed as part of the continued presence of a people on their landscape.

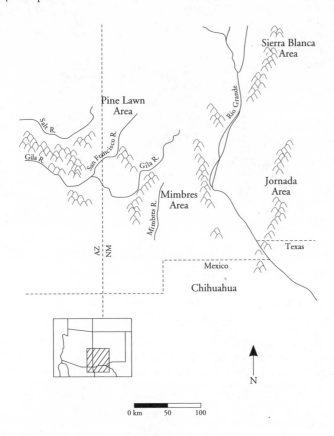

Figure 1.1
The Mimbres region in southwestern New Mexico.

The Mimbres region (fig. 1.1) is best known for outstanding naturalistic and geometric black-on-white pottery. This ceramic tradition grew over many centuries as people gradually settled into ever larger villages, cultivating adjacent floodplains and alluvial fans. By the early eleventh century, Mimbres ceramic producers occupied large masonry pueblos along the major drainages in southwestern New Mexico (fig. 1.2). These large villages dominated the landscape through the eleventh and into the twelfth century. In the middle of the twelfth century, many people living in large pueblos in the Mimbres region left them. This abandonment, which terminates the Classic Mimbres period, has received considerable attention. The black-on-white pottery ceased to be produced at large sites. Where the Mimbres people went and what happened to them have been of interest to lay people and archaeologists for decades. Most have assumed

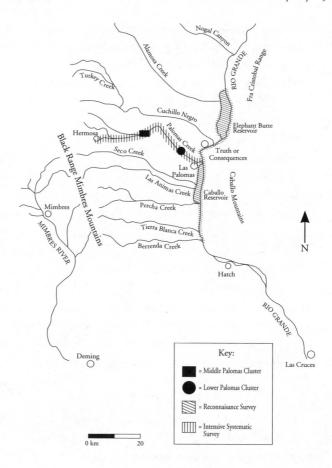

Figure 1.2
The Eastern Mimbres area.

that the Mimbres region was abandoned and the Mimbres people became ac-culturated into other aggregated population centers. Abandonments, such as the Mimbres, have been thought of as mysteries to be solved: What happened to the Mimbres people?

Village abandonment has received considerable attention in archaeological research throughout much of the world. The greatest attention is paid to causes for abandonment, sometimes referred to as "collapse" (Berman 1989; LeBlanc 1983; Lekson 1992b; Minnis 1985a; Tainter 1988; Yoffee and Cowgill 1988); processes and strategies of abandonment are just beginning to be examined (Cameron 1995; Cameron and Tomka 1993). The study of cause and process, especially the focus on abandonment as a movement strategy, emphasizes that village abandonments are not mysteries; they do not represent the disappearance of people. Two perspectives within archaeology have promoted the "mystery" theme. First, a focus on large sites as the nodes of residence for cultivators has led to the conclusion that when village centers are abandoned, regional abandonment follows. In fact, cultivators reside in a range of different kinds of settlements that are arranged in patterns from dispersed to aggregated. Culture histories of the Mimbres identify a temporal hiatus between the final occupation of Mimbres phase villages by large aggregates and the establishment of the large villages of the next period, assuming that the Mimbres region was thus abandoned. Continuity of regional occupation following depopulation of large villages, however, has not previously been explored. Second, the static nature of archaeological information has led to the careless equating of pottery types with people. When styles disappear from the archaeological record, it is easy to equate their absence with the disappearance of a people. Ceramic styles are traditions for making and decorating pottery that result from histories of learning and social identity. When the social landscape changes, we should expect changes in styles. People may adopt ceramic styles or discontinue them as they change their identities. It is no mystery that styles are replaced.

Just as the notion of the disappearance of a people is inaccurate, the equation of village abandonment with collapse is misguided, at least for nonstate or middle-range societies. The concept of collapse in archaeology has developed in part because we tend to focus our attention on the process of growth and development (Carneiro 1967) and the complex factors that contribute to the demise of centers. As a consequence, our view of social and economic organization and change is truncated, excluding changes that occur with the abandonment and reorganization of economic and social adaptations (for exceptions see Cameron 1995; Cordell 1984:317–325; Hegmon, Nelson, and Ruth 1998; Nelson 1993a, 1993b; Upham 1984). Processes of population amalgamation and strategies for maintaining population clusters influence abandonment and reorganization strategies. Abandoning groups establish new ways of living, depending on the social and environmental conditions to which and from which they move. Thus, abandonments may be more profitably viewed as transformations. Use of the concept "collapse" has, unfortunately, been interpreted as indicating the demise of a social group. In the Southwest there are clear indications of continuity of groups, ideas, and behavior. The notion of "abandonment" has also carried with it the implication that social groups disappeared or gave up using an area (Ferguson 1995). The case of Mimbres abandonment is an excellent example.

Abandonment of the large Classic Mimbres villages has been viewed as the end of the Mimbres people. While the composition and organization of social groups changed, as did ideas and behaviors, recurrent practices of movement, aggregation, and dispersion were common in the Southwest and frequently involved changes in land use rather than absence of use.

Understanding abandonment processes, then, contributes to our understanding of the complexities of land use among cultivators in nonstate societies. Examining abandonment as a process of changing landscape use allows refocusing the phenomenon to be explained. No longer is the question Why did they disappear? but rather How does movement play a role in the use of landscapes by prehistoric people? Why is movement important to arid landscape use? What are the varied movement strategies that cultivators employ? The mobility theories that apply to foraging groups and the collapse theories that explain state-level abandonments are not appropriate to settled cultivator-hunter-gatherers. Not only are middle-range societies different from foragers and state-level societies, their structures and practices are highly variable both among and within communities. In this book I explore how population dispersion to small settlements served as a strategy that allowed people to continue to occupy a region rather than abandoning it. Abandonment of large villages is viewed as a shift in population distribution on a continuously occupied landscape.

The long-term land-use strategies of cultivators in the prehistoric Southwest can be understood in terms of several variables. The first is *movement*, which includes both organizational aspects of mobility (logistical and residential) and scalar aspects of movement (local reorganization as contrasted with migration to another region). The second is *ownership and access*, which influences the extent to which occupational continuity or abandonment is expected. The third is *flexibility of social groups*, a variable condition among Southwestern communities that must be understood in terms of leadership and household autonomy. These factors intersect in a model of land-use practices in which regional occupational continuity and reorganization may be expected under some circumstances and from which expectations about patterns of shifting land use can be proposed.

Movement

The subject of movement is more commonly treated in studies of foraging societies. The differences between foragers and cultivators make foraging models problematic as a basis for understanding movement within and between groups of cultivators. The role of movement among foragers is immediately evident; foragers depend on movement on a daily basis, as well as seasonally. In contrast, the role of movement among cultivator-hunter-gatherers is not immediately evident and has been oversimplified. Cultivation has been perceived as a sedentary practice and contrasted with mobile foraging. In arid landscapes, sedentism, or more accurately residential stability, does depend in large degree on cultivation or other artificial means for increasing the productivity of plants and animals (but see Fish, Fish, and Madsen 1990). In the North American Southwest, residential stability is correlated with cultivation, although initial cultivation was not associated with sedentary village life (Minnis 1985b; Wills 1988). But the equation of hunting and gathering with mobility and of cultivating with sedentism, although common in archaeological research, is far too simple (Carmichael 1990; Rocek 1996; Upham 1984; Whalen and Gilman 1990). All groups are sedentary to some degree, and all incorporate different kinds of mobility strategies into their land use (Rocek 1996). Cultivators have considerations of resource tending, land modification, storage, and ownership. While these are considerations for some hunter gatherers with abundant, localized resources (such as the classic example of salmon fishing on the Northwest Coast [Ames 1985]), they are less central to the movement strategies of foragers.

Movements among cultivators may be logistical or residential, residential movement involving patterned movement within a subsistence cycle, local reorganization, and migration. Logistical movement is by groups crosscutting communities and involves travel to acquire resources and transport them to a residential locus (Binford 1980). Whether to hunt, gather, fish, or trade, these trips provide information about places and people, reconfirm access to land and resources, and consolidate social ties. Understanding these patterns can be important to understanding the abandonment process because people tend to move to those places and join those groups with which they have ties (Cashdan 1983; Stone 1996; Watson 1970).

Residential mobility may involve temporary moves as part of a regional strategy for accessing resources and people, leaving some residences temporarily abandoned. Archaeological and ethnoarchaeological research documents patterns of residential mobility among cultivators (Graham 1993; Hard and Merrill 1992; Horne 1993; Kohler 1992; Mills and Ferguson 1993). Intra-annual moves are made to acquire wild resources, to farm in distant fields, to avoid social conflicts, and to respond to cycles of environmental change and ritual activities.

Hard and Merrill's (1992) observations of Tarahumara intra-annual movements document the degree to which households and individuals move residence in order to take advantage of available resources. The Tarahumara subsist primarily on cultivated foods, and by traditional notions they should be quite sedentary. The primary residence of a household is in a cluster of households forming a village. Two extended residential moves are made by some households in a village group each year. During the growing season, many households move residence to their field areas as far as 8 km away from the main village (Hard and Merrill 1992:606). During the winter, some households move to isolated rock shelters to protect their sheep and goats from the cold and dampness. These moves depend on the availability of land, the number of domestic animals and weather conditions. The less land held by a household, the more likely members are to move away from their village and remain in their field houses. Brief moves are also made to the main center within the region for participation in major ceremonies. Households establish temporary residence in these centers; the length of their stay partially depends on their role in the ceremonial activities.

Horne (1993) discusses the fluidity of land use in the Khar o Tauran region of arid northeastern Iran. Among cultivators, even relatively permanent villages are not occupied continuously. Time is spent in winter stations to tend animals and in summer camps to herd cows, to milk, and to process the milk. Not all village residents have winter or summer camps. Those who do occupy winter camps tend to be groups of men, while more complete households live in summer camps. Tomka (1993) describes a similar pattern for agropastoralists in Bolivia, which involves seasonal movement and periodic or episodic abandonment of sites.

Thus, intra-annual movement by cultivators is a strategy for adjusting to the physical and social contexts in which they live. In particular, cultivators may move to expand their agricultural base (Kohler 1992; Preucel 1988). People move to farming hamlets in order to extend farming productivity beyond the areas immediately around large villages and as a mechanism to relieve the social tensions that develop in large-group contexts. Decline in conditions of population-resource balance as well as social stress, both of which ultimately lead to village abandonment, may contribute to more frequent and longer moves away from the main village. Thus, abandonment of large villages may, in part, be an extension of the practice of occupying secondary farming settlements.

More permanent residential moves, or abandonments, occur at different scales (Cameron and Tomka 1993; Cordell 1984:314–324). Local moves reorganize groups within a region; distant moves shift occupational focus away from a region. First, I discuss local moves and the process of reorganization. Within

Southwestern archaeology, studies of shifts from dispersed to aggregated settlement abound. Fewer studies consider shifts from aggregated to dispersed settlement or the movement of village groups within regions (Adams 1989; Hegmon, Nelson, and Ruth 1998; Nelson and Anyon 1996; Preucel 1988; Reid et al. 1996; Schlanger and Wilshusen 1993; Upham 1984).

Examining the relationship between aggregation and dispersion is useful in understanding reorganization. Both are strategies of land use appropriate to different economic, social, and environmental circumstances. They may be combined within annual cycles as well as over longer periods of time. Within an annual cycle, some people aggregate year-round, with segments of the population periodically dispersing to special resource areas as did the Huron in the eastern Great Lakes region (Heidenreich 1971); in other contexts, people aggregate during some seasons and disperse during others as on the Northwest Coast (Mitchell 1971) and in the Great Basin (Larsen and Kelly 1995; Steward 1938); and in still different contexts people live in a dispersed pattern throughout the year, aggregating briefly for ceremonial reasons as in northern Mexico (Hard and Merrill 1992).

These two settlement poses, aggregation and dispersion, may be incorporated into longer-term strategies of regional occupational continuity that involve periodic reorganization. Aggregation offers many advantages. Group living facilitates the definition and control of landownership (Yellen and Harpending 1972), reducing competition for land (Kohler 1992), and facilitating defense (Bluhm 1960; Mills and Ferguson 1980). Aggregation is an effective way of responding to population pressure (Adler 1990), resource stress (Cordell and Plog 1979:417; Hill 1970), and localized abundance of critical resources (Graves, Longacre, and Holbrook 1982:194–197; Reid 1989). It is also a strategy for assuring the existence of social support networks (Graves, Longacre, and Holbrook 1982:198–199; Kohler and Van West 1996) and a response to conflict (Brooks 1993). In an aggregated village context, cooperative labor investments are possible; social networks can be established within and between villages to address economic, social, and political needs: to hedge against the risk of shortfall in production, for protection against others, for finding mates, and for meeting ritual obligations.

Anthropologists have discussed a variety of negative consequences of aggregation. In arid climates, population clustering may lead to environmental degradation and food stress (Berman 1989; Kohler 1992; Kohler and Matthews 1988; Minnis 1985a). The presence of large numbers of people also creates organizational demands (Johnson 1982). Intracommunity stress may develop in large villages (Adler 1993; Cameron 1991; Cordell 1975:189; Lipe 1995; Titiev 1944:97–99; Whiteley 1987) and be difficult to resolve, particularly where ranking is not institutionalized. Dispersed settlement distributes population more evenly over landscapes and may create less impact on resources. People living in small settlements, however, have fewer village dwellers upon whom to depend and with whom they can share the labor and obligations of subsistence, social, and ideological practices (Hegmon, Nelson, and Ruth 1998). In addition, small communities are vulnerable to raiding and other encroachments (Fish et al. 1994); the frequent burning of structures on small sites in some regions of the Southwest may be attributable, in part, to this vulnerability (e.g., pithouse structures in the northern part of the Southwest [Mobley-Tanaka 1996], although it has also been attributed to other factors [Cameron 1990; Wilshusen 1986], and small settlements in the Grasshopper region [Fish et al. 1994]).

Shifts between aggregation and dispersion change the distribution of people within a region and shift the organization of social and economic use of the landscape. Upham (1984) proposes a model of cyclical change between aggregation and dispersion. He argues that dispersion is concomitant with a change in resource base from one that is primarily agricultural to one derived from hunting and gathering. Agriculturalists, however, commonly occupied small, dispersed settlements throughout Southwestern prehistory; small sites vastly outnumber village centers (McAllister and Plog 1978). Dispersion of groups into small hamlets and continuation of an agricultural focus may have been more common than not. The common view that village abandonments represent failed attempts at aggregation may misrepresent an effective strategy of shifting land use to sustain regional occupational continuity.

We lack a thorough picture of the relationship between aggregation and dispersion because Southwestern research has predominantly focused on large sites (for exceptions see McKenna and Truell 1986; Powell 1983; Varien 1997; Ward 1978.) This practice has been criticized because it has led to the construction of cultural sequences that ignore periods of population dispersion and strategies of dispersed land use concurrent with large village settlement (Carmichael 1990; Nelson 1993a; Tainter 1985:146 in Berman 1989; Upham 1984). When the periods of occupation of large settlements in a region do not overlap in time, archaeologists argue for occupational hiatus. During periods in which no large sites are evident, archaeologists argue that regions were not occupied. Regions may never have been completely abandoned in the past, but until considerable research is directed toward understanding the occupational histories of small settlements and the organization of land use that produced them, the nature and context of dispersed land use and its relationship to aggregated settlement in the Southwest will remain poorly understood. Small settlements need not imply short occupation spans (Kent 1992), nor must large settlements imply long periods of occupation (Lekson 1990a). One of the important, and as yet unanswered, questions is how dispersed agricultural land use was organized. Were small hamlets occupied for long periods of time—decades or centuries? Were they seasonally occupied across different environments? Were they occupied regularly on a cycle of movement and reoccupation?

Movement over long distances, or migration, shifts the focus of residence away from a region but does not necessarily entail giving up ownership or use of abandoned land. Migration is a transformation in land use of a different sort than regional reorganization. Migration studies have recently returned to favor in North America and are a major focus of current research in the Southwest (Cameron 1995; Lipe 1995). The processes of migrating away from a region are variably paced (Cameron 1991), and conditions in present and future homelands influence these processes. Lipe (1995) discusses the relationship between push factors within the home region and pull factors from potential future homelands that draw people to migrate. Environmental change, resource depletion, and social stresses influence decisions to move, while the prospect of new land, new ideologies, and new trade relations in growth areas attract migrants. These migrations may involve few people or many. Some movement of large groups over fair distances has been noted within the Southwest: the historic Tewa move to Hopi and movement of some Hopi to Havasupai (Schlegel 1992), and prehistoric movements to Hopi mesas from the Upper Little Colorado, Tsegi Canyon, Canyon de Chelly, and Mesa Verde (Upham 1984:247, referencing an unpublished paper by S. Plog 1969), but as Upham notes (1984:247–248), documentation of mass movement in the Southwest is rare.

Migrations, however they were accomplished, resulted in shifts in the way the abandoned areas were used, but cessation of residential use does not necessarily imply no use. Within the Southwest, modern Hopis and Zunis continue to visit places where they once resided in large villages, and they use them for collecting resources and performing rituals (Ferguson 1995). Adams and Adams (1993) and Reid (Fish et al. 1994:162) argue that residents of previously densely occupied regions in the North American Southwest continued to collect resources after they had abandoned them as loci of residence. The regional networks of those who continued to occupy these depopulated regions shifted toward other centers of growth. From a strictly functional and ecological perspective, "continued utilization of land would have extended the duration of claims on the best lands" (Adler 1996:355). Adler argues that continuity of access and claim is related to previous investments. From the perspective of identity and community integrity, people maintain contact with their home-land because it is part of their essence and their history. Adams (personal communication, 1997) documented the continued use of an abandoned farming village in the Homolovi area in northeastern Arizona for the ritual burial of birds. Many native people state that prehistoric sites are not abandoned; their buried ancestors still occupy those places. Return to those "living" places to communicate with ancestors and bury relatives may be more common than we currently perceive it to be (see, for example, Blake 1998). Continued use for different purposes is more pervasive and extensive when moves are not across great distances (Adler 1993). But even at the level of regional abandonment, people return to use their former homeland and retain rights to the land (Fish et al. 1994:145).

Those who have been interested in the processes of movement and the aban-donment of villages in the North American Southwest describe them as recur-rent and complex phenomena (Cordell 1975; Graves, Longacre, and Holbrook 1982; Kidder 1962; Parsons 1939; Reid 1982; Schlegel 1992). Cordell (1975:190) and Ahlstrom, Van West, and Dean (1995) state that site-level aban-donment was frequent in areas of the prehistoric Southwest; Parsons (1939:14) went so far as to refer to Pueblo dwellers as seminomadic. Within the South-west, movement by individuals, households, and communities was frequent because, as Johnson (1989) and Reid (1982) argue, mobility is an important survival strategy in marginal environments and was a recurrent response to natural and social variables. Identifying the role of logistical and residential mobility in land use over short and long periods of time increases our understanding of the potential for using arid landscapes and of the varied strategies of cultivators in this context. Movement plays a role in the occupational continuity of regions through reorganization of people on landscapes.

Ownership and Access

Issues of ownership and access affect land-use decisions, including movement strategies. In foraging societies population densities are low and strategies of resource use are extensive rather than intensive (Cashdan 1983, 1984, 1990; Halstead and O'Shea 1989; Kelly 1983). Among cultivators, some population packing is frequently evident and land use targets specific places (true for some hunting and gathering strategies, as well). Farming promotes a degree of landownership resulting from the limited distribution of arable land and investments in preparing land for cultivation (Bender 1990; Kohler 1992; Preucel 1988).

Aggregation offers advantages of control over ownership claims, or at least centralization in the contestation of claims to land and resources (Fish et al. 1994; Kohler 1992; Yellen and Harpending 1972). Reid describes the aggregation process during the thirteenth century in the Mogollon uplands as a defensive move responsive to uncertainty and competition over access to resources (Fish et al. 1994:157–161; Reid et al. 1996). Ownership issues may not have been resolved by aggregation, but their resolution was focused. Villages of cultivators in the Southwest tended to be located near the most abundant agricultural land; however, all members did not share equally in access to farmland and other resources. Kohler (1992:619) believes that, in the context of declining access to adequate farmland and the degradation of fields, the establishment of field houses at some distance from villages was an overt symbol of ownership by some village members. Hegmon (1989), modeling Hopi agricultural productivity and variable returns within a village, argues that the best strategy is not to share widely or pool and redistribute food. Households would maximize their potential survival and success by sharing only their surplus. Her model suggests that issues of access to the best land and to limited surpluses would have been constant in the villages of cultivators.

Movement may help to resolve issues of access to resources. Migration out of an area reduces immediate demands on available resources; reorganization may either redistribute existing patterns of ownership and access or actually open new resource areas. However, movement may also entail giving up ownership or the potential for claim on a resource. Thus, decisions to move are not simple.

Flexibility and Leadership

The nature of leadership and the flexibility of group integration influence movement. Middle-range societies, such as those in the prehistoric Southwest, have been characterized as having relatively flexible social arrangements (Adler 1990; Horne 1993; Johnson 1989; O'Shea 1989; Upham 1984); people are relatively autonomous, or at least can "vote with their feet" (Netting 1993:276). Power relations in middle-range societies may be more often negotiated and more easily undermined than in more complex societies (e.g., Bender 1990; Brandt and Spielmann 1998; Earle 1977; Potter 1997; Whiteley 1988).

Argument about the nature of leadership in middle-range societies has persisted for many years, dominating Southwestern archaeology in the 1980s (e.g., Reid 1989; Upham, Lightfoot, and Jewett 1989), but the relationship of forms of power to movement has received little attention. Power may derive from the control of resources (examples from the Southwest include Brandt 1994, Hantman 1989, and Judge 1979), of people (Vivian 1970), and of ritual knowledge (Brandt 1994, Brandt and Spielmann 1998, and Potter 1997), each having different implications for the ability of individuals and groups to move and to negotiate access. In middle-range societies, there is "considerable variability in the ways leadership positions are transferred from one generation to the next" (Feinman and Neitzel 1984:61), suggesting that negotiation is a constant and crucial dimension in community social relations. Access to resources and options is derived through social mediation (Adler 1996:339); this would include the option to leave or stay. In addition to community-level negotiation, power relations within households and kin groups influence the options available to individuals. For example, heads of households or kin groups, if they are perceived as the holders of land, may have the authority to slough off members (i.e., cause them to abandon their homes) under difficult economic circumstances (Wilk 1991). Gender and age relationships impact this process in the sense that they are integral to owning and controlling resources, people, and knowledge.

Considerable variation is found in perceptions about the nature of leadership and the flexibility of social forms. Aggregation requires some degree of social organization in the form of leadership and conformity. Following Carneiro (1967) and Johnson (1982), it is clear that as the size of a coresidential social group grows, need for managed decision making increases. The degree of social complexity that developed in the prehistoric Southwest has been of considerable debate, with a particular focus in the Mogollon region on the late prehistory of the western area (Graves, Longacre, and Holbrook 1982; Plog 1983; Reid 1989; Upham 1982; Upham, Lightfoot, and Feinman 1981; Whittlesey 1978, 1984, 1989). Some have argued that the relatively egalitarian organization of contemporary pueblos is not an appropriate model for understanding prehistoric social organization (e.g., Upham 1982); others have challenged the notion of egalitarianism within contemporary Puebloan social relations (Schlegel 1992; Whiteley 1987, 1988).

Aggregation into villages in the Southwest takes various forms, representing a variety of ways of structuring the social lives of those in large settlements. Figure 1.3 illustrates different settlement plans. The town sites in Chaco Can-

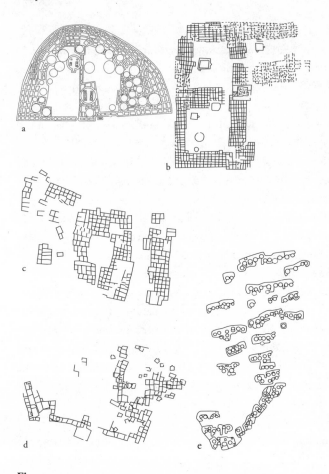

Figure 1.3
Patterns of village organization in the prehistoric Southwest:
  a. Pueblo Bonito (adapted from Cordell 1984)
  b. Kuaua (adapted from Stuart and Gauthier 1984)
  c. Grasshopper (adapted from Longacre and Reid 1974)
  d. Galaz Ruin (adapted from Anyon and LeBlanc 1984)
  e. Yellowjacket (adapted from Ferguson and Rohn 1987)

yon, for example, are constructed on a preconceived plan, with all rooms facing
a central plaza area. As Lekson and Cameron (1995) argue, their use as residential sites would have required change toward a more socially integrative ideology. Similarly, some of the late prehistoric and protohistoric pueblos in the
northern Rio Grande are planned settlements with interior plazas where every-

one working or performing in the plazas is in sight of those within the structures. In the Mogollon area, Grasshopper Pueblo grew into a few large-room blocks, one of which was accessible only through a passageway and had an interior plaza (Reid 1989). In contrast, Mimbres villages are amalgamations of rooms into blocks that are only loosely clustered to form the village (Anyon and LeBlanc 1984; Shafer 1991a, 1991b).

Mimbres village form does not indicate that control was established through the structure of the village itself. Detailed studies of construction sequences of two large villages in the Mimbres Valley have documented village formation into loosely clustered room blocks (Gilman and LeBlanc 1998; Shafer 1991a, 1991b). Not all residents were in sight of a single plaza, and people could not view all residential areas simultaneously, as is possible in villages built around plazas. Thus, architectural indices of integration do not suggest visual controls. Analysis of styles, however, indicates considerable conformity. Hegmon, Nelson, and Ruth (1998) compared architectural and ceramic styles in the aggregated villages to those in small, hamlet settlements and found considerably greater conformity in the styles at the aggregates. In the Mimbres region, village dwellers conformed to standard styles, but there is no indication of levels of management of village life that would be consistent with strong, centralized authority.

Given the leadership demands of aggregated settlement, how might people disengage from the village? Most models of population movement derive from studies of foragers, who lack multiple levels of social identification and ranking (Cashdan 1983, 1984; Halstead and O'Shea 1989; Minc and Smith 1989). It could be argued that the prehistoric farmers of the Southwest were sufficiently sedentary and socially stratified to rule out the sort of social flexibility necessary for short-term residential mobility; but a range of opinions are expressed about the kinds of movement that would occur among cultivators (Rocek 1996). Some researchers emphasize the flexibility of social groups that allows for dispersal and the splitting of groups (Adler 1990; Cordell and Plog 1979; Horne 1993; O'Shea 1989; Upham 1984), yet others emphasize the integrity of social structures established in the context of aggregation (Fish et al. 1994; Graves, Longacre, and Holbrook 1982; Schlegel 1992). O'Shea (1989:58–64) argues generally that in poor agricultural years, farmers may resemble hunter-gatherers. He notes that in times of resource stress, historic Huron living in large villages dispersed into small groups that ranged widely to collect food. Among the Plains groups, individuals, families, or whole villages moved in response to shortages (O'Shea 1989:58, 61, 64). For the Southwest, Upham (1984) and Cordell and Plog (1979) argue that population dispersion is an appropriate response to failed attempts at aggregation but that archaeologically it is difficult to see because the remains of mobile groups do not accumulate sufficiently. The more substantial remains resulting from periods of sedentism have been the focus of archaeological research and chronology building in the past. These authors suggest that in the centuries after cultivation was established in the Southwest, prehistoric social groups alternated between aggregated and dispersed social arrangements.

In contrast, others view pueblo social organization as less flexible and abandonment as the movement of social groups to other contexts of aggregation. Schlegel (1992) argues that movement in the Southwest was by groups rather than by individuals or household, but she does believe that larger social institutions were quite flexible in their acceptance of immigrants into villages. She observes that Hopi have flexible phratries that allow for the "segmentation, merging, and incorporation of immigrating groups" (385). Kinship could be changed within a phratry and was often changed among the members of migrating groups in order to establish their claim to common ancestry (383–388). This flexibility, she argues, made it possible for groups to move easily in response to both natural and social conditions. Johnson (1989) states that in the agriculturally marginal Southwest, cultivators needed to maintain a degree of flexibility in social relations in order to be able to respond to conditions of abundance and dearth. Rigid, higher-order social arrangements would interfere with the long-term adaptability of social groups; thus, while ranking may have occurred in certain times and places, according to Johnson, it must have been short-lived.

If social flexibility is so important, how did large aggregates stay together for as long as they did? I have argued earlier that under some conditions, aggregation is an important strategy, and we know that it did occur in many times and places in the Southwest. Adler (personal communication, 1992) identifies the persistence of small residential units within some of the largest thirteenth-century Anasazi farming villages. He argues that the small residential units comprised of a few households persisted over time, sometimes forming large villages and other times small hamlets. The structures of large and small villages in southwest Colorado illustrate this consistent organizational unit that allows for social flexibility in a variable environment (Adler 1990; Lightfoot 1994; Varien 1997). Adler (personal communication 1992) believes that at times when aggregation was important, the political and religious roles held by leaders of each small residential unit were integrated to hold the larger group in place. Graves, Longacre, and Holbrook agree with Johnson that institutionalized social ranking did not develop in the aggregated villages of the Mogollon region, but they emphasize the importance of regional and interregional networks. Graves, Longacre, and Holbrook argue that when the five-hundred-room pueblo of Grasshopper in the Mogollon highlands was abandoned in the 1300s, people moved to areas where nucleated settlements existed or re-created smaller settlement systems elsewhere (1982:203). Once large pueblos have formed inter- and intraregional networks of trade and exchange, "it is difficult to revert to a system of dispersed hamlets"; the "system no longer exists as an independent entity in the area," and "the set of mutually supporting relations had been organized among larger numbers of individuals under the new settlement system" (1982:202). They believe that "to return to a successful dispersed system, it would have been necessary to re-create those links" of ceremony, marital exchange, and resource exchange (Graves, Longacre, and Holbrook 1982:202–3). Stone (1993), from his studies of the Kofyar and Tiv on the Nigerian savanna, concurs that social arrangements influence the flexibility of social groups. The social history of mobilizing human resources is as much an influence on land-use strategies as are the conditions of the natural environment.

Because movement may change social organization, it may also influence, or be influenced by, ideas about ordering and integration. New ideologies may be created or adopted when people form new communities (Adams 1991; Adler 1993; Fish and Fish 1993; Herr, Mills, and Newcomb 1996; Lipe 1995). Mills and her students discuss the adoption of great kiva architecture as a way to integrate disparate communities such as those that moved into the Silver Creek area just north of the Mogollon Rim in east-central Arizona (Herr, Mills, and Newcomb 1996). Fish and Fish similarly find developments in communal architecture with reorganization within the Hohokam region in southern and central Arizona during the Classic period. Adams (1991) accounts for the development of the kachina cult as an example of this integration. Each group within a village holds an important element of the religious cycle so that it cannot be complete without participation by all. This new ideology of ancestor worship emerged as a means of integrating unrelated groups that came together to form large communities in the late prehistoric Southwest. All of the above are examples of ideologies that were associated with movement toward aggregation. Ideologies related to dispersion have received little attention by researchers, although Hegmon, Nelson, and Ruth (1998) do suggest that dispersion is associated with a shift in the ways in which communities are defined. Styles that once integrated village communities were replaced by styles that align individuals or households to new regional centers.

Thus, movement in the prehistoric Southwest was possible, even promoted, by the relative autonomy of small groups. Flexibility would have been necessary in the ideas that define relationships, obligation, and access. Movement, however, creates issues of redefinition at a local and regional scale. Leadership roles, community structures, and regional networks may be challenged by decisions to move, while at the same time they provide the social links along which mobility decisions are negotiated and implemented. Highly structured communities are evident only relatively late in the prehistory of the Southwest; prior to that time movement probably was relatively easy. As village and regional structure became more complex, movement was increasingly difficult.

Autonomy and Variability

Household organization and composition varies within communities as a product, to some degree, of different strategies of production and consumption. "Every economic system has a diverse set of roles available, and households adopt different strategies to take advantage of them" (Wilk 1991:28). The strategies appropriate for one community, kin group, household, or individual may not be suitable for another. We should expect a varied and complex array of behaviors.

Independent domestic groups that manage their own production are typical in prestate societies (Rocek 1995:5; Sahlins 1968:74–75), although they vary in composition and size (Cameron 1992:178; Rocek 1995) and in their functions (Wilk and Rathje 1982). Hegmon (1989) argues that within agriculturally based villages, households survive best by maintaining a considerable amount of economic autonomy. Sharing only surplus is the strategy most suited to the variability of the Southwest environment. Kohler (1992) notes that in the Northern Anasazi area, the frequency of field houses increased with population growth and competition for farmland. Aggregation increases communal control, but the increased presence of field houses indicates "practical control" by households. Kohler notes, however, that there are fewer field houses than expected if all households in the aggregated settlements claimed farmland in the region. He suggests that only a limited number of households had the right to claim land and establish field houses, indicating that an overt, landholding, leadership class developed (Kohler 1992:630–31). It is also possible that the lack of congruence between the number of households in the villages and the number of field houses may indicate that a range of options were employed in addressing the problem of limited resources for a growing population. Some people may have supplemented shortages by diversifying farming, others by trading, and still others by increased hunting or gathering.

This diversity is evident in the contemporary Maya community of San Mateo Ixtatan in the highlands of northwestern Guatemala (1979, personal observation, Coxoh Ethnoarchaeology project, directed by Brian Hayden). Among the seven hundred or so households of contemporary subsistence farmers, no one depends entirely on cultivation of their plots in the village. A few families hunt extensively, while others have distant farm plots and field houses, many produce items for exchange or sale in local and regional markets, and still others leave the village for wage labor. This varied economic mix supports the continuity of the community, making possible the aggregation of the many households in the agriculturally marginal highlands. The diversity of subsistence strategies by households implies different practices and sets of daily interactions as well as the formation of different networks. These strategies contribute to defining the options available to people for moving from one place to another as well as to the difficulty of making decisions to move. Were San Mateo Ixtatan to come apart, I would expect the current residents to make different decisions regarding their movements.

Julie Lowell's 1991 study of households in a large prehistoric village documents the kind of variability described for the Maya. She documents variation in the size and structure of households within the large prehistoric community of Turkey Creek Pueblo in east-central Arizona. Based on analysis of artifacts within rooms, she argues that settlement in the village and abandonment of the village was a household-level decision, although household groupings representing small villages may have migrated together to the site. Thus, to view a community as a single-minded social entity creating and responding to social, political, and environmental change ignores variability among the basic social units within which many decisions are made.

This is not to argue that households are isolated, autonomous entities, or that they are rigidly constituted. The household exists within a broad social and economic network (Wilk 1991:34) and within an ecological context. These circumstances set limits on the options available to all households. However, within these limits households are composed differently, and the members act in a variety of ways, depending on their specific situation. Wilk documents considerable change in the composition of households and in the ways that they respond to economic and political change over time among the Kekchi Maya in the Toledo district of Belize, a phenomenon which probably occurs in many societies. Kent suggests that during the Pueblo II period in the northern

Southwest, "there may have been diversity in the settlement pattern. . . . Some people might have resided permanently . . . in small family camps . . . while others lived in aggregated communities elsewhere and seasonally visited the . . . area" (1992:653).

Just as social and economic strategies among aggregated people are diverse and flexible, as shown by Johnson (1989), Kent (1992), Schlegel (1992), and Watson (1970), those employed by abandoning populations are varied even within a community (Brooks 1993; Tomka 1993). Household economic autonomy facilitates diversity in the decisions of households. Returning to Kohler's observation about the limited number of field houses in relation to the total number of households forming a village community, if only some households had ownership over field areas distant from village centers, then only the households having possession had the option of moving to those hamlets when the village was abandoned. The cost of moving may also have been greater for those holding land into which they had invested their labor than for those who placed more emphasis on hunting, gathering, or trading.

Anthropologists have argued at length about the definition and recognition of households (see introduction in Netting, Wilk, and Arnould 1984). Regardless of the conceptual and analytical problems, there is no question that households exist and that the members perform a variety of domestic and nondomestic activities in concert (Lowell 1991; Wilk 1991). Within this book, households are recognized through repetition in domestic architecture and artifact assemblages. The important aspect of "households" here is not their precise composition but rather their existence as small corporate groups of decision-making individuals who responded to and molded the immediate economic and ecological conditions in which they lived (Wilk 1991).

Changing Land Use

Movement, therefore, is a strategy of resituating, both socially and ecologically, and perhaps even ideologically. It can take various forms, occur at various scales, and promote continuity or sever relationships among people and between people and their land. Movement is made possible by flexibility in social arrangements within communities and regions, but it is limited by commitments to ideas that successfully bind people in communities. Movement strategies vary with the role of individuals and groups within communities but are important dimensions of arid landscape use. As Horne argues, populations can cope with social, political, and environmental change by maintaining settlement flexibility; fluidity or instability in occupation is "part of an intentional production strategy typical of arid land occupations" (1993:43).

Cultivation is associated with some degree of residential stability because of the patchy distribution of arable land, the need for tending crops over multiple seasons, investment in land modification, the need for storage, and the potential for ownership. Differential investment in cultivation should influence the costs of moving within regions and out of regions. Early cultivation in the Southwest, with limited investment in fields and reliance on cultivated foods, may have had limited impact on movement (Minnis 1985b), although it promoted longer use of some resource areas (Wills 1988). As cultivated foods became a major portion of the prehistoric diet, the requirements of farming and the investments in fields influenced movement potential. Demands on land, access to land, and investments in land contribute to the development of ownership claims.

Taking the view that village abandonment does not imply regional abandonment and that claiming land is important to cultivators, the reasons for continuity and the form which continuity may take can be explored. Within villages of cultivators, some members are first-comers, while others are recent immigrants; similarly, some are leaders, and others are followers; some are members of newly formed families, and others are in aging families. Within this variation, claim to land will not be evenly distributed, and the economic and social strategies of families will vary. Thus, we should expect that strategies for abandonment of a village would vary. For those who derive their influence from controlling land and resources, moving away from a region might be much more costly than for those not holding such control. For those who derive control from people or ideas, keeping a group together might be more important than remaining at a particular place. Thus, residential moves that maintain regional occupational continuity may be expected by those who claim land. I have argued that cultivation practices increase claim and ownership. Thus, I would expect continuity of regional occupation to be accomplished through continued cultivation by those who control arable land.

This notion can be explored by examining the potential relationship between logistical and residential movement. Village-dwelling cultivators in the prehistoric Southwest maintained secondary field sites, which, as Kohler (1992) suggests, established ownership of fields. The field structures constructed at secondary field sites may have served as much to mark ownership as to shelter the temporary occupants. Their use was not only to supplement the productivity of primary fields near the village, but also to escape the social stresses of aggregated village life. Movements away from village settings may have extended for longer periods of time and been more frequent as the conditions that promoted these moves were amplified (Minc and Smith 1989:10; O'Shea 1989:58). The pattern of moving away to adjust to conditions in the main village is familiar to small-scale cultivators (see Cameron 1992 for the Hopis; Mills and Ferguson 1980 for the Zunis). Logistical use of field sites may have increased during times when food was scarce or there were social stresses, but it would only have provided options for those who had access to these secondary places. Others in communities may have relied on hunting or trading. For them, movement to the best hunting areas or to trading partners could have alleviated stresses developed within any community (nutritional and social). Logistical trips to farm fields, game locale, or trading partners would have established a baseline of relationships and access outside the village and perhaps for some beyond the immediate region. Movement would more likely have been to familiar places and people rather than to unknown situations (Cashdan 1983:55; Stone 1996). These logistical moves could have been transformed to residential moves, through gradually extended trips and greater reliance on the resources and networks of these secondary places. Thus, an entire village would be unlikely to have remained intact, or to have moved together, because of the different options available to its members. Large-scale movement of entire village groups should have been unusual.

Regional occupational continuity and reorganization should have been structured around access and ownership, which among cultivators is primarily centered on agricultural land. Dispersion within the region should have been associated with the continued occupation of that region by cultivators. This notion is contrary to models by Upham (1984) and others such as Carmichael (1990) and Stuart and Gauthier (1984), who argue that dispersions were associated with shifts to hunting and gathering. Some portion of a dispersing population may have shifted toward hunting and gathering, but the factors promoting continuity of regional occupation derive from access and ownership of agricultural land. Occupational continuity within a region was accomplished by a shift in the location and organization of cultivation, not through a shift to a different resource base—hunting and gathering. Gathering is not only a more dramatic shift for cultivators, but it has little basis in the land-use practices and the social dynamics of preceding cultivating populations. Movement to secondary field camps through gradually longer trips away from the village simply extended intra-annual movement to permanent occupation. Stone describes two settlement patterns of different groups living on the Nigerian savanna; the pattern of the Kofyar is of interest here. Kofyarian farmers moved onto the savanna first "on a seasonal basis, living in ephemeral compounds" that eventually became permanent residences (Stone 1993:75). These compounds grew and became residentially stable farming villages. Similarly, Adams describes the late-nineteenth-century shift from the village center at Walpi to Polacca as beginning with a small temporary settlement by a few Tewa families (1989:179). The Oraibi split in the early twentieth century was accomplished by some families establishing residence at the locale of a seasonal farming village (Cameron 1992:174, 181). Thus, movement and shifting land use within a region were common and effective strategies of adjusting to variation and change in arid landscapes and were practiced by cultivators.

As I have noted, some members of a cultivating village were likely to have shifted toward greater investments in hunting and gathering. Those individuals or households with little or no claim to field areas, perhaps because they were latecomers to the settlement, may have shifted toward increased hunting and gathering. Other members are more likely to have left the region altogether, based on their previous contacts outside the region.

This book explores the dispersion of Classic Mimbres village dwellers to their farming hamlets and the associated reorganization of their land use from an economic and social perspective. I offer here one of many possible strategies of change that could have been employed during the mid-1100s. The model of reorganization has been formulated by exploring the role of "movement" among cultivators; the social and economic patterns that promote, restrict, and shape movement; and the variation that can be expected among communities of cultivators. This exploration of movement stands in contrast to studies of migration, exploring how people manage to maintain occupational continuity through movement.

Chapters 2 through 6 document various aspects of reorganization. In particular, Chapter 2 explores our current understanding of the traditions and materials that are "Mimbres." Through analysis of survey data, chapter 3 establishes population dispersion by people in the Eastern Mimbres study area. Chapter 4 uses excavation data on architecture and artifact assemblages to look at the nature and timing of settlement formation following village abandonment, and at the autonomy and mobility of households in the new settlements. Shifts toward occupation of secondary field sites have implications for the economy and society of the reorganized groups. Secondary fields are presumably less productive than the former primary fields. A shift toward greater reliance on nondomesticated resources or on maintenance of multiple fields is explored in chapter 5, using ethnobotanical, faunal, and settlement data. In chapter 6 we learn that dispersion to small settlements required some changes in the social dynamics within those settlements, as well as within local areas, and across the Mogollon region. This study provides an overall basis for examining movement as a strategy for sustaining people in arid landscapes and shows that the fascinating aspect of abandonment is not in "mysterious disappearance" but rather in the way people use movement to achieve continuity.

The Mimbres

Southwestern New Mexico was an integrated cultural region, which archaeologists refer to as the Mimbres, occupied by thousands of village dwellers by A.D. 1000. People were concentrated in groups of two hundred or more, living in masonry pueblos formed as blocks of contiguous rooms or "room blocks" and clustered on the first terraces above the most productive farmland to be found in the area. These were among the largest villages in the Southwest at that time. People of the Mimbres region made white-slipped bowls and jars on which they painted intricate, black, naturalistic and geometric designs, the complexity of which, many would argue, was never rivaled in the prehistory of the Southwest. As with all traditions, this one eventually changed. Villages were depopulated and the pottery style replaced by other styles. Although abandonment of many of the villages and discontinued production of Mimbres pottery may appear to indicate a dramatic occurrence in Mimbres history—a disappearance—in reality, it does not.

The depopulation of villages was actually a transformation of Mimbres cultural traditions. Faced with issues of providing sustenance for an ever-larger population and of maintaining order both within villages and in the region at large, people shifted away from village-focused land use. In this chapter, I describe the Mimbres region, the Mimbres cultural traditions, the formation and organization of villages, and the conditions that promoted movement away from villages. The Mimbres region provides an excellent context for examining the flexibility of land use and social organization among small-scale societies that occupied a relatively arid landscape.

Delimiting and Describing "Mimbres"

The Mimbres cultural region encompasses much of what we know today as southwestern New Mexico (fig. 1.1). It may even extend into southeastern Arizona (Douglas 1997; Gilman 1997); possibly western Texas (Lekson 1988), although Whalen (1980) notes that Mimbres ceramics are rare on these sites; and probably northern Mexico (DiPeso, Rinaldo, and Fenner 1974). "Mimbres" is defined by the distribution of a complex of pithouse and stone masonry architecture and Mimbres plain and painted wares that were produced between A.D. 200 and at least the middle of the twelfth century (Anyon, Gilman, and LeBlanc 1981; Brody 1977; Brody, Scott, and LeBlanc 1983; Haury 1936; LeBlanc and Whalen 1980; Lekson 1988). The pithouse architecture shifted from a round structure to a rectangular one. Toward the end of the pithouse sequence, extended side-entry ramps were replaced by entry through the roof (Anyon, Gilman, and LeBlanc 1981; Shafer 1995). Pithouse residences were generally replaced with surface-stone masonry room blocks by A.D. 1000. Lekson (1992a:28) describes the river cobble masonry as "a lot like stacking ball bearings," although some walls are quite carefully constructed, especially on sites in the southern Mimbres Valley. The painted ceramics shift from redware to red-on-brown to black-on-white ware through the pithouse sequence. From A.D. 900, when people were living in rectangular pithouses, through the Classic Mimbres period, the black-on-white ceramic style changed in design form, design layout, and design execution in a fairly consistent way throughout the region (Anyon, Gilman, and LeBlanc 1981; Brody 1977; Scott 1983; Shafer and Taylor 1986). Toward the edges of the Mimbres region, however, these associations break down, so that any boundary is difficult to delimit; I base my determination of the region on the dominance of Mimbres architecture and ceramics on particular sites. The boundary also fluctuates depending on the time period under consideration. For this study, the Mimbres area refers to the distribution of Classic Mimbres sites. During the 150 years that are recognized as the Classic Mimbres period (A.D. 1000–1150), Mimbres architecture and ceramics dominated this portion of the Southwest.

The Mimbres Valley has traditionally been considered the core of the Mimbres region. To the west, Mimbres sites are densely distributed along the Gila River and its tributaries in New Mexico (Chapman, Gossett, and Gossett 1985; Fitting 1972a; Lekson 1990b); farther west, Sauer and Brand (1930) and Gilman (1997) have documented sites with Mimbres ceramics in the San Simon region, and Douglas (1997) reports Mimbres plain and painted wares in the San

Bernardino Mountains of southeastern Arizona. To the east, Lekson's (1984, 1989) and Nelson's (1984, 1986, 1989, 1993b) surface surveys have provided evidence for extending the region at least to the Rio Grande. Laumbach and Kirkpatrick (1983) and O'Laughlin (1985) have documented Mimbres sites in the vicinity of the Rio Grande south to the border with Mexico; excavations at a few of these sites document the association between pithouse or surface-masonry architecture and Mimbres Black-on-white ceramics (Hammack 1962; Laumbach 1982; Lehmer 1948; O'Laughlin 1981). Minnis indicates that sites with Mimbres pottery occur just south of the United States—Mexico border in northern Chihuahua (Minnis, personal communication 1991).

The research described in this book is based on survey and excavation data from the Eastern Mimbres, although reference is made to the entire Mimbres region and adjacent centers of occupation with different traditions and histories (see chap. 5). The Eastern Mimbres includes the Rio Grande and its tributaries, which have their origin in the Black Range (fig. 1.2). These tributary drainages flow intermittently, with relatively permanent surface water in narrow sections of the floodplain and adjacent to springs. While the Rio Grande is one of the three large rivers in the region, its tributary drainages are less well watered than those to the west in the Mimbres region.

The topography, vegetation, and climatic conditions within the Mimbres region have been described in detail by Minnis (1985a) and summarized by Lekson (1992a, 1992b). In brief, basin-range topography dominates the area. North-south trending ranges extend from the Chihuahuan Desert in the south, to the Mogollon Rim and San Agustin Plains in the north. Vegetation zones are diverse, including the Lower and Upper Chihuahuan, and Transitional, which offer a range of vegetation from desert grasslands and shrub communities of creosote and mesquite, through piñon and juniper, to ponderosa pine and fir. Two aspects of the Mimbres regional environment are important to this research: aridity and distribution of water.

Aridity varies considerably within the Mimbres region. In the mountainous areas, both rainfall and snowfall are relatively abundant as compared with other regions of the Southwest (Bennett 1986a:42–43); but the growing season is short (Bennett 1986b:47), so plant foods are limited, and cultivation is problematic. Dry farming of maize requires a growing season of from 110 to 130 frost-free days minimum, although this varies with the type of maize (Berman 1989:162; Cordell 1975; Hack 1942:20–23; Minnis 1985a). The growing season is shorter than 110 days in most mountainous settings in the Mimbres region. The desert portions of the region are exceptionally dry, and again, plant resources are limited, although mesquite may have been relatively abundant (Minnis, personal communication 1998). Dry-farmed maize requires 20.32 cm (8 in.) rainfall in summer (Martin, Leonard, and Stamp 1976:327 in Berman 1989:160; Shaw 1977) and a total precipitation of 30 cm (Hack 1942:8), which is rare in the Mimbres desert areas. Prehistoric cultivation may have required watering technology, which in the Mimbres region included simple channels, check dams, and possibly reservoirs, as well as hand watering (Herrington 1982). Planting in low, moist areas may have worked without artificial watering (Minnis, personal communication 1998). Between the mountains and deserts, however, is an area with adequate growing season and water for production of cultigens during most years. The densest concentration of sites occurs in this band of relatively greater productivity. Although much of the Eastern Mimbres research area is within this band of higher productivity, the Eastern Mimbres is substantially drier than elsewhere within the band. The orographic effect of the high peaks of the Mogollon Mountains and the Black Range cause winter storms, moving east from the Pacific, to drop more precipitation west of the Black Range (Bennett 1986a:42). The creeks that drain the eastern slope of the Black Range carry little winter run-off from snowmelt. As would be expected, prehistoric occupation in the Eastern Mimbres region is less dense than in the Mimbres Valley to the west.

Water is a critical resource in this arid region, for farmers as well as for those who hunted and gathered food centuries ago. Assuming that small-scale horticulturists settled adjacent to their primary farmland, the distribution of water had significant influence on the distribution of settlements throughout the prehistoric and historic periods; the same is true in contemporary farming. The Mimbres and Gila Valleys receive more rainfall than does much of the periphery of the Mimbres region. Major rivers flow through these valleys, and the largest settlements are located along these rivers. The Rio Grande, on the eastern periphery of the Mimbres region, has the largest drainage system and should have been settled intensively and extensively. However, fewer large sites are found along the portion of the Rio Grande in the Mimbres region than along the other major rivers (Lekson 1992a, 1992b). At least two factors possibly account for this lower frequency of identified residential sites. First, the Rio Grande appears to have been a slow-flowing, meandering river, which may have supported a considerable marshland, and which flooded frequently. These characteristics created a floodplain not conducive to reliable farming. Thus, large, aggregated populations would not have established residence in much of this area. Neal Ackerly (personal communication, 1993) argues that some areas adjacent to the Rio Grande in this region were fairly well drained and that water could have been easily channeled for irrigation farming. He identifies these as the locales of the largest sites. However, Lekson (1992a:34) argues that the flow rate of the Rio Grande was far too great for prehistoric irrigation agriculture. The hydrology of the lesser Gila and Mimbres Rivers was better suited to prehistoric technologies of water control for farming. Second, the Rio Grande and its immediate surroundings were dramatically altered in the early twentieth century with the damming and irrigation programs supported by federal and local government agencies. Evidence of prehistoric sites has been eliminated in many areas adjacent to the Rio Grande floodplain. However, one of the surveyors for the dam project, Herbert Yeo, was interested enough in archaeology to sketch and record large sites around the area of Elephant Butte reservoir. His records (on file at the New Mexico Laboratory of Anthropology, Santa Fe) do not show site density as high as along the Mimbres River.

While the primary farmland in the Mimbres region is in the floodplain of rivers and creeks (Minnis 1985a), other sources of water and farmland also influenced settlement. Springs offer a dependable, yet relatively limited, source of water. Examination of sites in the Eastern Mimbres region indicates a close correlation between the location of springs and the clustering of sites (Lekson 1984). Water and farmland are also available in alluvial fans. The analysis of intensive and randomly sampled survey areas in the Eastern Mimbres region demonstrates that residential sites are located only along the creek channels, adjacent to springs, or adjacent to alluvial fans (Nelson 1986, 1993a). If farming was an important subsistence activity, the size of farmland and dependability of the water source in these areas should be related to the amount of time during an annual cycle and the number of years an area could have been occupied and farmed. Aspects of occupation duration and continuity are evaluated in chapter 4.

Mimbres Village Formation and Cultural Traditions

In the Mimbres region, village settlement is associated with considerable reliance on cultigens, as it was throughout much of the prehistoric Southwest. By A.D. 600, residences were concentrated at some of the best farming locales along the major rivers; cultigens are ubiquitous in features on these sites (Diehl 1994; Minnis 1985a). These pithouse villages appear to have grown in size through the next few centuries (LeBlanc 1983). Considerable disagreement exists over how residentially stable these pithouse occupants were. Gilman (1987) and

Lekson (1988) argue that pithouse dwellers moved seasonally; the pithouses were winter residences in Gilman's model. In contrast, LeBlanc (1980) and Anyon and LeBlanc together (1984) argue that pithouse village formation marks permanent residence. Resolution to this argument influences population estimation (if each household had multiple residences, estimates based on a model of permanence would be too high), explanations of land use, and models for the formation of villages. Currently, data on occupational history of pithouses do not resolve the dilemma.

Large clusters of pithouses occur in the Gila and Mimbres Valleys, although many are partially beneath later Classic Mimbres surface-masonry pueblos. While it is difficult to impossible to estimate the number of pithouses on these multicomponent sites, various suggestions regarding the scale and number of sizable villages have been made. LeBlanc (1983:75) argues that "[b]y A.D. 800, at least fourteen villages had been established in the Mimbres Valley proper." Most are the locales along the Mimbres Valley where the major villages of the subsequent Classic Mimbres period were built. Two large pithouse villages in the Mimbres Valley are not covered by substantial Mimbres pueblos: Harris Site (Haury 1936) and Three Circle Site. Others are primarily beneath Classic room blocks: Cameron Creek (Bradfield 1931), Swarts (Cosgrove and Cosgrove 1932), NAN (Shafer 1995; Shafer and Taylor 1986), and Galaz (Anyon and LeBlanc 1984; Bryan 1931) are among the largest of these in the Mimbres Valley. In the Gila Valley, Woodrow Ruin, Saige-McFarland (Lekson 1990b), Fort West (Lekson, personal communication, 1998), Wind Mountain (Woosley and McIntyre 1996), Lee Village, and the earlier Mogollon Village on the tributary San Francisco River (Gilman et al. 1991; Haury 1936) are among the largest clusters of pithouses, although size estimates for Woodrow Ruin and Saige-McFarland are severely restricted by the overlying pueblo structures (Lekson 1990b:86–87). In the Eastern Mimbres, no large pithouse villages or clusters have been documented (Laumbach and Kirkpatrick 1983; Lekson 1984, 1989; Nelson 1986, 1989)

Whether pithouse villages were integrated socially is again difficult to assess. The largest clusters of pithouses have great kivas and lack smaller kivas, an index of possible village or intervillage integration (Anyon and LeBlanc 1980). This is true for the Mimbres Valley (LeBlanc 1983) as well as the Gila Valley (Lekson 1990b). Creel (1995) and Lucas (1996) note pithouse clusters within the site of Old Town, where pithouse rampways face into a central area, but LeBlanc (1983:75) suggests that pithouse sites have little evidence of formal planning.

The ceramics associated with pithouse sites were first painted early in the A.D. 700s (Gilman 1988; Lekson 1992b; Powell 1996). This earliest painted ware, Mogollon Red-on-brown, may be more common in sites on the Gila and its tributary, the San Francisco River, than in the Mimbres Valley (Powell 1996). Red-on-brown was transformed to red-on-white by the addition of a white slip and was subsequently modified to black-on-white through a change in firing technology (LeBlanc 1983). The black-on-white color combination continued to be produced through the end of the pithouse periods and into the Classic period. The similarity in pithouse ceramics throughout the region suggests considerable regional interaction (LeBlanc 1983), although Powell (1996) notes an eastern and western design set for Mogollon Red-on-brown.

Panregional interaction during the pithouse periods seems strongest with groups to the west. Items of Hohokam origin, shell and palettes, occur on many pithouse sites. Brody (1977) and LeBlanc (1983) suggest that the use of naturalistic and figurative design motifs on black-on-white ceramics was adopted from the people of the Hohokam region. LeBlanc (1983:77) also notes the appearance of Hohokam vessel form in the Mimbres ceramic assemblages. Hohokam ceramics have been reported from Old Town (Lucas 1996) in the Mimbres Valley and from Saige-McFarland (Lekson 1990b) on the Gila. This relationship did not continue into the Classic Mimbres period. By the early eleventh century, social interaction was primarily within the Mimbres region (Hegmon, Nelson, and Ruth 1998; Minnis 1985a).

By A.D. 1000, most residential architecture within the Mimbres region was stone-masonry construction in blocks of contiguous rooms. Why and how the transition from pithouses to pueblos occurred have absorbed many pages, years of thought, and numerous hours of debate. In brief, arguments range from economic to social and ideological. Gilman (1987) argues that the transition is from seasonal to more permanent residence, with greater reliance on cultigens. She views population increase as responsible for increased need to produce food and store it. Surface architecture is both better suited to year-round occupation and to storage by individual households. Lekson (1992a) also emphasizes the mobility of the pithouse period, arguing a small, seasonally mobile pithouse population made "a rapid transition to full sedentism and full reliance on corn agriculture during the 150 years of the Mimbres phase" (meaning the Classic period) (Lekson 1992a:25); Lekson (1988) had earlier argued for considerable, seasonal, residential mobility during the early Classic Mimbres period. Diehl's research (1994, 1996) on the history of maize cultivation through the Late Pithouse periods in the Mogollon region shows a shift toward substantial investment in maize cultivation prior to the Classic Mimbres period, indicating that increased investment in maize cultivation may not have been responsible for the shift to surface pueblos (see also Wills and Huckell 1994 for increased maize production in the Southwest about A.D. 200). LeBlanc's view (1983) of the transition to surface pueblos places emphasis on the economics of adaptation without reference to a shift in mobility. In his model the transition did not involve a shift toward less mobility (by the Late Pithouse period, LeBlanc believes, occupation of villages was permanent) but involved more pooling of labor and resources among extended kin. The room blocks and their growth represent the cooperating kin group in LeBlanc's model, which he states does not represent a substantial sociological change from the Late Pithouse period. LeBlanc refers to the shift away from "great kivas" to "kiva rooms incorporated into room blocks" as an index of the integration of the kin group within a room block. However, each room block does not have such a kiva. Feinman argues that the transition is a significant social one. He suggests that the individual decision making of households was replaced by a more integrated, "corporate form of political action with little initial or associated increment in political complexity" (1997:28). Corporateness is seen in the formation of contiguous room-block architecture and shifts toward ritual structures both incorporated into room blocks and constructed for community use. Feinman argues that even distribution of wealth and storage support the view that complexity was not immediately increased. Finally, Shafer (1995) presents the transition from pithouses to pueblos as a shift in ideology. He examines common themes in Chichimec, Pueblo, and Central Mexican beliefs and uses these to understand elements of the material changes that accompany the transition to pueblo architecture. Focusing on changes to roof entry, burial beneath room floors, and the placement of hearths of standard form directly beneath roof entryways, Shafer argues that the shift to pueblo architecture symbolizes the multilayered universe in which death is perceived as a continuation of life, and emergence is from the underworld. The rectangular hearth is a portal to the underworld, constructed into the floor of each room; beneath the floor, the dead are placed as a starting place to their entry into the other world. The roof entryway creates daily reenactment of the symbolism of emergence from below. These various explanations may account for different aspects of the changing society and land-use patterns of people occupying the Mimbres region. While archaeologists differ considerably in the models they accept, I believe all would agree that the shift was toward a more place-focused settlement practice, with accompanying changes in the organization of households and village structure, including ceremony.

The growth pattern of Mimbres villages is important to evaluating the transition from pithouses to pueblos. Although Lekson (1992a) argues that Classic Mimbres pueblos could have developed with little continuity of occupation from the pithouse periods, Shafer (1995) demonstrates gradual shifts and occupational continuity at the NAN Ruin in the Mimbres Valley. An important perspective is derived from distinguishing between the initial and final sizes as well as organization of these pueblos. Those who have dissected the occupational histories of large, Classic-period sites agree that room blocks began with a few contiguous rooms (Gilman 1989; Gilman and LeBlanc 1998; LeBlanc 1983:105–15; Shafer 1982, 1990, 1991a, 1991b, 1991c). The Mangus phase in the Gila area is viewed as the initial surface architectural manifestation of small room blocks (Lekson 1990b; Woosley and McIntyre 1996). In LeBlanc's reconstruction of the history of Swarts Ruin, six small room blocks grew accretionally, eventually merging to become two, with a sizable population. LeBlanc argues that the two massive room blocks at Swarts Ruin are unique, rather than typical, as the site was once described (Cosgrove and Cosgrove 1932); their massiveness, he believes, results from efforts to compress occupation into a small area so that arable land was not used for residence. (Swarts is one of the few Mimbres sites on the floodplain.) Gilman for the Mattocks Ruin and Shafer for the NAN Ruin similarly document growth from small blocks. Shafer (1996) suggests that over the history of the occupation of room blocks, rooms were added to the edges of room blocks to accommodate short-term occupants. Thus, some rooms were occupied continuously for long periods of time while others were briefly occupied. Gilman argues that with the growth of room blocks, the earliest or "core" rooms were abandoned for use as ritual spaces, with a shift in residence toward more peripheral rooms (Gilman 1989; Gilman and LeBlanc 1998). Each room block, she believes, was the residence of a family; the structures grew, and room use changed as the composition of the family changed. The patterns described by Shafer and Gilman would make the village population appear considerably larger than it was at any one time. Thus, if Gilman's and Shafer's arguments are correct, the transition from pithouse to pueblo architecture may not initially have involved a shift toward *substantially* greater population aggregation.

Change in population size through the Mimbres periods is a central theme of much Mimbres research. Lekson (1992a) cautions that knowledge of the size

and mobility of pithouse-period population is too limited for demographic comparisons to be made with the later Classic period. He further argues that Classic
and later population sizes may not be vastly different. Others use estimates of
room counts to model a population increase for the Mimbres Valley from the
earliest pithouse periods through the Classic Mimbres period, with a substantial decrease after the Mimbres period (Blake et al. 1986; LeBlanc 1980, 1983;
Minnis 1985a). One aspect of the difference between Lekson and others may
be the scale of their view of Mimbres population (although Lekson also questions some of the high estimates of population size by others). In his overview
of surface archaeology in southwestern New Mexico, Lekson compiled data on
room counts from all major surveys throughout this broad region. Surveys in
the Mimbres, Gila, Rio Grande, and Eastern Mimbres regions are extensive and
systematic (Accola and Neely 1980; Blake, LeBlanc, and Minnis 1986; Blake
and Narod 1977; Chapman, Gossett, and Gossett 1985; Fitting 1972a; Graybill
1973; Herrington 1979; Laumbach and Kirkpatrick 1983; LeBlanc 1975, 1976,
1977; Lekson 1984, 1989; Nelson 1986, 1989, 1993a; Nelson and LeBlanc
1986). Lekson is the only researcher to have gathered these data in one place,
attempted to convert them to a comparable form, and taken this broad-scale
view. In his words, the process "required hundreds of miles of travel, reams of
correspondence, hours of phone calls, weeks of ceramic reanalysis, and months
of Sisyphean archival work" (Lekson 1992a:15). I have converted these data to
examine relative shifts in population across drainages over time. Using room
counts from all recorded architectural sites along the three major drainages,
standardized by survey coverage, I have constructed an estimate of relative population size from Late Pithouse through immediate Postclassic phases (Postclassic
Mimbres, El Paso, Tularosa, Black Mountain) along the major rivers in the
Mimbres region (table 2.1). The room counts do not represent actual population, but the methods of calculation are comparable across drainages and over
periods.

The Gila has the highest number of structures dating to the Late Pithouse
and Late Pithouse-to-Classic periods among the three drainages. In the Gila,
Fitting (1972a) and Lekson (1990b) have argued that the multicomponent
Pithouse-to-Classic sites were occupied early in the Classic period. Classic
Mimbres room counts are highest in the Mimbres Valley. The room counts
from multicomponent Late Pithouse–Classic–Postclassic (LP-CM-PC) sites could
be added to the Classic samples; most are primarily Classic period in the Mimbres
Valley. With this addition the room count for the Classic Mimbres period is
vastly higher in the Mimbres Valley than in the other two drainages. Immedi-

Table 2.1[1]

The distribution of rooms by period across the major river drainages in the Mimbres region

Drainage	Rio Grande	Mimbres Valley[2]		Gila (Cliff/Redrock)	
Type of coverage	reconnaissance	intensive/sample		reconnaissance	
Linear distance[3]	95	60		87.5	
Mulitiplier[4]	1.0	1.6		1.1	
Number of rooms by time period:	N	N	IN[5]	N	IN
Late Pithouse	59	101	162	167	184
Late Pithouse-Classic[6]	149	700	1120	2393**	2632
Classic Mimbres	301	1696	2714	958	1054
Classic-Postclassic[7]	766	1047*	1675	0	
LP-CM-PC	0	1052	1683***	0	

*   Includes Lekson's "Mimbres—El Paso/Black Mountain" with his "El Paso/Black Mountain Tularosa"

**   Includes Lekson's "Pithouse—Mimbres" and "Mimbres I, II, III B/W"

***   This number should be added to the Classic Mimbres value because these are primarily Classic room blocks with some later ceramics on the surface (my understanding of the data).

[1]   These are adapted from Lekson (1992: table 4 and p. 9–15). Only those surveys along the channels of the major rivers and their tributaries are included.

[2]   The Mimbres Valley sample does not include the Upper Mimbres survey by Graybill (1975) or the Lower Mimbres survey (Blake and Narod 1977).

[3]   This is the linear distance covered by the survey, not the linear distance of the drainage.

[4]   Because survey coverage varied from drainage to drainage, an index was calculated to standardize the actual frequencies (N) for comparison. Each index was calculated by dividing the linear coverage of a drainage into the longest distance covered on all drainages. For the Mimbres Valley, the index is 95/60 or 1.6: the longest distance covered on a drainage (the Rio Grande) divided by the distance covered on the Mimbres drainage. This number is multiplied by the actual frequency to standardize room counts in relation to surveyed area.

[5]   IN are the standardized frequencies of rooms or structures (pithouses); actual room or structure count (N) was multiplied by the "multiplier index" calculated to compensate for differences in surveyed area.

[6]   Includes Lekson's "Pit House—Mimbres" and "Mimbres I, II, III B/W"

[7]   Includes Lekson's "Mimbres—El Paso/Black Mountain" and his "El Paso/ Black Mountain/Tularosa"

ately after the Classic period, room counts remain highest for the Mimbres Valley; no sites are recorded as late Mimbres and Postclassic for the Gila because this compilation does not include the later Salado occupation in that drainage. The Rio Grande has fewer rooms than the Mimbres Valley for the Classic to Postclassic, but the number of rooms is proportionally higher than during other periods of occupation within the Rio Grande drainage. The general pattern over time is a shift in population toward the south and east. Recognizing this pattern reinforces the value of examining the processes of Mimbres period village depopulation and reorganization in the Eastern Mimbres area.

Classic Mimbres period sites vary in size from single rooms up to a few hundred, but the majority of the population was living in multihousehold settlements. The smaller settlements are similar to initial room blocks on the large villages, but the nature of their occupation is unclear and probably variable. Lekson's compilation of survey data from all major surveys in southwestern New Mexico documents the high percentage of small sites in the three major drainages. In the Gila, Mimbres, and Rio Grande drainages, two-thirds to three-quarters of all Classic-period sites have fewer than ten rooms (Lekson 1992a:16–17, table 5). However, most of the population resided in the larger sites. The distribution of rooms across sites of various sizes indicates that only one-eighth to one-quarter of the population in the three major drainages resided in sites with fewer than ten rooms (Lekson 1992a:table 6). Many of these small sites may have been field houses of people who had residences in the larger villages (Nelson 1993b; Nelson, Rugge, and LeBlanc 1978), but some may be permanent residences (Laumbach 1982). Estimates of the number of large villages range from about twelve to eighteen in the Mimbres Valley and tributaries. We may never know how many large villages there were on the Gila or Rio Grande, with the impact of development on those sites bordering primary floodplain land. The large villages in the Mimbres Valley have been extensively documented (Anyon and LeBlanc 1984; Bradfield 1931; Bryan 1931; Cosgrove and Cosgrove 1932; Nelson and LeBlanc 1986; Nesbitt 1931; Shafer 1987, 1988) as have some in the Gila (Lekson 1990b).

The large villages are comprised of blocks of contiguous rooms. Extensive room-block excavation at the NAN Ruin has allowed Shafer and his students to identify room suites (Shafer 1982). These are comprised of two to four different kinds of rooms, including storage, cooking, and general residence. Room suites have also been recognized at the Saige-McFarland site on the Gila (Lekson 1990b) and at the Mattocks Ruin in the Mimbres Valley (Gilman 1989; Gilman and LeBlanc 1998). LeBlanc (1983) believes the combination of rooms that form the room block comprise the structures occupied by a resource pooling group. Cameron (1991) has warned against assuming that the occupants of pueblo room blocks share kinship or collaborate in any way. Especially large rooms are also incorporated into many room blocks; their size, features, and artifact composition indicate use as ceremonial structures (Anyon and LeBlanc 1980; Shafer 1982).

The room blocks are loosely organized in relation to each other and to open areas. A somewhat more formal arrangement may be present at the sites of Old Town and Cameron Creek, where rooms are arranged around a plaza. Elsewhere, plazas are open areas between room blocks or attached to the ends of room blocks. These plazas may have served as community gathering areas, replacing the great kiva used before A.D. 1000 (Anyon and LeBlanc 1980; Shafer 1995). The possibility of dual division within villages is raised by Creel (Creel and McKusick 1992) and Lekson (1982). Creel notes a pattern of macaw burials only on the north side of villages, and bowls with macaw and parrot representations only on the south side of villages at the three villages where macaw remains have been found as burials (Cameron Creek, Galaz, and Old Town in the Mimbres Valley). Lekson discusses separation of north and south room clusters by a plaza or open area at most large villages. Even if these patterns are the product of a structural separation, there is little evidence of class or hierarchical difference between or within groups. Gilman's analysis of burial and architectural data yielded variation but no evidence for differential access to resources or space (Gilman 1989, 1990). Community-level ceremonial facilities indicate, however, some leadership above the level of the household or room block. Sheer numbers of people would require it. The absence of material indices of hierarchy may result from absence of institutionalized positioning of individuals or groups. Shafer (1996) argues that differential access to agricultural land may have existed within villages as "first-comers" sought to control the best field areas. This proposition is consistent with the general trend toward ownership as people increasingly invest in modifying or maintaining land; Herrington (1982) documents a range of water-control features constructed in association with large Classic Mimbres villages.

Within the Mimbres region, there was considerable movement of goods and probably people but limited evidence of panregional ties. Within the region the broad distribution of design elements on painted ceramics (LeBlanc 1983), the homogeneity in technology of plain-ware ceramics (Shafer 1995), painted ceramics and architecture (Hegmon, Nelson, and Ruth 1998), and the exchange of either temper and clay or plain-ware ceramics (Minnis 1985a) can be explained by strong intraregional ties. No evidence, however, suggests hierarchy among large villages. They are relatively evenly spaced and generally similar in size. At least three villages have macaw burials, but these are extremely rare. The macaws are derived from contact with people to the south; Creel and McKusick (1992) argue that the birds were transported from the south as juveniles. Additional contacts to the south are symbolized in some of the naturalistic designs in Classic Black-on-white ceramics (Hegmon, Nelson, and Ruth 1998). These

southern connections are not strong; items and symbols derived from the south
are extremely rare (Woosley and McIntyre 1996). As Minnis (1985a) noted,
during the Classic Mimbres period, people intensified internal interaction rather
than their relationships with others outside the Mimbres region (but see Lekson
1993 for connections to Chaco).

Between A.D. 1130 and 1150, for a variety of economic and social reasons,
the large villages were depopulated; some may not have been completely abandoned as residences, particularly in the southern Mimbres Valley (Creel 1998).
Researchers have argued that village abandonment signaled regional abandonment in the middle of the twelfth century. Following a hiatus in occupation,
populations from the east and south (Black Mountain or El Paso phase) and
west (Salado and Tularosa phase) moved into the Mimbres region in smaller
numbers. This study in the Eastern Mimbres area demonstrates continuous
regional occupation from Classic to Postclassic. The latter occupations may be
thought of as Mimbres and include continued use of Mimbres Black-on-white
pottery and architectural style, at least for a limited time, with the addition of
new technological and stylistic traditions. Haury (1936:130) recognized this
late association several decades ago for areas east of the Mimbres Valley. To
understand the process of transformation, it is important to examine the causes
for Classic village depopulation.

The Conditions Related to Village Abandonment

In the Mimbres region, intensive cultivation and population growth are associated with aggregation during the Classic Mimbres period (Anyon and LeBlanc
1984; LeBlanc 1989; Minnis 1985a; Shafer 1991a, 1991b). One of the primary factors leading to abandonment was population-resource imbalance that
seems not to have been compensated by changes in land-use practices or social
strategies (Minnis 1985a; Nelson 1981). Depopulation of large villages was
ultimately the consequence. For this reason, I focus discussion on evidence of
resource stress and potential adjustments to resource stress, including movement of human groups.

Many anthropologists and ecologists have discussed human responses to resource stress, and general consensus has been found in the belief that human
cultural strategies are highly flexible (see, e.g., the papers in Halstead and O'Shea
1989 and in Netting, Wilk, and Arnould 1984). Human responses are depen-
dent on the social, technological, ideological, and biotic circumstances in which
groups live (Cashdan 1990; Halstead and O'Shea 1989; Horne 1993; Minnis

1985a; Wilk 1991; Winterhalder 1990). Economic responses may include specialization, diversification, and storage among other strategies (Schlanger 1988). Land-use practices may involve changes in logistical mobility or in residential mobility, changes in the scale of territory or region, in the ways in which territories are maintained (Cashdan 1983), and in the ways in which various resource areas are used. Movement is a common response to resource stress, especially under conditions of relatively low population density or where relatively unpopulated lands are adjacent to densely populated areas (Ahlstrom, Van West, and Dean 1995; Dean, Doelle, and Orcutt 1994; Minnis 1985a). Social responses may involve sharing and exchange (Schlanger 1988), which may range from local coresidents to panregional relationships; the scale of these relations depends on the characteristics of resources and the nature of the stress. (See Hegmon 1989 and 1991 for discussion of intervillage sharing and Minc and Smith 1989 and Rautman 1993 for discussions of regional exchange.)

Diversification, exchange, and movement are especially relevant to this study. Minnis (1985a) has shown that the Classic Mimbres village dwellers of the Mimbres Valley had denuded their natural riparian environment through extensive cultivation practices. His analysis involves evaluation of pollen, charred seed, and charred wood remains as they indicate the kinds of taxa present at different time periods. Riparian species were rare by the Classic Mimbres period, which he interprets as the product of field clearing. The assemblage of plants found in sites occupied during subsequent periods are characteristic of riparian recovery. This intensive use of field areas, coupled with both increases in population and periods of below-average precipitation, contributed to imbalances between provisioning potential and demand.

Evaluations of responses to potential imbalances indicate that diversification and intraregional exchange were primary. Settlement data for the Mimbres Valley document an expansion of villages and field houses into more diverse settings during the Classic Mimbres period (Blake, LeBlanc, and Minnis 1986; Nelson, Rugge, and LeBlanc 1978), which is interpreted as a change in land-use practices and a diversification of field areas. Nelson (1981) and Minnis (1985a) have shown through analysis of faunal and ethnobotanical data, respectively, that resource use was diversified during the Classic Mimbres period. Minnis, in discussing various social responses to increased resource stress, emphasizes the development of intraregional exchange during this period; ceramics and possibly other resources were exchanged among the large villages. Thus, diversification and exchange were identified as prehistoric strategies employed by people during the Classic Mimbres period in the Mimbres Valley to address their increasing food stress. Movement, in the form of village abandonment, was ultimately the strategy employed by many of these people. In the past, archaeologists working in the Mimbres region have argued for movement out of the region; I argue that within the Eastern Mimbres, movement by some entailed short-distance resettlement at small hamlets. Quite recently, Creel (1998) has suggested that occupational continuity exists in the lower elevations (below 6,000 ft.) of the Mimbres Valley as well. There, some people continued to occupy a few rooms in the Classic villages and eventually constructed new villages adjacent to the old. Creel also believes that during the final years of the Classic period, a few households did extend regional ties to adjacent areas.

Much later, west of the Mimbres region, in the Mogollon Mountains of central Arizona, large village settlements, such as Grasshopper Pueblo, formed and then were abandoned through a process that looks similar to the Mimbres but with different final results. In the Grasshopper region, diversification, exchange, and movement were employed to address changes in the population-resource balance (Graves, Longacre, and Holbrook 1982; Reid 1989; Zedeño 1994). The large, aggregated settlement of Grasshopper Pueblo was formed in the early fourteenth century around the rich farmland of Salt Water Draw Valley. As this pueblo grew to about five hundred rooms, subsistence was diversified to include more dependence on large-game hunting, and a regional community of pueblos established exchange links. Graves, Longacre, and Holbrook (1982:193) argue that the sociopolitical developments that would have held the aggregated population together in times of resource stress never occurred and that the population gradually moved away from the region, in much the same way as was once argued for the occupation and abandonment of the Mimbres region two centuries earlier. "The nearly synchronous abandonment of Grasshopper and other pueblos in the region was not coincidental. . . . The abandonment reflects the collapse of an entire system of interdependent communities" (Graves, Longacre, and Holbrook 1982:201).

The interrelationship between diversification, exchange, and movement has been discussed by Halstead and O'Shea (1989) and by Minc and Smith. Minc and Smith (1989:10) argue that diversification may imply both increased mobility and exchange. The use of nonlocal resources may require both logistical and residential moves. As the duration and intensity of stress increases, these residential movements may develop into extraregional migration. They state further that the scale of expansion of social networks is directly related to increased duration and extent of stress. Those expanding networks insure access to diverse resource areas.

While Minc and Smith apply this model to understanding the evolution of economic and social relations between Arctic hunters in the Alaskan coastal and interior regions, as a general model it is applicable to the nonstratified Mogollon pueblo societies described above. In both the Mimbres and Grass-hopper regions, wild resource acquisition was diversified just prior to abandon-ment, and in the Mimbres region, placement of field areas was diversified. Ex-change was most developed in the Grasshopper area in the period prior to abandonment. Graves, Longacre, and Holbrook (1982) and Zedeño (1994) describe development of a network of large pueblo communities that made possible the expansion of both intraregional and interregional exchange. In the Mimbres region, however, ceramic evidence indicates an internally focused sys-tem of interactions dominated by exchange of Classic Mimbres ceramics (Nelson and Hegmon 1996). Exotics, such as macaws, occur on Classic Mimbres sites but are extremely rare.

The contrast in development of external exchange relations between the Grass-hopper region and the Mimbres region may account for different abandon-ment strategies. Regional abandonment is posited for the Grasshopper area with the abandonment of the village centers, although Reid et al. (1996) posit a brief period of dispersed occupation before people move to other areas; for the Mimbres region, at least in the Eastern Mimbres area, I argue for population dispersion within the region as part of the abandonment process of village cen-ters and a subsequent reaggregation a century or two later. Following the mod-els discussed above, underdeveloped regional networks may have made it im-possible for all residents to move to new areas. Viewed another way, diversification of field areas may have provided sufficient cultivable land to sustain a number of small groups who could continue to reside in the area. Schlanger states that "[i]t may be possible to encompass relatively short moves within the short-term strategy of field dispersal such that what has been one of several outlying fields becomes the locus of a new habitation site" (1988:779).

Ecological studies of regional exchange may help explain the inward focus of the Mimbres region during the Classic Mimbres period. Rautman (1993) and others (Cashdan 1983; O'Shea 1989; Schlanger 1988) have discussed the ad-vantages of regional exchange and visitation as techniques for coping with stress. According to Rautman, for exchange networks to reduce the risk of shortfall effectively, reciprocal areas must have different and complementary patterns of resource abundance. When it is a bad year in one area, it must not be a bad year in the neighboring areas depended upon for support. Within the Mimbres re-gion, such diversity may have existed. The three major river systems within the

Mimbres region have separate watersheds. The portion of the Gila River in the Mimbres Region has a broad watershed, flowing from the mountains at the southern edge of the San Agustin Plains, from the east and west sides of the Mogollon Mountains, and off the west slopes of the Black Range. The Rio Grande is fed from an even broader area of the Colorado Plateau and mountains of northern New Mexico before it reaches southwestern New Mexico; the side drainages of the Eastern Mimbres area are fed primarily by summer rain. In contrast, the Mimbres River has its head in the southern end of Black Range and Pinos Altos Mountains, flowing into the desert basin of southwestern New Mexico. This is the smallest watershed of the three. Thus, the conditions that influence variation in water flow and resource abundance within the riparian resource zone over time should be somewhat independent between these drainages within the Mimbres Region. Sufficient paleoclimatic data are not yet available from these three areas of the Mimbres region to model potential networks of dependence.

If these three watersheds had different patterns of good and bad years, an internal system of exchange and dependence may have developed, as indicated by the dominance of one painted and one plain ceramic type in the region and the homogeneity of those forms throughout the area. This system of internal dependence would work as long as centers were present. When some of the centers were abandoned, the interdependence would have weakened. If the people in Classic Mimbres villages lacked strong external regional relations to facilitate long-distance movement or migration, it is possible that they remained in the region. As Lipe (1995) argues, for the abandonment of the Four Corners area in the late 1200s to have occurred, people had to have established ties to the other areas and to have had reasons that drew them to migrate. Moving in with relatives and trading with partners in other areas are good means of coping with the risk of local scarcity (Cashdan 1983:55; Halstead and O'Shea 1989:4; Watson 1970:114, 119), but those regional ties may not have been in place for the villagers of the Classic Mimbres period.

The diversity of the local landscape in the Eastern Mimbres area and field diversification for cultivation were advantageous to dispersing groups. While the eastern slope would not have provided abundant wild resources, as it is considerably drier than the Mimbres Valley (Nelson 1993a, 1993b), small springs adjacent to floodplains offer consistently well-watered though limited patches of farmland. These springs can be found on all drainages and are distributed from fairly high in the Black Range to within a few kilometers of the mouths of the drainages, an elevational variation of more than a thousand meters. Thus, a variety of farming conditions can be exploited, promoting diversification in land use. The productivity of springs is conditioned by precipitation patterns, which include winter snowfall, summer monsoons (southern tropical storms), and localized summer thunderstorms. The snowfall and monsoons are broad regional patterns, which influence the entire area in similar ways. However, summer thunderstorms, which provide the majority of precipitation in the area (Williams 1986), are extremely localized. Good farmland during one year might be poor the next. The diversification of field areas during the Classic Mimbres period laid the groundwork for population dispersion within the local area, as is explored in this study.

In the context of low population density, mobility is a common option for adjusting to resource and social stresses (e.g., Dean, Doelle, and Orcutt 1994; Halstead and O'Shea 1989). As population increases, however, frequent mobility is more difficult as a solution to these stresses, and aggregation is more common. Also, cultivation can create conditions that encourage permanency and increase risk of resource shortage. Farming promotes a degree of landownership that requires some presence by the owners (Kohler 1992; Preucel 1988). Fixing to land can restrict the range of subsistence resources accessible to groups, potentially increasing their susceptibility to resource shortfall. Social dependencies of the sort examined by Rautman (1993) may replace mobility as the means for addressing resource and social stresses under conditions of relatively greater population in an area. Intragroup and intergroup bonds provide for resource exchange, marriage partners, visitation (for alleviating resource or social stresses), and ceremonial activities.

Under conditions of low population density, dispersed groups face the problems of hedging against risk and of meeting ritual and social obligations, especially if they are farmers somewhat fixed to land. I have argued above that the transition from aggregated cultivator to dispersed cultivator is not as dramatic as a transformation to hunting and gathering, either economically or socially. However, problems arise in maintaining strategies to meet important social needs and for hedging against subsistence stress. The argument for regional abandonment in the Grasshopper area is compelling: "[I]t is difficult to revert to a system of dispersed hamlets"; the "system no longer exists as an independent entity in the area; . . . to return to a successful dispersed system, it would have been necessary to recreate those links" of ceremony, marital exchange, and resource exchange (Graves, Longacre, and Holbrook 1982:202–3). However, Minnis (1985a) and Berman (1989) have noted that abandonment of large villages in the Mogollon region occurred partially as a result of the failure of regional exchange systems to mitigate resource stresses. If existing regional ties were not effective, we should expect changes in regional relations. Dispersion and reorganization in the Mimbres region may have initiated these changes. With dispersion, new, strong ties would be needed with external trading partners because the village centers no longer existed as safety nets in time of need or as an organization through which regional and interregional bonds were maintained. As this occurred, shifts in styles should be evident from those that cemented the Classic Mimbres village centers together to those that express the increasingly important regional or interregional ties of Postclassic hamlets to new centers. Gradually, the types of ceramics and forms of architecture that archaeologists use to identify Mimbres would have been replaced with new styles that define the new networks of relationships at household, community, and panregional scales. Thus, the label "Postclassic" Mimbres is used for the period immediately following the depopulation of Classic Mimbres villages (Nelson and Hegmon 1993). The label denotes continuity as well as change. It is not the best label one could imagine, but given the history of labeling for the region, I believe it best carries the information.

The process of change to dispersed hamlet settlement during the Postclassic in the Eastern Mimbres area is examined in chapter 4 from the perspective of the growth of the hamlet sites and their transformation from field houses to residential settlements. The changes in resource selection and organization of land use are then explored in chapter 5, followed by a consideration in chapter 6 of the changes in social relations at various scales, including a perspective on how the processes developing in the Eastern Mimbres area are related to those in adjacent regions. Prior to these detailed discussions of process, I examine in the next chapter the surface evidence for Classic and Postclassic sites in the Eastern Mimbres area.

Evidence for Mimbres Occupation during the Eleventh through Thirteenth Centuries

3

Understanding land-use and abandonment phenomena in southwestern New Mexico involves varied approaches: analyses at the scale of site histories, local or valley patterns, and regional or multivalley patterns. These are the different scales of the social context in which the Mimbres system changed in the mid-1100s. Regional patterns in surface data from within the Eastern Mimbres area are discussed in this chapter. In chapter 4 I discuss the occupation histories of four sites that shed light on the reorganization that followed abandonment of centers. This reorganization is put into a broader regional framework in chapter 6.

Sites with Mimbres Black-on-white pottery scattered on the surface are abundant in the Eastern Mimbres region. The co-occurrence of Classic Mimbres Black-on-white with other painted ceramic wares on these sites indicates an occupation history that spans the Classic Mimbres period and abandonment of Classic Mimbres sites; these are the Postclassic Mimbres sites. Analysis of surface data from intensive survey along Palomas Creek in the Eastern Mimbres region suggests fundamental changes in land use with the abandonment of large Classic Mimbres villages. Villages with associated small sites are replaced by dispersed residential settlements. Villagers from the large Classic Mimbres settlements may not only have been drawn into other large centers, such as Casas Grandes to the south (LeBlanc 1989), they may have dispersed to their farming villages and secondary field sites. This alternative is consistent with patterns of field-house use that develop with the growth of population in large residential centers, increased conflict, and greater demand for resources.

In this chapter, survey data from fifteen surveys in the Eastern Mimbres region are discussed. Changes in the size of structural remains, the size of room blocks, the density of artifacts, and the materials of structure construction are identified. These data provide a baseline of local information on site forms and distributions. From the surface record, six sites have been selected for excavation, among which four are reported in this study; research at the other two is in progress. The excavations on these sites and others (Hegmon and Nelson 1994; Mayo 1994; Nelson and Hegmon 1993, 1995) document the continuity of regional occupation following abandonment of large Classic Mimbres sites and the Postclassic process of population dispersion. The four excavated sites are briefly described at the end of this chapter.

The Surveys

The most extensively studied area along the eastern slope of the Black Range is Palomas drainage (fig. 1.2). Between 1982 and 1989 more than six hundred sites and isolated artifacts were recorded through systematic surface survey (Lekson 1983, 1984; Lekson and Nelson 1984; Mills 1983, 1986; Mills and Lekson 1983; Nelson 1984, 1986, 1989, 1993a). Three other related surveys have been conducted: a sample survey by Laumbach and Kirkpatrick (1983) of 2 percent of state land in western Sierra County, which includes much of the eastern slope of the Black Range (fig. 3.1, area 3); a reconnaissance survey directed by Lekson (1986a, 1986b, 1989) of the Rio Grande Valley and lower 8 to 10 km of its tributaries from Alamosa Creek on the north to Tierra Blanca Creek on the south (fig. 3.1, area 2); and a sample survey and historic reconnaissance survey of National Forest land directed by Nelson (Hunt 1990; Kralick 1990). A few other surveys provide more limited information about prehistoric sites along the eastern slope of the Black Range: the Ojo Caliente reconnaissance survey (fig. 3.1, area 1) by Laumbach (1992), the Cuchillo Negro survey (fig. 3.1, area 4) by Enloe et al. (1981), the Arizona Interconnection Project Transition Line Corridor Survey (fig. 3.1, area 5) by Fowler (1989), and various small surveys (Brethauer, Paul, and Hoyt 1977; Bussey and Naylor 1975; Harkey 1981; Kirkpatrick and Duran 1982; Laumbach 1974, 1980, 1981, 1982; Smith 1985; Weyer and Strong 1976).

The Palomas and Rio Grande surveys provide the most extensive information on eleventh- to thirteenth-century occupation. Architectural sites, those with surface and pit structures, are combined from these survey data sets, and patterns of changing land use they identified are discussed. The Rio Grande

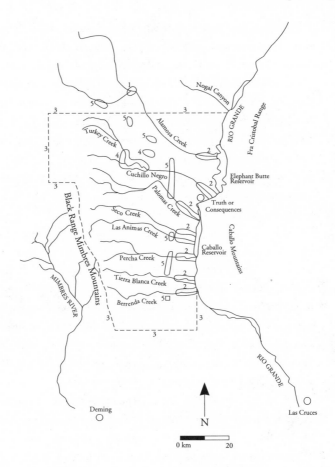

Figure 3.1

Limited surveys in the Eastern Mimbres area:

1. Ojo Caliente Reconnaissance Survey (Laumbach 1992)
2. Rio Grande Reconnaissance Survey of side drainages (Lekson 1989)
3. State Land Sample Survey (Laumbach and Kirkpatrick 1983)
4. Cuchillo Negro Sample Survey (Enloe et al. 1981)
5. Transition Line Corridor Survey (Fowler 1989)

data were graciously supplied to me by Stephen Lekson. The analysis presented here represents my interpretation of his data and does not necessarily represent his views. I attempt to identify differences in our inferences about land use in the Eastern Mimbres region; details of Lekson's views can be found in chapter 6 of this volume and elsewhere (Lekson 1986a, 1986b, 1989, 1992a). Fewer data are available from the other surveys, but I discuss information and inferences about eleventh- to thirteenth-century occupation as relevant to the Palomas and Rio Grande data, especially the views of Laumbach and Kirkpatrick (1983; Laumbach 1992), who have worked for many years in this area.

The Palomas study area extends from the crest of the Black Range to the Rio Grande Valley. At its peaks, the Black Range extends to about 3,350 m (11,000 ft.). The mouth of Palomas stands at about 1,280 m (4,200 ft.) where it enters the Rio Grande near the historic town of Las Palomas. Between its ends, Palomas Creek passes through steep mountain slopes covered by ponderosa pine and fir at the upper elevations, piñon pine and juniper woodlands at lower forest elevations, and then through dissected mesas and terraces formed from alluvial and colluvial deposits between the mountains and the Rio Grande. This open, lower country is a grassland with clumps of mesquite and creosote dominating. Sites were recorded during an intensive survey of nearly all accessible low terraces and ridges along approximately 53 km (32 miles) of Palomas Creek (south fork), from the historic town of Hermosa at an elevation of 1,880 m (6,110 ft.) to its confluence with the Rio Grande (Lekson 1984; Nelson 1986, 1989). In addition, a 2 percent stratified random sample of much of the drainage area was surveyed. All sites, from isolated artifacts to masonry architecture, were recorded. Surface recording and surveying procedures are documented in Hunt 1990, Lekson 1983, Lekson and Nelson 1984, and Mills 1983.

The archaeological record of the segment of the Rio Grande in the vicinity of Palomas Creek is less intensively studied than is Palomas drainage, although Herbert Yeo was recording sites in the early 1900s (Lekson 1989). Many sites may have been lost owing to damming of the Rio Grande to form two reservoirs in the area, Elephant Butte and Caballo. Lekson's recent reconnaissance survey (1989) is the most complete record of the terraces above the Rio Grande on both the east and west banks and of limited segments of the lower portions of drainages flowing from the Black Range (fig. 1.2). His survey includes portions of the Rio Grande Valley from Nogal Canyon on the north to Berrenda Creek on the south. The riparian zone adjacent to this stretch of river is poorly developed. Cottonwoods and other riparian trees hug the edge of the riverbank in a thin line. Away from this thin belt of trees are dry, fairly barren terraces covered in some places with creosote and mesquite. Much of the floodplain below Truth or Consequences is irrigated farmland, but the riverine habitat has been dramatically altered by damming to form reservoirs and by clearing and building for modern settlement and recreation. The contour lines on topographic maps of the area indicate that the Rio Grande was a meandering river. Slow-moving water may have created a marshland, such as can be seen in a segment of the Rio Grande north of the study area that has been somewhat protected from building and damming and in which there are current efforts to return the land to its natural form.

The Sites and Ceramics

All of the sites discussed in this portion of the book are known through surface evidence of prehistoric occupation. In the Eastern Mimbres, as in much of the Southwest, sites are assigned temporal designations based on types of ceramics present in their assemblages. Ceramic assemblages reported from surface surveys of sites along the eastern slope of the Black Range and the Rio Grande Valley date from the Early Pithouse to the late historic Apache occupation (Lekson 1984, 1989; Mills 1986; Nelson 1986, 1989). This study is focused on the Classic Mimbres (A.D. 1100–1150) and Postclassic Mimbres in the Eastern Mimbres region. Thus, only sites with Classic Mimbres Black-on-white Style III associated with contemporary and later forms will be discussed (Scott 1983). Details on earlier and later occupations are available in Laumbach and Kirkpatrick (1983), and Laumbach (1992), Lekson (1983, 1984, 1989), Hegmon and Nelson (1994), Nelson (1984, 1986, 1989, 1993a, 1993b), Lekson and Nelson (1984), Nelson and Hegmon (1993, 1995), and Schutt, Chapman, and Piper (1991).

Ceramic assemblages on the surfaces of the sites contain few sherds from painted or slipped wares, but the range of types is considerable. Within the Palomas and Rio Grande study area, fourteen painted slipped types, contemporary with or thought to have been produced after Classic Mimbres Black-on-white Style III, occur on sites with Mimbres Style III: Chupadero Black-on-white, Wingate Black-on-red and Polychrome, St. Johns Black-on-red and Polychrome, El Paso Bichrome and Polychrome, Reserve Black-on-white, Tularosa Black-on-white, Socorro Black-on-white, Red Mesa Black-on-white, Magdalena Black-on-white, Ramos Polychrome, and Playas Red. The period of production of each type is presented in table 3.1 along with references to detailed descriptions and illustrations of each type.

There are fifty architectural sites with Classic Mimbres Style III recorded along the Palomas drainage and thirty-one on the Rio Grande. The surface assemblages on some of these sites have one or more of the other fourteen painted ceramic types. Initially, the sites were divided into two groups on the basis of the ceramic samples recorded from the site surfaces: those with ceramics that indicate occupation contemporary with the Classic Mimbres period (A.D. 1000–1150) in the Mimbres Valley and those with Classic Mimbres ceramics and

Table 3.1

Temporal ranges for ceramic types present on Classic Mimbres and Postclassic Mimbres sites in the study area

A.D.	1. Classic Mimbres B-on-w Style III	2. Chupadero B-on-w	3. El Paso Bi- and Polychrome	4. Wingate Bi- and Polychrome	5. St. Johns Bi- and Polychrome	6. Playas Red	7. Reserve and Tularosa B-on-w	8. Socorro B-on-w	9. Magdalena B-on-w	10. Ramos Polychrome
1000	X		.				?			
	X		.				?			
1050	X		.	.			?	X		
	X		.				?	X		
1100	X		.	.			?	X		
	X		?	.			.	X		
1150	X	X	X	X		X	.	X		X
		X	X	X		X	.	X		X
1200		X	X	X		X	X	X		X
		X	X	?		X	X	X		X
1250		X	X	?		X	X	X		X
		X	X	?		X	X	X		X
1300		X	X	?		X	X		X	X
		X	X			X	?		X	X
1350		X	X			X			X	X
		X				X			X	X
1400		X				X			X	X

Notes corresponding to columns:

B-on-w = Black-on-white

1. From Anyon and LeBlanc (1984); Laumbach and Laumbach (1989); LeBlanc (1977); Mills (1986); Scott (1983); Shafer and Taylor (1986). Sudar-Laumbach (1982:140) suggests a begin date of A.D. 900, and Gilman and LeBlanc (1998) report the presence of small amounts of Classic Mimbres Black-on-white in excavated contexts that date as early as A.D. 900. McGregor (1965:364) suggests an end date in the thirteenth century; Breternitz (1966:86) suggests that Classic Mimbres persisted until after A.D. 1250; Laumbach and Kirkpatrick (1983) and Carmichael (1983, 1986:67) suggest an end date in the late 1100s. (Also includes a rare polychrome form; see Carlson 1982).

2. Carmichael (1986); Human Systems (1971:337); Laumbach and Laumbach (1989); Mills (1986); tree ring evidence strongest A.D. 1250–1400 (Breternitz 1966:72). Wiseman (1982, 1986:4) suggests a beginning date of A.D. 1100 based on association with Classic Mimbres Black-on-white; Kelley and Peckham (1962) suggest even earlier initial production at A.D. 1050.

3. * From Human Systems Research (1973); Carmichael (1986); El Paso Bichrome rare and short-lived (Human Systems 1973). LeBlanc (1982:117) suggests that the El Paso series did not begin much before A.D. 1150.

X Ck Marshall (1973), LeBlanc and Whalen (1980). El Paso Polychrome end dates from Hawley (1936); Breternitz (1966:74); Human Systems (1973); Whalen (1981) extends the end date to A.D. 1400, and Carmichael (1986:67) indicates that this late date is possible. El Paso Polychrome begin date from Mills 1986; Mills notes that the straight-rimmed variety was made only until A.D. 1250; Way (1979) dates the straight-rimmed variety slightly earlier, between A.D. 1100 and 1250. LeBlanc (1982:117) states that El Paso Polychrome was not made much before A.D. 1150; Carmichael (1986:67) holds out the possibility of an early 1100s date but agrees that El Paso Polychrome was produced by A.D. 1150.

4. * Wingate Bichrome (Black-on-red) dates from Carlson (1970:15–17); Human Systems (1973:358).

X Wingate Polychrome dates from Carlson (1970:23–25); the A.D. 1200–1300 extension is for Tularosa style.

5. St. Johns Bichrome (Black-on-red) and Polychrome date ranges are the same, from Carlson (1970:31); Mills (1986:173) suggests a begin date of A.D. 1200 for St. Johns Polychrome.

6. Mills (1986:174)

7. * Martin and Rinaldo (1950a:552) estimate that the Reserve phase and initial production of Reserve Black-on-white pottery in Pine Lawn Valley was ca A.D. 1000. LeBlanc (1982:116) concurs with this date. Laumbach and Laumbach (1989) suggest that initial production may have been as early as A.D. 940 and that production extended into the early 1100s.

X Rinaldo and Bluhm (1956:184) and Breternitz (1966) estimated initial production of Tularosa Black-on-white at A.D. 1100–1250. This date is revised by Tuggle and Reid (1982) to after the twelfth century. The end date is placed by Mills (1986) in the 1300s. The new range is A.D. 1200 to 1300 or 1325 (Mills 1986:174).

8. Smiley, Stubbs, and Bannister (1953:58 referenced in Breternitz), Breternitz (1966:96), Human Systems Research Technical Manual (1973:355).

9. Gallinas Spring Pueblo (LA1178), seventy-five miles north of the study area, is the type site for Magdalena Black-on-white (Knight and Gomalak 1981, 1987). The type is described and discussed in these sources and in Lekson (1986c; 1989). Lekson (1989:27) places it in the range of 1300–1400.

10. DiPeso, Rinaldo, and Fenner (1974:77–84) date the production of Ramos Polychrome to the Medio period at Casas Grandes, which DiPeso argues is A.D. 1060 to 1340 based on tree-ring and radiocarbon dates. LeBlanc (1980) and Lekson (1985) have re-evaluated these dates, and they argue that the period begins after A.D. 1130 and ends by early A.D. 1400.

ceramics that post-date the mid-1100s. The former are classified as Classic Mimbres sites, the latter as Postclassic Mimbres. The term "Mimbres" appears in both labels because of the occurrence of Mimbres ceramics on all sites and its implications for continuity of occupation in the region. "Postclassic" used in this sense refers only to sites with Classic Mimbres Black-on-white and later ceramics, not to later sites lacking Classic Mimbres Black-on-white.

Where Classic Mimbres Black-on-white Style III co-occurs with forms that were produced after A.D. 1130, it is possible that the sites were abandoned by people at the end of the Classic Mimbres period and subsequently reoccupied by makers of the other ceramics. This is the interpretation offered for such ceramic co-occurrences on Mimbres Valley sites (Gilman 1980; LeBlanc 1976:5). While reoccupation may have been the case at some sites, occupation of other sites was continuous through the period of abandonment of large Classic Mimbres settlements. Subsurface evidence from small structural sites in the Eastern Mimbres area shows that they continued to be occupied through the A.D. 1100s (see chap. 4), indicating regional occupational continuity. In contrast, Mimbres village excavations document ceramic and architectural evidence of discontinuity, with abandonment by the mid-1100s. This latter conclusion is drawn from analysis of excavated materials from the Anderson site (Nelson 1984), Las Animas village (Hegmon and Nelson 1994; Nelson and Hegmon 1993, 1995), and the Rio Vista Site (Mayo 1994). Thus, Classic Mimbres Black-on-white appears to have been used, and may have continued to be produced, after the end of the Classic Mimbres period, at least in the Eastern Mimbres area (Hegmon, Nelson, and Ruth 1998; Mills 1986:180; Nelson 1993a).

Analysis of the surface evidence cannot be used to evaluate occupational continuity. The distinction between those sites occupied through the period of large village abandonment (the mid-1100s) and those occupied, abandoned, and later reoccupied cannot be made on the basis of ceramics found on the surfaces of the sites. The survey data, thus, provide a base from which to select sites for excavation, and they offer a preliminary view of settlement shifts during the 1100s.

Regional Patterns Identified from Surface Data

Several characteristics of the surface features of the Classic and Postclassic sites indicate organizational changes in the land use. In an earlier analysis of surface data (Nelson 1993a), I concluded that Classic occupation in the Eastern Mimbres area was ephemeral, becoming more residentially stable in the Postclassic pe-

Table 3.2

Classic Mimbres and Postclassic Mimbres sites of different sizes on Palomas Creek drainage (revised from Nelson 1993a)

		NUMBER OF ROOMS ON A SITE				
		1–3	4–6	7–10	11–14	15+
Classic	fo	21	8	3	0	3
	fe	16.1	7	7	2.8	2.1
	X^2	1.49	0.14	2.29	2.80	0.38
Postclassic	fo	2	2	7	4	0
	fe	6.9	3	3	1.2	0.9
	X^2	3.47	0.33	5.33	6.53	0.9

$$N = 50$$
$$X^2 = 23.66$$
$$df = 4$$
$$p < 0.05$$

riod. This conclusion is correct if one looks only at the small sites; most of the Classic sites have one to three rooms, while nearly half of the Postclassic have seven to ten rooms (table 3.2). In addition, excavation shows a shift from special to residential use of the small Palomas hamlets (Nelson 1993b; Nelson and Hegmon 1996; and chap. 4 in this volume). However, I had previously classified one of the largest sites on Palomas Creek as Postclassic. Excavation data from this large site, with mixed ceramic assemblages, has changed my view of the settlement pattern; Classic Mimbres ceramics are not mixed with Chupadero and other later forms in floor and roof contexts on the site. All of the later ceramics are in the top few centimeters of fill. Thus, the site must be reclassified as Classic Mimbres, leaving no sites of more than fifteen rooms in the Postclassic category. In another Black Range drainage to the south, Las Animas Creek, a larger village of sixty to eighty rooms has a mixed surface assemblage that would be classified from the surface as Postclassic; excavation has revealed a Classic Mimbres village abandoned in the mid-1100s and reoccupied in the late 1200s or early 1300s (Hegmon and Nelson 1994; Nelson and Hegmon 1993, 1995). With this reclassification, the Classic Mimbres pattern is of a few large villages and many relatively small sites, while the Postclassic pattern is weighted toward the middle range. Table 3.2 is the revised classification of sites[1] showing the shift toward medium-sized settlements. Classic Mimbres sites are more frequent, but as a group they have fewer structures than do the Postclassic sites.[2] The low-

Table 3.3

Classic Mimbres and Postclassic Mimbres sites of different sizes on the Rio Grande
(revised from Nelson 1993a)

		ROOMS PER SITE						
		1–3	4–6	7–10	11–14	15–35	50	100+	N
Classic	N	8	2	5	1	2	1	1	20
	%	40	10	25	5	10	5	5	
Postclassic	N	2	1	1	2	3	0	0	
	%	22	11	11	22	33	0	0	9

cell chi-square values for large sites in both the Classic and Postclassic samples could be interpreted as a lack of difference or a difference that is the product of the sample size representing each period. But these counts are not *samples* of the sites on Palomas Creek; they are *all* of the architectural sites of these periods on terraces and ridges above the floodplain of the creek. Large sites are present only during the Classic Mimbres period.

The sample from the Rio Grande must be similarly revised from my earlier interpretation (Nelson 1993a), with the advantage of excavation data. Initially, I interpreted the Rio Grande data as showing a shift toward larger sites from Classic to Postclassic. I disagreed with Lekson (1989:62), who suggested that the mixed assemblage sites (assemblage "H" in Mills 1986 classification) were Classic Mimbres with later reoccupation; these are the largest sites, and I had classified them as Postclassic. Recent study of excavation data from one of these large sites led Mayo (1994) to conclude that it is Classic Mimbres.[3] Lekson (1989) suggested that some of the large sites with Classic Mimbres ceramics were reoccupied rather than continuously occupied. Based on these new excavation data from the Rio Grande and the two large villages on Palomas and Las Animas Creeks, I agree with Lekson regarding the large sites with mixed assemblages; they may all be Classic Mimbres. I have reexamined all of the site data for the Rio Grande sites with Classic Mimbres Black-on-white pottery; table 3.3 is the revised classification[4]; the original analysis is reported in Nelson (1993a:table 5). The result of this reanalysis is a pattern on the Rio Grande similar to that on Palomas Creek. The largest sites are Classic Mimbres as are most of the smallest; more than half of the Postclassic sites are in the "medium-size" range from eleven to thirty-five rooms. The data in table 3.3 are too sparse to evaluate statistically, but the pattern is clear; even with the small sample size for the Postclassic, at least one large site should have been found. Examining the largest of the Postclassic sites more closely, we find that among the three sites with fifteen to thirty-five rooms, two have adobe room blocks and only one is stone masonry. The one with stone masonry may be the only site contemporary with the Postclassic sites on Palomas. Those with adobe room blocks may represent a slightly later immigration from the southern Jornada region (see chap. 6).

The difference in Rio Grande and Palomas Creek data is in the size of the largest sites. On the Rio Grande, the largest Classic Mimbres sites have at least fifty rooms, and the medium-sized Postclassic sites are up to thirty-five rooms; on Palomas the large Classic sites have twenty to thirty rooms, and the medium-sized Postclassic are up to twelve rooms. On Palomas Creek, one large site with Classic Mimbres ceramics has about one hundred rooms (including pit structures); the massive masonry room blocks and carbon-painted ceramics probably date to the A.D. 1300s (Lekson 1989:27), although there may be a Classic Mimbres component (see chap. 6).

Survey Results from Other Black Range Drainages

Fifteen other surveys on the eastern slopes of the Black Range have been reported. Three are fairly large areas of one or more side drainages, and two cross all of the side drainages but cover a small area on any one. These five surveys offer sufficient data for comparison to the Palomas and Rio Grande patterns. In addition, ten small surveys have been conducted from which only two sites relevant to this research have been recorded. The majority of sites recorded from these surveys are assignable to the Classic Mimbres period. Most of the sites from both temporal categories are small.

Three large surveys cover limited areas of the side drainages: Lekson's survey of the lower portions of all side drainages, Laumbach's survey of Ojo Caliente on the Alamosa, and Enloe et al. record search and survey of Cuchillo Negro (fig. 3.1). Lekson (1989) reports on reconnaissance survey of the lower 8 to 10 km of the side drainages west of the Rio Grande that drain the Black Range, including lower portions of Alamosa, Cuchillo Negro, Seco, Animas, Percha, Tierra Blanca, and Berrenda Creeks. These segments of side drainages have relatively wide floodplains but are quite dry except when creeks flood during the rainy season. Low terraces and flat ridges adjacent to the main channel were checked for sites. Reconnaissance survey on the side drainages yielded twenty-two sites that have Classic Mimbres ceramics. Associated later ceramics are as

Table 3.4

Classic Mimbres and Postclassic Mimbres sites of different
sizes on the side drainages to the Rio Grande

		ROOMS PER SITE			
		1–3	4–6	7+	N
Classic	N	10	4	3	17
	%	59	23	18	
Postclassic	N	1	2	2	5
	%	20	40	40	

described above for the Palomas and Rio Grande surveys. The sample from
these side drainages is so small that only suggestions about patterns can be
offered (table 3.4). All of the sites are fairly small, which is the same pattern as
found on Palomas Creek. On Palomas, the closest architectural sites to the Rio
Grande are a cluster of four sites about 6 km upstream; the largest of these is a
nine-room Postclassic site. The current coverage in Lekson's survey of side drainages is consistent with Palomas data but offers a limited view of settlement
pattern.

Laumbach (1992) conducted a record search and reconnaissance survey
around Ojo Caliente, at an elevation of 1,198 m (5,900 ft.) to 2,187 m (7,177
ft.), on Alamosa drainage (fig. 3.1). Ojo Caliente is a warm spring that provides
water to Alamosa Creek directly upstream from the box canyon on Alamosa
Creek. The surveyed area includes terraces and ridges overlooking the wide
floodplain of Alamosa Creek above the box. Laumbach reports twenty-four
sites from the reconnaissance survey and records search as having a Classic
Mimbres component. However, some of these sites have no painted ceramics,
so inferences about period of occupation were based on architecture; other sites
have painted ceramics but no architecture. I have included only those architectural sites that have Classic Mimbres Black-on-white in the surface ceramic
assemblage; fifteen of these were recorded. In contrast to the reconnaissance
survey of the lower end of the drainage (Lekson 1989, described earlier), this
sample from the foothills of the Black Range has some large sites, although
most are quite small (table 3.5).

Nearly all of the sites, twelve of fifteen, can be classified as Classic, with
Classic Mimbres Black-on-white, Socorro Black-on-white, Reserve Black-on-
white, Red Mesa Black-on-white, and Puerco or Wingate. One of these sites is

Table 3.5

Classic Mimbres and Postclassic Mimbres sites of different sizes within the Ojo Caliente survey area

		ROOMS PER SITE					
		1–3	4–6	7–10	11–14	15+	N
Classic	N	4	3	2	0	4	13
	%	31	23	15	0	31	
Postclassic	N	0	1	0	0	1	2
	%	0	50	0	0	50	

fairly sizable, with more than forty rooms. Only two sites can be described as Postclassic. One is a six-room pueblo with Mimbres and Tularosa ceramics. The other has three hundred to five hundred rooms and a diverse ceramic assemblage, including Classic Mimbres Black-on-white, St. Johns Polychrome, Wingate Black-on-red, El Paso Polychrome, Chupadero Black-on-white, Tularosa and Reserve Black-on-white, and Socorro Black-on-white. The largest site in the area, this pueblo has the massive architecture of late pueblos; Laumbach argues, on the basis of ceramic associations, that the site was occupied during the period A.D. 1100 to 1200 and is "affiliated with the Cibola branch of the Mogollon rather than the Mimbres branch" (Laumbach 1992:11). It may be either the largest Postclassic settlement in the area or a later Tularosa phase (A.D. 1200s) immigration into the Eastern Mimbres area from the west, with the large Tularosa pueblo constructed over a Classic Mimbres room block (see chap. 6). Three other large Tularosa phase settlements (with 55 rooms, 80 rooms, and 150 rooms), lacking Classic Mimbres ceramics, were recorded by Laumbach in the Ojo Caliente area.

Enloe et al. (1981) report on a Laboratory of Anthropology records search and a limited surface survey on Cuchillo Negro Creek. All of the sites on which architectural remains and Classic Mimbres ceramics were evident occur between 1,750 m and 2,000 m elevation around the historic towns of Winston, Chise, and areas to the east. This area is primarily piñon-juniper woodland dominated by terraces, ridges, and mesas. Two sites with possible architectural remains were reported from the mouth of Cuchillo Negro at the Rio Grande; these are also reported by Lekson, who notes no clear evidence of structures, although he suspects they once existed. Excluding the two sites at the mouth of Cuchillo Negro, twenty sites with Classic Mimbres ceramics are reported. Two

Table 3.6

Classic Mimbres and Postclassic Mimbres sites of different sizes within the Cuchillo Negro survey area

		ROOMS PER SITE						
		1–3	4–6	7–10	11–14	15+	50+	N
Classic	N	9	0	0	0	0	0	9
	%	100	0	0	0	0	0	
Postclassic	N	2	0	0	2	0	4	8
	%	25	0	0	25	0	50	

of these have no record of whether architecture is present, and one is a cave. The remaining seventeen sites are summarized in table 3.6, although estimates of room counts on some sites are not accurate; they are based on sketchy statements about site size.

All of the Classic Mimbres sites are small, with one to three rooms. These sites have Classic Mimbres Black-on-white and Socorro Black-on-white. The Postclassic sites have a range of ceramic wares including Classic Mimbres, Chupadero Black-on-white, Ramos Polychrome, Tularosa Black-on-white, Wingate Black-on-red, St. John's Polychrome, El Paso Bichrome and Polychrome, and Three Rivers Red-on-terra cotta. Among the Postclassic sites, most are large, with eleven or more rooms. The four largest probably have more than fifty rooms each. Laumbach (1991, personal communication) believes that one is a Tularosa phase occupation built over a Classic Mimbres room block of unknown size. The other three also may be Tularosa phase occupations similar to those recorded by Laumbach (1992) in the Ojo Caliente area of Alamosa Creek to the north. Excavation is needed in this area to understand the occupation pattern and the relationship that developed in the late A.D. 1100s and 1200s between the Mimbres and Tularosa areas.

Two surveys cover a broad area but a small portion of the land area on the eastern slopes of the Black Range: the State Land Sample Survey by Laumbach and Kirkpatrick (1983) and the Transmission Line Corridor Survey by Fowler (1989). The State Land Sample Survey covered 2 percent of New Mexico State land in western Sierra County. This area subsumes all of the drainages that flow from the Black Range. Small sampling units were placed in creosote lowlands, grasslands, piñon-juniper foothills, and the ponderosa pine mountain slopes. The Transmission Line Corridor Survey is far more extensive than the area on

Table 3.7

Classic Mimbres and Postclassic Mimbres sites of different sizes within
the State Land and Transmission Line Corridor Survey areas

		ROOMS PER SITE				
		1–3	4–6	7–10	11+	N
Classic	N	12	2	0	0	14
	%	86	14	0	0	
Postclassic	N	1	1	0	2	4
	%	25	25	0	50	

which this study is focused. The transect along the eastern slope of the Black
Range trends north to south, passing through all of the drainages within 5 to 15
km west of the Rio Grande, although at the north end of the area, it parallels
the side drainages, trending east-west between Alamosa and Cuchillo Negro. At
the northern end it passes through the piñon-juniper uplands, but most of the
transect passes through mesquite-covered low terraces and ridges. Both surveys
complement smaller surveys on side drainages with coverage of the same side
drainages but coverage of more-varied land areas, especially off the main
floodplain of each creek.

The State Land survey yielded information on eighteen sites with visible
architectural remains and Classic Mimbres Black-on-white pottery. These are
found in all of the major environmental zones sampled. The only painted ceramic on fourteen of the sites is Classic Mimbres Black-on-white; the other
four sites have Classic Mimbres along with Reserve-Tularosa Black-on-white,
St. Johns Polychrome, El Paso Polychrome, and Playas Red Incised. Most of the
sites are small (table 3.7). The two largest are Postclassic with approximately
twenty-one and eleven masonry rooms. All others have six or fewer rooms. This
survey did not detect the large Mimbres sites but otherwise has results consistent with other surveys; small sites are predominantly Classic and medium-
sized sites are Postclassic.

Seven clusters of sites were recorded from the Transmission Line Corridor
Survey along the eastern slopes of the Black Range: Antelope Canyon, Iron
Mountain, Roque Ramos, Cuchillo-Palomas, Las Animas, Percha–Tierra Blanca,
and Berrenda. Within these clusters, ten architectural sites are identified as
Mimbres. One of these was reported in discussion of the Palomas survey, and
three have no ceramic data. Only six can be included in this analysis. Classic

Mimbres ceramics are found on all of the sites. Other ceramics include Red Mesa Black-on-white, Reserve-Tularosa Black-on-white, and St. John's Bichrome and Polychrome. Five of the sites can be classified as Classic Mimbres and one, which has the St. Johns Polychrome, as Postclassic. All sites are small; those with estimated room counts are one or two rooms. Again, this is consistent with the State Land survey (Laumbach and Kirkpatrick 1983) and with Lekson's (1989) data from the lower portions of the drainages.

Ten small surveys cover limited areas on one or more drainages (Brethauer and Hoyt 1977; Bussey and Naylor 1975; Harkey 1981; Kirkpatrick and Duran 1982; Laumbach 1974, 1980, 1981; Smith 1985; Weyer and Strong 1976). Only two architectural sites with Classic Mimbres ceramics were recorded from these surveys. Laumbach (1980) briefly notes the presence of two habitation sites on Las Animas Creek, one of which may be the large Classic Mimbres component at Las Animas village (Hegmon and Nelson 1994; Nelson and Hegmon 1993, 1995) and both of which may have been included in Lekson's side drainage survey described above.

These additional surveys provide data consistent with those from Palomas but add an additional dimension of the large Tularosa phase site. On upper Cuchillo Negro and Alamosa Creeks a group of large village settlements may be contemporary with the Palomas hamlets. Alternatively, they may represent immigration into the Eastern Mimbres area as the result of new regional relations that were developed by hamlet dwellers with the Tularosa population center to the northwest. The revised range for Tularosa Black-on-white and St. John's Polychrome, beginning after A.D. 1200 (Mills 1986; Reid et al. 1996; Tuggle and Reid 1982), suggests that the Tularosa phase began in this century. If strong regional ties had developed between the dispersed Postclassic population in the Eastern Mimbres and the village centers to the northwest by A.D. 1200, immigration and the development of local village centers are reasonable consequences. Until further data on the large sites in the Cuchillo Negro and Alamosa drainages are available, I favor the view that these settlements developed as a result of new, Postclassic regional ties established by those who remained in the Eastern Mimbres region after Classic Mimbres villages were abandoned. The hamlet sites are clearly residential (as described in chap. 4) and were continuously occupied through the twelfth and into the thirteenth centuries, representing a local continuity. The ties to the northwest are a Postclassic phenomenon in the Eastern Mimbres.

Site distribution is difficult to evaluate except on the Rio Grande and Palomas drainages, and even on the Rio Grande, reconnaissance data do not provide a full picture of occupation. In addition, development, looting, and collecting cause archaeologists to record only a part of the original archaeological record and to misclassify sites. Site distribution on Palomas is discussed in chapter 6, where questions of intravalley social relationships are evaluated. Similarly, the distribution of Rio Grande sites is discussed as part of the regional analysis of social networks, also in chapter 6. Both are discussed in the context of the broader area of southwestern New Mexico.

Discussion

Survey data have limited application in understanding occupational history in a region but can be used to identify patterns of change that can be more fully evaluated through excavation. In the Eastern Mimbres region, east of the crest of the Black Range, surface evidence is abundant for prehistoric occupation during the Classic Mimbres period and immediately after. The abandonment of large Mimbres pueblos throughout the Mimbres region in the mid-1100s would have had consequences for those who continued to use or occupy the region. Analysis of the occupational history of the Eastern Mimbres area during this period can contribute to understanding the reorganization that occurred and the strategies of small-scale social groups in using arid lands.

Surface survey data indicate the Classic pattern of a few large village centers supplemented by many small sites (1 to 3 rooms). The small sites may be special-use locales or small settlements. Excavation data to be discussed in chapters 4 and 5 support the former interpretation. The Postclassic sites appear to be primarily "medium-sized" (7 to 25 rooms), a change that excavation data demonstrate was a shift toward more residential use of previously occupied Classic Mimbres farming camps. A few large sites are difficult to place temporally. Some on the Rio Grande and Las Animas Creek are large Classic Mimbres villages with much later reoccupations. A few on upper Cuchillo Negro and Alamosa Creeks appear to be Tularosa phase occupations (A.D. 1200s) overlaying Classic Mimbres sites. None is a convincing Postclassic village center, although further research may reveal that the small Postclassic, residential hamlets were contemporary with large settlements. Currently, the Postclassic pattern appears to be dispersed occupation in medium-sized pueblos.

Evaluation of these ideas about use of the Eastern Mimbres region, both patterns of change and variation, require excavation data. None of the sites along the Rio Grande have been systematically excavated. On Palomas drainage, six Postclassic hamlets have been partially excavated, and the data from four of these sites can be used to evaluate the patterns and processes of Mimbres reorganization in the twelfth century.

Along the drainage channels that flow from the slopes of the Black Range to the Rio Grande are patches of permanent surface water flow attributable both to the uplift of impermeable geological formations, which force water to the surface, and to the presence of springs and seeps. (These features are closely related in the study area.) As with nearly all of the architectural sites in Palomas drainage, the four excavated Postclassic sites included in this study are located on low terraces above the floodplain of the main drainage. The Rio Grande is about 11 to 32 km to the east (downstream), and the peaks of the Black Range are about 29 to 50 km to the west. Three of the sites are in the lower portion of Palomas drainage—Buckaroo, Lee, and Ronnie; the fourth, Phelps, is in the middle portion of the drainage and is one of three excavated sites in that area. Some data from the other two are available for dating and land-use analyses discussed in chapters 4 and 5, but only Phelps is discussed in detail because work at the other sites is ongoing (Hegmon and Nelson 1994; Nelson and Hegmon 1993, 1995). Phelps and the other two sites are about 16 to 21 km upstream from the three sites in the lower reaches of Palomas Creek.

These sites were selected for this study because they have ceramic assemblages produced before and after A.D. 1150, the accepted reference date for Classic Mimbres village abandonment (table 3.8). The four excavated sites provide detailed information on the nature of organizational changes in site occupation (chap. 4), economic strategies (chap. 5), and social interaction (chap. 6).

Buckaroo Site (LA70259, field number 85NM613)

From the surface the Buckaroo site appears as a cobble masonry pueblo of from eleven to twelve rooms with two or three pit structures to the north and west (fig. 3.2). The area of surface scatter is approximately 4,000 m², while the area of masonry architecture is approximately 320 m². The masonry is substantial, indicating full-height stone walls; the rooms, which are well outlined by the stone rubble, appear similar in size, with two exceptions. Surface ceramics are dominated by plainwares, as is common throughout the study area on sites of all periods. Among the painted ceramics on the site surface, Classic Mimbres Black-on-white, Style III, is the dominant type, with a few rare occurrences of Chupadero Black-on-white. Classic Mimbres has been firmly assigned a beginning date of A.D. 1000 and an end date in the Mimbres Valley of A.D. 1130 to 1150 (Anyon, Gilman, and LeBlanc 1981; Shafer 1990). Chupadero is generally believed to date between A.D. 1150 and 1400, and to have been made

Table 3.8

Postclassic Mimbres sites and their associated ceramics within the study area

Field No.	LA No.	No. Rooms	Rmblks.	Classic	Chup B/w	El Paso Pt	Wt Mt Red	Playas	Tula Fil	R/T B/w	R/T Corr
226	44997	9	1	X	X				X	X	
273	45028	5	2	X	X						
2	37691	7	2	X	X	(X)	X	X	X	(X)	(X)
44	37728	7	1	X	X	X	X	X	X	(X)	(X)
40	37726	12	2	X	(X)	X	X	X	X	X	(X)
43	37727	12	1	X		(X)	X	(X)	X	X	(X)
77	37763	9	1	X			X		X		X
294	45046	8	1	X	X	X	X				
400	45103	7	2	X	X	(X)	(X)		X	(X)	(X)
460	45158	11	4	X	X	X	X		X		
610	70256	2	1	X	X				X		
612	70258	4	1	X	X		X		X		(X)
613	70259	12	1	X	X	(X)			X	(X)	X
621	70265	2	1	X							
617	70263	9	2	X			X				

Notes:

(X)   = Ceramic types found only through excavation.

Field No.   = Site number assigned in the field.

LA No.   = Site number assigned by the Laboratory of Anthropology, New Mexico State Museum.

No. Rooms = Number of rooms visible on the surface of site.

Rmblks   = Number of room blocks visible on the surface of site.

Classic   = Classic Mimbres Black-on-white (III)

Chup B/w   = Chupadero Black-on-white

El Paso Pt   = El Paso Painted

Wt Mt Red = White Mountain redwares

Playas   = Playas Red

Tula Fil   = Tularosa Fillet Rim

R/T B/w   = Reserve/Tularosa Black-on-white

R/T Corr   = Reserve/Tularosa Textured Corrugated Wares (except Tularosa Fillet Rim)

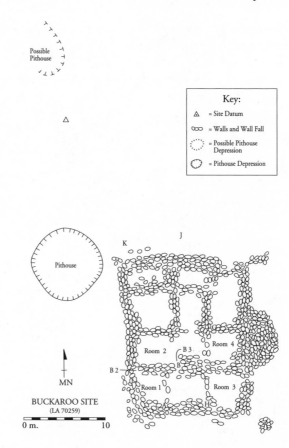

Figure 3.2

Site plan for the Buckaroo Site (LA70259). Excavated rooms are numbered. Datum points are lettered.

mostly to the east of the study area (Breternitz 1966:72), although it is widely distributed. Based on surface evidence, the Buckaroo Site was initially interpreted as a single occupation, small, Classic Mimbres residential site, with perhaps an earlier pithouse period occupation and some ephemeral use after A.D. 1150. Excavation yielded a more complex picture of the history of site occupation, with three or four different kinds of occupation beginning at least by the A.D. 900s (possibly as early as the A.D. 300s) and ending possibly as late as the early 1300s. This range spans the growth and abandonment of large Classic Mimbres villages. Excavation has been conducted in four of the surface rooms of the final occupation, in one earlier surface structure, and in three pit structures.

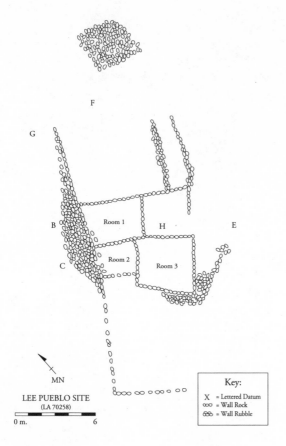

Figure 3.3

Site plan for Lee Pueblo (LA70258). Excavated rooms are numbered.

Lee Pueblo (LA70258, field number 85NM612)

Lee pueblo has several small room blocks, pithouse depressions, and rock clusters visible on the surface. Four cobble room blocks, four isolated cobble rooms, and five pithouse depressions were noted during the surface survey. The largest room block does not exceed 90 m² and was estimated to contain seven rooms (fig. 3.3). The artifact scatter, however, extends over an area of 75,000 m². All of the rooms appear to be small, much smaller than those on the Ronnie and Buckaroo sites. Enough surface rubble is evident to indicate that some of the walls were full-height masonry. Painted ceramics are extremely rare on the site, but Classic Mimbres Black-on-white Style III, Chupadero Black-on-white, and St. John's Polychrome were found in small numbers. The latter two types are traditionally thought not to overlap the temporal range of Classic Mimbres

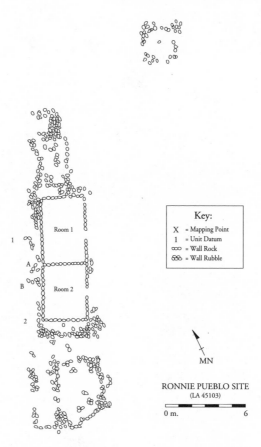

Figure 3.4

Site plan for Ronnie Pueblo (LA45103). Excavated rooms are numbered.

Black-on-white styles. Thus, the site was originally recorded as Classic Mimbres with later reoccupation. The area around the largest room block, designated "Area B" during preliminary surface reconnaissance, was the focus of excavation. Excavation of three rooms and a limited amount of area immediately outside the room block yielded evidence of occupation beginning sometime in the 800s, with final use possibly as late as the 1300s.

Ronnie Pueblo (LA45103, field number 83NM400)

Surface evidence on Ronnie Pueblo is less substantial than at the Buckaroo site. A mounded room block area of five to six rooms is covered by large and small cobbles (fig. 3.4). To the northeast of the room block is one cobble room. The area of the room block is 324 m², while surface scatter extends over an area of

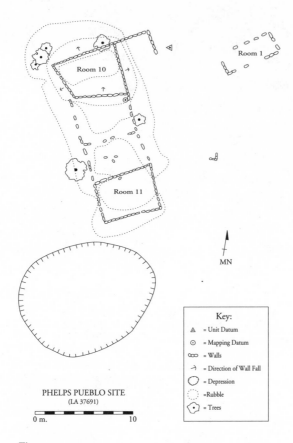

Figure 3.5

Site plan for Phelps Pueblo (LA37691). Excavated rooms are numbered.

approximately 3,000 m². The masonry is not substantial enough on the surface to indicate full-height cobble walls, but the mounding suggests substantial construction. Room dimensions were difficult to determine from surface rubble, but the rooms appeared to be larger than any others excavated on Palomas. Surface ceramics are dominated by plainwares with a few pieces of Classic Mimbres Black-on-white Style III and Chupadero Black-on-white, indicating an occupation beginning sometime in the 1000s or 1100s. As noted above, Mimbres Black-on-white Style III and Chupadero Black-on-white are traditionally assumed not to have overlapping temporal ranges, although they occur together on the surfaces of many sites. This surface evidence indicates that the site is appropriate for investigation of the transition from Classic to Postclassic land-use patterns.

Excavation of two rooms in the room block yielded information on the apparent contemporaneity of the ceramics and on the occupation history of the site. Classic Mimbres bowls and a Chupadero jar were found associated near the floor of one of the rooms. The construction of this room is dated to the early 1000s, with a possible abandonment date in the 1200s.

Phelps Site (LA37691, field number 82NM002)

The Phelps site is located on the second terrace and consists of two room blocks, two pithouse depressions, and a large ceramic and lithic scatter (fig. 3.5). The larger room block is visible on the surface as a mound of cobbles, indicating full-height masonry construction that includes five to six rooms. The smaller room block, with two rooms, has less cobble debris and does not appear to be constructed with full-height masonry walls. The surface area of the large room block is 180 m², indicating that the rooms may be quite large, as they are on the Buckaroo and Ronnie sites. The scatter is estimated at 13,000 m², larger than the Buckaroo and Ronnie sites. Painted ceramics on the surface of the site include Mimbres Black-on-white wares, Chupadero Black-on-white, and St. Johns Polychrome as at Lee Pueblo.

Three rooms were excavated, yielding a limited amount of information that indicates possible contemporaneity among the ceramics. The occupation is dated as within the range of the early 1000s to the late 1200s.

Occupational Histories of Four Postclassic Hamlets

4

From the moderate-sized Postclassic sites along Palomas drainage come the data that provide an understanding of Mimbres reorganization. The surface ceramics of the sites indicate occupation both before and after the mid-century depopulation of large villages. How these sites were occupied through this period provides the basis for examining how people in the Eastern Mimbres region moved and reorganized their lives. To answer the larger questions about the region, questions about site-level data need to be answered, because fine-grained information derived from excavation is the basis for examining reorganization and continuity. We must know whether the use of the sites was continuous, how site use changed over time, and how households were reorganized in the process. All of these questions require information on the timing of construction, remodeling, and abandonment. Toward these ends, I analyze the occupational history of the four sites that were introduced at the end of the previous chapter. Chronometric and relative dating procedures are applied to examine timing; architectural and artifactual details are employed to assess the continuity and organization of site occupation.

The four sites that form the excavated data on Mimbres reorganization are stone masonry room blocks, with rooms arranged in linear or square fashion. The sites range in final size from about six to twelve rooms. While two sites have more than one room block, the second block is small (1 or 2 rooms). Within each excavated room block, at least 25 percent of the rooms were excavated. This sample represents a sizable portion of each site but is relatively small with respect to the total number of rooms for a site. The location and number of excavated rooms are indicated on the site maps (figs. 3.2–3.5).

The earliest surface architecture at three of the four sites is Classic Mimbres. These structures are primarily ephemeral, made either as tri-walled stone structures or with lighter construction materials (jacal). A few rooms are more substantial. The Classic period rooms form the initial construction from which the small pueblos grew. I first describe the pueblos and the probable range of dates within which their occupation may be placed. My purpose is to establish the general time frame for occupation of these sites. I then dissect the information from the sites to examine the nature of the earliest occupation, evidence for occupational continuity from the early structures to the later, larger pueblo room blocks, and shifts in the nature of site use. These analyses form the sections that follow the general description of the sites and their occupation ranges. First, however, I describe the analytic procedures used for all of the analyses of the sites and their occupational histories.

Analytic Procedures

Analyzing the occupational histories of sites requires placing them into the most probable time range as well as determining the meaning of changes in architectural form and the composition of artifact assemblages. In the Southwest, dating the construction, use, and abandonment of structures can be accomplished fairly easily because of the successes of dendrochronology (e.g., Lightfoot 1994; Schlanger and Wilshusen 1993). However, in southwestern New Mexico, dendrochronology has had limited application, primarily because the datable species were not commonly used for construction and firewood. In the study area, not a single wood sample could be dated by the Tree Ring Laboratory at University of Arizona, Tucson. Thus, less precise procedures for chronometric dating were employed. The plan devised for dating sites and the parameters of each technique are described in the following pages. Occupational histories can be interpreted from the changes evident in architectural features and artifact forms. The basis for these analyses is discussed following the dating procedures.

Procedures for Chronometric and Relative Dating

The concern of this analysis is to place in time the construction, use, and abandonment of surface architecture; any earlier semisubterranean structures are not dated, although their presence impacts the analysis, which is noted. The earliest ceramics associated with surface architecture in the Mimbres region are Mimbres Classic Black-on-white, Style III, initial appearance of which has been dated to about A.D. 1000. [Lekson (1990b) argues that Style II, which is slightly earlier, is found with surface architecture in the western portion of the Mimbres region, along the Gila River drainage.] Based on this ceramic association, the earliest Mimbres stone masonry architecture is understood to have appeared at about A.D. 1000. The end point of the sequence cannot be determined from ceramic associations. Painted wares made well into the 1400s occur on the sites, although these wares also were made centuries earlier. The sites were not occupied for four hundred years, as discussed below, but determining the date of final abandonment is difficult.

The dating program designed for the Eastern Mimbres has two goals with respect to the occupation of surface structures. First, a probable temporal range must be determined for the earliest surface architectural components on the excavated sites; at issue is whether they were contemporary with large, nucleated Classic Mimbres villages in the region, A.D. 1000 to 1150. Radiocarbon and obsidian hydration data have been examined and recorded here from the early floors as were ceramic data from the early structures. Second, a probable range must be determined that encompasses the occupational history of each site, and an effort has been made to determine whether the use of each site was continuous through the twelfth century, at least. Toward these ends, grouped distributions of age ranges from radiocarbon and obsidian hydration samples are examined. Occupational continuity is also determined through analysis of architecture (see methods that follow). The dating, thus, provides a baseline for investigating the processes of economic and social reorganization, which are explored in subsequent chapters. They are most useful in setting ranges and evaluating occupational continuity and least useful for dating specific structures.

Chronometric dating techniques have varied application to archaeological deposits, depending on the kind of samples dated, the context of the sample, and the dating procedure. Age determinations on roof timbers, for example, should indicate construction and renovation of structures. Those on hearth wood might identify the timing of final occupation, as would age assessments of small obsidian artifacts on the floors of structures. Room abandonment is estimated by dating the timing of room burning (archaeomagnetic dating of walls), if the abandonment can be associated with the burning event. Thus, the archaeological context and inferred systemic context of items are crucial for interpreting how each age determination contributes to understanding the occupational history of each site (see Schiffer 1972).

Radiocarbon samples, obsidian hydration samples, tree-ring samples, and archaeomagnetic samples were submitted for analysis. All but the tree-ring samples, as noted above, yielded age determinations. From the age values, it is theoretically possible to suggest a time range within which structures were most likely constructed and abandoned. The actual dates are not especially precise because of the nature of the random error inherent in radiocarbon and obsidian hydration dating. A computer program, designed by Keith Kintigh (1994) is used to construct probability distributions for site occupations by combining multiple age ranges from similar contexts. The results of this analysis are also used to evaluate whether occupational continuity of sites is likely from initial construction prior to A.D. 1150 to abandonment after A.D. 1150. Most of the information about the timing of construction, occupation, and abandonment of the sites is from the final occupations, which are the largest, most substantial, and least affected by scavenging. They are also the structures from which most of the datable samples were recovered, because many were burned.

Radiocarbon Dating. Construction dates are derived from radiocarbon assessments of roof timbers, posts, and reeds used in roof construction; occupation dates are from hearth wood and maize associated with the occupation of structures. Some construction and hearth wood may have been scavenged from earlier structures on the same sites, or on other nearby sites, or stockpiled before use, leading to earlier values than apply to actual construction and occupation (Schiffer 1982). Some maize may have been tossed into abandoned structures and have an age range later than the actual occupation. These effects are evaluated for the dates presented.

A more difficult problem is the actual evaluation of probability distributions of radiocarbon ages. The radiocarbon ages, expressed with symmetrical standard error values, were determined by two different laboratories, Beta Analytic and University of Arizona Laboratory of Isotope Geochemistry (table 4.1). Dates from maize, which exhibits delta C13 values, were adjusted by the radiocarbon laboratory (see discussion in Taylor 1987:48, 95–102). Radiocarbon age determinations were calibrated using the dendrochronological calibration curves derived by Stuiver and Becker (1986) and Stuiver and Pearson (1986), among others (see Watkins 1975 for discussion of calibration). Calibrated ages were reported for some of the Beta Analytic samples by Buekens of the IsoTrace Radiocarbon Laboratory, Accelerator Mass Spectrometry Facility at the University of Toronto, and for others by Long of the Laboratory of Isotope Geochemistry, University of Arizona. The calibrated ages, expressed in years A.D. have nonsymmetrical standard errors reported as means and one sigma ranges (see table 4.1). For some of the samples, the one sigma range on uncalibrated and

Table 4.1

Radiocarbon samples, contexts, and dates from sites in the study area

SAMPLE	SITE	ROOM	CONTEXT	C14 AGE	SD	TYPE	CAL MEAN	1SD LOWER	1SD UPPER
42837	Buckaroo	1	floor	720	60	wood	1298	1272	1303
42839	Buckaroo	1	lower floor	1030	60	ewood	1014	978	1032
42840	Buckaroo	2	fill above floor	600	60	wood	1316 48 89	1287	1407
42841	Buckaroo	2	hearth	680	60	hwood	1283	1270	1305
6655	Buckaroo	3	roof	605	30	reed	1324 57 89	1300	1394
6651	Buckaroo	3	roof	835	35	owood	1214	1162	1275
6652	Buckaroo	3	fill above floor	880	40	wood	1161 85	1042	1214
6653	Buckaroo	3	fill above floor	845	40	wood	1210	1158	1256
6656	Buckaroo	3	fill above floor	485	60	reed	1434	1408	1451
6640	Buckaroo	4	roof	1035	65	owood	996	904	1026
6639.2	Buckaroo	4	roof	1025	55	owood	998	980	1026
6638.2	Buckaroo	4	roof	930	45	owood	1040 95	1023	1160
6637	Buckaroo	4	hearth	670	50	hwood	1283	1278	1387
6641	Buckaroo	4	roof	685	70	reed	1282	1263	1388
42838	Buckaroo	1	floor	740	60	maize	1270	1244	1283
6654	Buckaroo	3	roof	585	30	maize	1329 48 92	1315	1407
6648	Ronnie	2	roof	800	50	wood	1230 43 56	1193	1276
6649.1	Ronnie	2	roof	1040	40	owood	995	980	1020
6650	Ronnie	2	roof	1020	50	owood	999	982	1026

SAMPLE	SITE	ROOM	CONTEXT	C14 AGE	SD	TYPE	CAL MEAN	1SD LOWER	1SD UPPER
6645	Ronnie	2	roof	1080	40	reed	981	897	996
7263	Ronnie	2	storage pit	1065	80	wood	993	892	1027
7262	Ronnie	2	floor	1180	85	wood	883	774	976
6646	Ronnie	2	roof	1100	60	maize	973	888	1011
6644	Lee	1	fill	560	30	wood	1134 1138 1403	1326 1390	1351 1414
6643	Lee	3	floor	1240	60	reed	782	689	883
8205	Lizard U	30	roof	565	75	wood	1410	1306 1384	1356 1432
8207	Lizard U	30	roof	1030	80	maize	1013	892	1158
8210	Lizard U	30	roof	0	0	maize	0	0	0
8209	Lizard U	30	roof	815	35	reed	1230	1221	1271
8250	Lizard L	10	fill between floors	760	35	ereed	1281	1253	1292
8325	Lizard L	10	lower floor posthole	725	35	ewood	1290	1271	1300
8246	Lizard L	10	roof	695	155	lwood	1294	1218	1410
8247	Lizard L	10	roof	595	195	lwood	1397	1262	1473
8249	Lizard L	10	hearth	820	305	lwood	1229	897	1423
8310	Mt Lion	1	fill between floors	840	95	jacal	1225	1054 1122	1082 1283
8063	Mt Lion	1	lower floor posthole	715	40	maize	1290	1275 1360	1304 1380
8059	Mt Lion	1	fill above floor	745	155	maize	1280	1060 1160	1070 1400
8060	Mt Lion	1	fill above floor	610	65	maize	1320 55 80	1302 1378	1364 1402
8061	Mt Lion	1	fill above floor	710	90	maize	1290	1241 1342	1318 1394
8062	Mt Lion	1	lower floor posthole	810	235	jacal	1245	1010	1400
8064	Mt Lion	1	lower floor posthole	750	215	jacal	1285	1040 1110	1100 1410

Table 4.1 continued

SAMPLE	SITE	ROOM	CONTEXT	C14 AGE	SD	TYPE	CAL MEAN	1SD LOWER	1SD UPPER
8123	Mt Lion	1	roof	850	60	lwood	1220	1072	1286
8124	Mt Lion	1	roof	785	45	maize	1280	1232	1410
8125	Mt Lion	1	roof	890	115	lwood	1170	1030	
8126	Mt Lion	1	lower floor hearth	880	50	ewood	1170	1048 1118	1310 1375
8127	Mt Lion	1	lower floor hearth	825	80	ewood	1225	1066 1128	1310 1385
113672	Phelps	10	posthole	610	60	wood	1325 40 90	1300	1405
113673	Phelps	10	warming pit	690	50	hwood	1295	1280 1365	1310 1375
113674	Phelps	10	in floor	680	50	wood	1295	1285 1355	1435
113675	Phelps	10	fill between floors	1100	120	ewood	975	800	1030
113676	Phelps	11	floor	630	60	maize	1310 55 85	1295	
113677	Phelps	11	floor	530	50	maize	1420	1400	
113678	Phelps	11	posthole	690	50	wood	1295	1280 1365	

Notes:

All mean calibrated ages are A.D.

Within the category "type": owood = outer ring

ewood = wood from a structure beneath another

hwood = wood from a hearth

lwood = wood from a late construction event

Multiple entries for "1sd lower" indicate the beginning points of different ranges on the calibration curve; similarly, multiple entries for "1sd upper" indicate multiple ending points.

calibrated ages is quite narrow, as low as forty-four years in one case of a calibrated age. For others, the radiocarbon age, when calibrated, yielded multiple solutions from the calibration curve and a very broad one sigma range, as high as 390 years. Some of these less precise ranges are useful for analysis because they identify a general time frame before and after which the events of concern are unlikely to have occurred, although this range is so broad in some cases that it is not useful.

The samples vary in interpretive potential as well. Those with least potential are small pieces with multiple growth rings. For these samples, the average of the life of the wood is being dated, and the relationship of the piece to the life history of the tree is unknown (Taylor 1987). Samples of outer rings from construction wood offer better interpretive potential because the age determination may more closely approximate the time of cutting of the tree (Aiken 1990:90–91; Taylor 1987:45). Best are the samples of annuals, reeds and maize, that have been dated. These have only one growth year (Taylor 1987:46–48). The type of sample is identified in table 4.1.

The contexts of samples vary in quality. Some of the rooms were substantially burned, thereby preserving sections of roof and segments of posts. These samples can be identified most confidently as construction material. Most reeds were taken from such contexts. Maize samples from the floors of structures offer a fairly good context for dating final occupation, if they are de facto refuse left behind by structure occupants. Some of the wood samples, however, were taken from contexts that are less easily interpreted. The wood samples from hearths were in contexts that also contained burned roof material; thus, the samples may derive from roof material that fell onto the hearth when it burned or from wood actually used in the hearth for cooking and heating. Most construction samples are at least from contexts in which roof adobe dominates the soil matrix. Most samples from which occupation dates are inferred are from roof or floor contexts. The type of context is identified in table 4.1.

Thus, the radiocarbon samples most clearly attributable to the timing of construction of structures are those from reeds or outer rings of construction wood, in preserved sections of roof or in situ posts, from which calibrated radiocarbon ages with narrow standard error ranges have been determined. Those that best date the final occupation of structures are maize samples from the floors of the structures that also have yielded calibrated radiocarbon ages with narrow standard-error ranges. This complex set of criteria makes interpretation of radiocarbon ages difficult but not impossible. Most dates do not meet all of the best characteristics for clear interpretation, but multiple dates from the same contexts and dates derived from other analyses contribute to the interpretive potential of dated samples.

Radiocarbon age determinations with standard error of one sigma, and mean calibrated ages and one sigma ranges are presented in table 4.1. Samples from all four sites (Phelps, Buckaroo, Lee, and Ronnie pueblos) were submitted for radiocarbon assessment. Preliminary information also is available from two ceramically and architecturally comparable sites, Lizard Terrace Pueblo and Mountain Lion Hamlet, which are in the middle portion of Palomas drainage.

Obsidian Hydration. Hydration measurements and age assessments were made on obsidian artifacts. Christopher Stevenson of Diffusion Laboratories (1993) analyzed the samples and determined the chronometric age of each piece using information on its geological origin (Stevenson and Klimkiewicz 1990), water content, thickness of the hydration rim (Scheetz and Stevenson 1988), hydration rates simulated at elevated temperatures or predicted from equations (Mazer, Stevenson, and Bates 1991), and soil temperature and relative humidity in the deposits from which the artifacts were recovered (Lynch and Stevenson 1992; Mazer, Stevenson, and Bates 1991). Simulated hydration rates are experimental and may be altered in the future, resulting in reassessment of chronometric ages. Nevertheless, the relationship between the ages of the pieces should remain the same.

Obsidian dates are interpreted as information about the occupation of sites. Many obsidian samples were recovered on or near the floors of structures. These may have been discarded at any time during the use of each room; they are small and could easily have become embedded in floors or swept into corners. Some of the obsidian may be de facto trash from the final occupation of the structures. If the samples are deposited over the life of the structure, the range of dates may be fairly broad; if they are only from the final occupation, the range may be fairly narrow. Obsidian, however, may have been scavenged from earlier deposits on any sites in the area. Obsidian does not occur locally, so obtaining it from its source rather than from the discards of earlier occupants in the area would have had an added cost. Scavenging may be indicated by some of the extremely early ages of samples.

Some obsidian samples were taken from the roof contexts and from the fill of structures to supplement the samples from floor deposits. Interpretation of their contexts is less clear; they are used primarily in grouped form when generally discussing the time frame of site occupation.

Obsidian hydration samples were submitted from five sites: Phelps Site, Lizard Terrace Pueblo, and Mountain Lion Hamlet in the middle Palomas cluster, as well as Lee Pueblo and Buckaroo Site in the lower Palomas cluster (fig. 1.2). Hydration dates and their contexts are presented in table 4.2.

Archaeomagnetic Dating. Archaeomagnetic samples were submitted to aid in determining the dates of occupation and abandonment of the Buckaroo, Ronnie, Lee, and Phelps sites. These sites had some severely burned rooms, with adobe features scorched by the fires. The Lee and Phelps sites had adobe collared features substantial enough to be sampled. None of the assessments provided ranges narrow enough to be of much use in discussing either occupation or abandonment. This is attributable to the nature of the samples and to the magnetic pattern within the occupation spans of the sites.

Archaeomagnetic samples are extremely difficult to collect from the excavated sites. Adobe features include wall segments, hearths, and mealing bowl holders. The quality of adobe is poor in that sand content is relatively high, with some small pebbles. Thus, the adobe is not homogeneous and is extensively cracked. Samples are difficult to cut around sand and pebble intrusions and around cracks. The number of samples submitted from each feature ranged from six to nine. Possible movement of sampling loci further affects the precision of the results from this technique. The samples from burned walls could have shifted with the deterioration of the structures. One sample from the Phelps site yielded a result that does not coincide with any portion of the curve for the North American Southwest. It is from a wall segment that apparently shifted as the roof collapsed onto the floor.

The pattern of magnetic polar change over the 1000s to 1400s further confounds precise archaeomagnetic dating. Movement is slight and follows a pattern of backtracking on itself, beginning at about A.D. 1125.

Samples from two wall segments and three collared floor features were submitted for analysis. The results from only one sample were useful for this research; for others, the age ranges were too broad.

Ceramic Cross-dating. Ceramic data potentially offer the least precise but most abundant information relevant to the construction, occupation, and abandonment of sites. Sherds found as wall chinking may help to establish the range of time during which structures were constructed. Those from in situ assemblages on room floors may help to identify the range of time during which structures were occupied, while sherds in postoccupation fill may identify the time period before which abandonment must have occurred. In the data presented from the six sites, some unexpected associations of ceramics occur. The archaeological

Table 4.2

Obsidian hydration samples, contexts, and dates from sites in the study area

Sample #	Site	Room #	Context	Mean Age	S.D.
DL96218	Phelps	11	fill	1419	57
DL96219	Phelps	11	roof	1683	42
DL96220	Phelps	11	roof	1432	57
DL96222	Phelps	10	roof	1560	53
DL96223	Phelps	10	roof	1275	72
DL91126	Buckaroo	1	floor	1205	72
DL91124	Buckaroo	1	fill between floors	974	82
DL91125	Buckaroo	1	fill between floors	917	85
DL91117	Buckaroo	2	floor	788	89
DL91118	Buckaroo	2	floor	1236	71
DL92435	Buckaroo	3	roof	925	84
DL92436	Buckaroo	3	roof	1283	68
DL92437	Buckaroo	3	floor	1256	69
DL92438	Buckaroo	3	floor	1263	69
DL92439	Buckaroo	4	roof	1283	68
DL91119	Buckaroo	pithouse 2	fill	892	86
DL91120	Buckaroo	pithouse 2	fill	331	105
DL91122	Buckaroo	1	fill between floors	950	84
DL91123	Buckaroo	1	fill between floors	900	85
DL92440	Buckaroo	pithouse 4	fill	900	85
DL92428	Lee	1	beneath floor	863	91
DL92429	Lee	2	fill	1357	68
DL92430	Lee	3	roof	1274	73
DL92431	Lee	3	floor	1323	69
DL92432	Lee	3	floor	1155	57
DL92433	Lee	3	floor	1021	61
DL92434	Lee	3	beneath floor	840	92
DL96175	Lizard-L	1	fill	1156	71
DL96176	Lizard-L	1	fill	1242	65
DL96177	Lizard-L	1	fill	1218	69
DL96178	Lizard-L	10	hearth	1256	70
DL96179	Lizard-L	19	roof	1135	76
DL96224	Lizard-L	19	fill	1382	58
DL96225	Lizard-L	19	fill	1406	58
DL96227	Lizard-L	19	fill	686	87
DL96228	Lizard-L	19	fill	671	91
DL96180	Lizard-L	19	fill between floors	827	63
DL96181	Lizard-L	21	floor	1044	79

Sample #	Site	Room #	Context	Mean age	S.D.
DL96182	Lizard-L	21	floor	462	104
DL96183	Lizard-L	21	floor	1137	79
DL96184	Lizard-L	21	floor	1236	70
DL96186	Lizard-L	21	floor	1149	79
DL96188	Lizard-L	21	floor	536 BC	130
DL96229	Lizard-L	21	roof	1411	61
DL96230	Lizard-L	21	roof	1501	57
DL96231	Lizard-L	21	roof	1538	56
DL96232	Lizard-L	21	roof	44	118
DL96233	Lizard-L	21	roof	1108	76
DL96234	Lizard-L	21	roof	1349	67
DL96235	Lizard-L	21	roof	1346	67
DL96236	Lizard-L	21	roof	1344	70
DL96237	Lizard-L	21	roof	925	87
DL96238	Lizard-L	21	roof	486	106
DL96239	Lizard-L	21	roof	1473	62
DL96240	Lizard-L	21	roof	15 BC	117
DL96241	Lizard-L	21	roof	1038	83
DL96217	Lizard-U	32	fill	1304	66
DL96216	Lizard-U	32	fill	1400	61
DL96215	Lizard-U	32	roof	1404	62
DL96214	Lizard-U	32	roof	1277	73
DL96190	Lizard-U	32	floor	1578	54
DL96192	Lizard-U	32	floor	1559	55
DL96193	Lizard-U	32	subfloor	1123	75
DL96211	Lizard-U	32	subfloor	687	93
DL96212	Lizard-U	32	subfloor	1726 BC	163
DL96204	Mt. Lion	1	mixed	1103 BC	74
DL96205	Mt. Lion	1	mixed	691	88
DL96203	Mt. Lion	1	fill	1049	80
DL96194	Mt. Lion	1	roof	1337 BC	84
DL96195	Mt. Liom	1	floor	1119	76
DL96196	Mt. Lion	1	floor	1496	60
DL96206	Mt. Lion	2	fill	893	79
DL96207	Mt. Lion	2	fill	1396	60
DL96208	Mt. Lion	2	fill	178	102
DL96209	Mt. Lion	2	floor	1051	77
DL96210	Mt. Lion	2	floor	1533	23
DL96198	Mt. Lion	2	floor	887	38

Note: Mean ages are A.D. unless otherwise indicated.

and systemic contexts of these associations are discussed and reference is made to related chronometric information.

In the ceramic assemblages from the surfaces of all sites, painted ceramics are rare. The painted ware component was dominated by Classic Mimbres Black-on-white, indicating construction and occupation within the period A.D. 1000–1150. Within each of the surface assemblages are later ceramics, suggesting site use after A.D. 1150. The specific ceramic types and dates assigned to those ceramics in other regions are presented in table 3.1, as introduced in chapter 3.

Ceramic data from fill, roof fall, floors, and between floor levels are discussed. Nearly all rooms, whether burned or not, collapsed roof first, followed by the walls. Some wall material is mixed with roof material at the upper roof-fall levels. All of the rooms that form the masonry room blocks appear to have been filled by natural processes of sheet wash and room decay.

Procedures for Analysis of the Nature of Occupation

This history of changing site use focuses on the function and regularity of structure use. Architectural and artifactual information is analyzed to determine (1) whether the structures were modified to accommodate different and/or more intensive uses; (2) whether their use continued throughout the history of the surface architectural portion of the sites, either actively through occupation on the site or passively through maintenance and regular reoccupation; and (3) the pattern of growth and abandonment of the pueblos.

Room function is inferred primarily from the presence of fixed features. In addition, artifact assemblages and construction data are considered in identifying room use. Longevity, regularity, and continuity of room use are evaluated from the construction characteristics of rooms, their condition when abandoned (roofs, walls, floors), and the condition and types of fixed furniture. Investment in architecture has been correlated with the length of time over which use of a structure was intended (Binford 1990; Diehl 1992; Horne 1993; McGuire and Schiffer 1983). All of the structures examined in this study were constructed of stone, adobe, or jacal with adobe plastered floors. Most have flat roofs that could have served as activity surfaces. However, the structures vary in how substantially the walls, floors, roofs, and fixed furniture were constructed. They also vary in the extent to which they deteriorated during use and were repaired or remodeled.

Walls. Wall construction varies across the rooms and pueblos in the amount of adobe used, the placement of footing stones in trenches, and the fitting of stones against one another within each wall. Information from wall construction is used primarily to identify the intended use and use-life of structures and the history of construction of each pueblo. Bonding and abutting patterns at the intersections of walls indicate the sequence through which rooms were planned within each pueblo. The kind of materials used for wall construction is considered an index of intended occupation length (Binford 1990; Diehl 1992). Lighter materials indicate less lengthy intended occupation or seasonal use during warmer portions of the year.

Floors. Nearly all of the room floors are packed mud and adobe, but they vary in slope, thickness, and evidence of remodeling and replastering. Floors were examined for evidence of extensive or intensive use of interior space; indicators of use include depression of floors in primary traffic or work areas, replastering around primary traffic or work areas, and construction of new floors. These data support inferences about the length of room use, the intensity of room use, and any occupational hiatus.

Roofs. Most roofs were constructed in similar fashion to walls and floors, but they vary in how substantially they were supported. This variation is indicative of how effectively roofs would have served as activity areas. It is often difficult to distinguish secondary roof support posts from furniture posts or other less substantial items that create floor depressions. This distinction is important to the analysis, because substantial roof support in puebloan rooms allows the roof to have been used as an activity area, expanding the domestic space for residence. As the length of occupation increased or the size of households expanded, more domestic space would have been needed (Kent 1992; Wilk 1983). Thus, the extent of roof support relative to room size has been evaluated on the basis of number and size of roof support posts, roofing material, and the presence of a roof assemblage, indicating the use of the roof as an activity area. The deterioration of roofs during the history of room use can be evaluated through analysis of the number, distribution, and replacement of roof support posts. Clusters of roof support posts indicate sections of deteriorating roof; plastering over the holes from roof support posts indicates remodeling and repair. Roof deterioration and repair result from extended occupation and regular reuse of structures. They are evidence that structures were being maintained over time. Finally, identification of posts from fixed furniture (tables, cribs, racks, screens, tripods, etc.) supports inferences about investments in work stations and commitment of space to specific activities, both of which occur when lengthy periods of use or regular reuse are anticipated (Kent 1992).

In an effort to sort through the post and floor-depression records in a way that allows comparison between rooms of different sizes (needing different sizes of roof support posts), I avoided establishing a standard size value for distinguishing roof support posts from furniture posts. Instead, I plotted the depths (y-axis) and diameters (x-axis) of all postholes and floor depressions for each room.[1] Primary roof supports were clustered toward the upper right side of the graph, furniture posts near the lower left. The large shallow depressions resulting from vessels (such as water jars) or other somewhat heavy, wide-based objects resting on the floor were outliers on the lower right side of the plot.[2] In some rooms the primary and secondary roof supports were tightly clustered and were easily distinguished from the very shallow, small supports of furniture. However, in other rooms the secondary roof supports were not easily distinguished from the furniture posts, in which case I placed some of the smaller postholes in a separate group that could be interpreted as either the remains of roof supports or furniture supports.

These data from postholes and fallen roofing material, the substance of roof construction, deterioration of roofs, roof remodeling, and furniture construction and remodeling are the bases for evaluation of occupational histories of rooms.

Fixed Furniture. Investment in fixed furnishings, as in architecture, indicates intent to occupy a residence over an extended period of time. Formalized facilities are interpreted as evidence of fairly long, regular reuse or permanent residential occupation. This expectation can be understood in terms of the efficiency of work and use of space. The most efficient tools are those designed precisely for a task (Nelson 1991; Torrence 1989), which is true for facilities as well. Further, structuring the use of space on sites eases the potential for conflict over work areas. Graham found that among the Raramuri, maize cultivators in northern Mexico, "as intensity of occupation increases—either through increased length or duration of occupation, or through increased number of inhabitants at the site—the placement of activities and the nature of maintenance becomes [sic] more formalized" (1993:38). Grinding may be one of the first activities to be fixed in space, because it requires extended periods of time, must be done often, and employs some equipment that is not easily moved. Graham (1993:38) observes that fixed mealing features occur in residences with the longest periods of use. Cooking is another activity that can take considerable space and must be done often. A cooking hearth with a collar will contain the ashes from heating and will concentrate the heat from a fire. This type of hearth should be more efficient in constraining cooking activity and in actually heating food. But, it may not serve as well for keeping people warm or providing light by which to work, because the fire is set down into a collared pit. Graham (1993:38) argues that multiple hearths provide flexibility in space use. Storage is also expected to become formalized with increase in the length of occupation (Graham 1993:32–33; Horne 1993; Kent 1992:638–642) because of the importance of effective storage for long-term occupation in a seasonal environment. The amount of space required to store necessary food may also influence the formalization of storage features and structures.

The presence and kinds of fixed furnishings also point to activities that were central to the occupation of the site. Those that are fixed have dedicated space assigned to them to assure that the tasks could be performed effectively. Changes in the kinds of facilities that become fixed furniture result from changes in site activities and subsequently the nature of occupation. Within the excavated rooms, comparisons are made in the presence of mealing, cooking, and storage features including tables and racks made from wood and indicated by post impressions.

Artifact Assemblage. The depositional context of the artifacts within the rooms varies within and between sites. None of the rooms are trash-filled, suggesting that they may all have been abandoned at the same time. They were not, however, abandoned in the same way. Some of the rooms are burned, and some are not. While pithouse structures may have been "difficult to ignite and slow to burn" (Lightfoot 1993:168), pueblo rooms might have burned more easily. Possible storage of plants hanging from the roof beams and the ease with which air can be drawn into above-ground structures would have made them more susceptible to catching fire. However, the relatively small size of the hearths and the limited extent of burning within the hearths does not support the conclusion that house fires were common. Further, construction material was primarily stone and adobe, which would not burn. Thus, I would argue, as Lightfoot (1993) did for Duckfoot Pueblo in southwestern Colorado, that some of the rooms were probably burned intentionally. However, there is variation in the extent of burning, which may simply indicate that some fires were not started as well as others.

The significance of intentional burning is that it may indicate some planning involved in the abandonment of rooms, although raiding may also be responsible for burned rooms (Mobley-Tanaka 1996). Consequently, the collections of artifacts from floors and roofs in the burned rooms do not necessarily represent the entire de facto assemblage of interior and rooftop activities. Brooks

(1993) has suggested other measures of planned abandonment, including lack of large items, absence of refit sequences, and peripheral distribution of artifacts on room floors. Tomka (1993) points to the importance of considering the condition of each item to determine its curation value. Items that are not expensive to replace may have been left at abandoned sites (Tomka 1993:22). Montgomery (1993) uses a ratio of reconstructible ceramic vessels on floors to ceramic fragments in fill as an index of the rate of abandonment as well as timing of abandonment. In this analysis, the condition of artifacts, their functional types, and their frequencies in fill, roof-fall deposits, and on floors are discussed with regard to the activities conducted in rooms and the abandonment processes at the sites. Rooms with partial to full-floor assemblages are easy to distinguish from those that were cleared out at abandonment. Cleared rooms have essentially nothing in them; rooms with "in-use" assemblages have abundant reconstructible and whole items.

Inferences regarding the functions of items are general and based exclusively on form. More research is needed on the temper, type of clay, and other properties of the vessels, on the wear patterns and residues on grinding tools, and on the edge properties of chipped stone in order to evaluate inferences regarding their specific uses.

Placing the Sites in Time

The most general way to examine the dating of the sites is to combine all radiocarbon dates and all obsidian hydration dates from the excavated sites. I have included not only the sites described in this study, but the two others from the study area with comparable architecture and ceramic assemblages. The inclusion of the two additional sites helps boost the sample size and does not change the overall pattern or its temporal placement.

Lists of chronometric information, as presented in tables 4.1 and 4.2, can be misleading and difficult to interpret. Samples with different standard deviations are problematic to compare. Those with large standard deviations may influence interpretation toward longer occupation ranges than are accurate. Kintigh (1994) has designed a computer program that combines sample distributions from the same context. The combined distribution represents the summed probability ranges for the dating of that context. This technique is preferable to others because it gives equal weighting to each sample; where the actual age range for the context is rather narrow, redundant dates and ranges will produce a pronounced, single mode; where there is little redundancy and

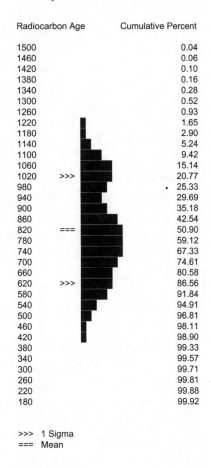

Radiocarbon Age		Cumulative Percent
1500		0.04
1460		0.06
1420		0.10
1380		0.16
1340		0.28
1300		0.52
1260		0.93
1220		1.65
1180		2.90
1140		5.24
1100		9.42
1060		15.14
1020	>>>	20.77
980		• 25.33
940		29.69
900		35.18
860		42.54
820	===	50.90
780		59.12
740		67.33
700		74.61
660		80.58
620	>>>	86.56
580		91.84
540		94.91
500		96.81
460		98.11
420		98.90
380		99.33
340		99.57
300		99.71
260		99.81
220		99.88
180		99.92

>>> 1 Sigma
=== Mean

Figure 4.1
The combined distribution of radiocarbon one-sigma probability ranges from all sites;
forty-three samples.

probably a range of real ages, the curve will be fairly flat or have multiple modes. To combine radiocarbon age determinations, the uncalibrated age distributions must be used, because the technique requires an assumption of normal distribution, which does not apply to calibrated age ranges.

Combining all radiocarbon dates (fig. 4.1) from the Palomas sites produces a very flat distribution within which the one-sigma range is from A.D. 930 and A.D. 1330 (uncalibrated).[3] The distribution of uncalibrated radiocarbon ages in figure 4.1 represents the entire range of variation among dates that may be accounted for by actual variation in the death dates of wood and annuals, as well as by the random error in measurement of those true ages. The early end takes in pithouse construction; final surface structure remodeling should be at the later end. The distribution of aggregated obsidian hydration dates is similarly flat, with a broader one-sigma range of A.D. 700 to 1450. Again, the early end represents pithouse occupation; final use of the surface structures should have occurred toward the end of the ranges represented by these combined probability distributions. The timing of occupation of each site cannot be determined from these distributions, nor is it possible to determine the true age range within the distributions, although occupation probably occurred within the period of the one-sigma range of radiocarbon ages, A.D. 930 to 1330 (uncalibrated), which is consistent with ceramic data (table 3.1). The broad range of both the radiocarbon and the obsidian hydration distribution reinforces the difficulty of assigning ages precisely. However, some greater precision is achieved at the level of sites.

Buckaroo Site

The Buckaroo Site (fig. 3.2) has a series of occupations beginning with pit structures. The focus, here, is on surface structures. Beneath a twelve-room, stone masonry pueblo is at least one, less substantial, three-walled structure with associated outside features, including a hearth and pit. Excavation on this site included four of the rooms in the twelve-room pueblo, one earlier room beneath Unit 1, and one complete (also beneath Unit 1) and two partial pithouses (beneath units 2 and 3) (Nelson 1993b). It is possible only to assign a fairly broad range of time to the occupation of this site (not to be confused with the length of occupation). The distribution of radiocarbon age ranges from Buckaroo Site is quite flat and broad (uncalibrated one sigma from A.D. 970 to 1370) (fig. 4.2). This wide range is produced by the range of true dates of the specimens and the random error inherent in the radiocarbon. As Cowgill (1996) argues, it is likely considerably broader than the true age range. The radiocarbon age distribution as a whole is not inconsistent with the argument for continued construction through the 1100s and 1200s; neither does it confirm this dating. Obsidian hydration dates have a different distribution and range, which help interpret the radiocarbon data. In figure 4.3 I have included only those obsidian samples from activity areas (floors and roofs) and beneath floors, excluding pieces from general fill, the behavioral source of which cannot be identified. The samples from activity areas should represent the final use of rooms, and those from below floors should represent preconstruction, thus bracketing occupation length. The distribution is strongly bimodal, with one mode around A.D. 900 and the other around A.D. 1250 (these modes are separated by 350

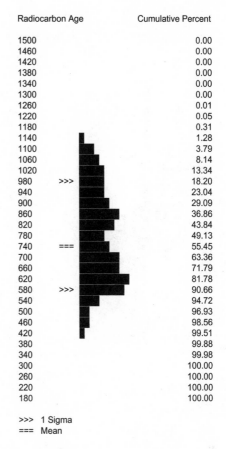

Radiocarbon Age		Cumulative Percent
1500		0.00
1460		0.00
1420		0.00
1380		0.00
1340		0.00
1300		0.00
1260		0.01
1220		0.05
1180		0.31
1140		1.28
1100		3.79
1060		8.14
1020		13.34
980	>>>	18.20
940		23.04
900		29.09
860		36.86
820		43.84
780		49.13
740	===	55.45
700		63.36
660		71.79
620		81.78
580	>>>	90.66
540		94.72
500		96.93
460		98.56
420		99.51
380		99.88
340		99.98
300		100.00
260		100.00
220		100.00
180		100.00

>>> 1 Sigma
=== Mean

Figure 4.2

The combined distribution of radiocarbon one-sigma probability ranges from the Buckaroo Site; sixteen samples; mean radiocarbon age = 772.

years, which greatly exceeds the one-sigma range of any sample). The early mode is consistent with use by pithouse dwellers; the late mode probably represents abandonment. If the latter is true, remodeling and additional construction would precede the mid-1200s. Also, the range for the obsidian dates is not as late as the radiocarbon probability distributions. If the latest obsidian dates represent abandonment, the late tail of the radiocarbon distribution is a product of random error.

The earliest rooms in this pueblo may have been constructed in the eleventh century. Among the four rooms excavated, the earliest construction of Room 1 (sample number 42839) may represent the earliest surface architecture on the site, with a calibrated, one-sigma, radiocarbon date range from the 900s into

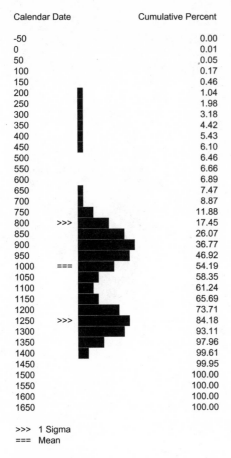

Calendar Date	Cumulative Percent
-50	0.00
0	0.01
50	,0.05
100	0.17
150	0.46
200	1.04
250	1.98
300	3.18
350	4.42
400	5.43
450	6.10
500	6.46
550	6.66
600	6.89
650	7.47
700	8.87
750	11.88
800 >>>	17.45
850	26.07
900	36.77
950	46.92
1000 ===	54.19
1050	58.35
1100	61.24
1150	65.69
1200	73.71
1250 >>>	84.18
1300	93.11
1350	97.96
1400	99.61
1450	99.95
1500	100.00
1550	100.00
1600	100.00
1650	100.00

>>> 1 Sigma
=== Mean

Figure 4.3
The combined distribution of one-sigma probability ranges for obsidian hydration dates from the Buckaroo Site; fifteen samples.

the 1000s; the upper end of the two-sigma range extends to the mid-1100s, placing the room firmly in the Classic Mimbres period. Room 4 has three samples (sample numbers 6638.2, 6639.2, 6640) with similarly early ranges, but two others have much later age ranges, and the ceramics in this room are consistent with the later range. The latest occupation was probably sometime in the 1200s, although three of the five dates on annuals (reeds and maize) have calibrated means later than the 1200s (sample numbers 6654, 6655, 6656). Wood from the only hearth sample, however, does have a calibrated mean in the late 1200s (sample number 6637). All rooms appear to have been abandoned at the same time; all were burned, many have extensive floor and roof assemblages, and none was trash-filled.

Ceramics from Buckaroo Site are consistent with the overall chronometric age range. Classic Mimbres Black-on-white, Style III, is the only painted ceramic associated with the early three-walled room, which places its occupation before A.D. 1150. In the later pueblo, sherds of Classic Mimbres Black-on-white, Style III, are associated with sherds of El Paso Bichrome and Polychrome, Chupadero Black-on-white, Cibola white wares (probably Tularosa), Wingate and St. Johns Polychrome, and two types of Reserve and Tularosa textured-corrugated wares. The painted sherds are rare but occur in all depositional contexts (table 4.3). Reconstructible vessels from the final occupation include El Paso Polychrome, Chupadero Black-on-white, and various Reserve and Tularosa textured-corrugated wares, including Tularosa Fillet rim. These are the last styles made or used at the site. All of these painted and textured wares were made during some portion of the twelfth and thirteenth centuries.

Buckaroo Site thus has a moderate-sized, one-room block pueblo as the final phase in a fairly lengthy occupation, which began with a pithouse settlement. By the eleventh century, pithouses were being filled with trash, and the occupants had built at least one surface structure, which was more ephemeral than the later room block. By the end of the 1200s, a twelve-room pueblo was constructed, occupied, and then abandoned.

Lee Pueblo

This pueblo is a small block of seven rooms within an extensive scatter of artifacts, small room blocks, and isolated rooms (fig. 3.3). All rooms are small in comparison with those on the other excavated sites in the study area. Their range is well within the size for Classic Mimbres rooms in the Mimbres Valley (Gilman 1980), and their construction is more similar to Mimbres Valley cobble masonry than are others in the project area. The pueblo is constructed on the fill-deposit of an earlier occupation, for which no architectural remains are present. Numerous pits appear in the gravel bedrock from this earliest site use. The lack of temporally diagnostic ceramics and datable materials on this site make placing it in time difficult. None of the structures at Lee Pueblo was burned, and the roofs and posts appear to have been removed at abandonment. This conclusion is based on the lack of adobe roof material in the fill of rooms, extreme weathering of the floors, and disturbance of the postholes. Thus, the site lacks organic remains that can be dated, and those that were recovered are

Table 4.3

The distribution of painted ceramics by analytic unit within the rooms excavated at each site

SITE	ROOM	AU	M2	M3	IM	CH	EPB	EPP	W	SJ	IW	P	T	RT
Buckaroo	1	F	8	80	70	12								
		R	3	46	10	21		1						
		FL	2	50	13	8								
	2	F	4	52	57	2	2		1		1			
		R		62	35	1	7			3				
		FL		27		3								
	3	F	9	50	41	36	24	14						
		R		25	5	65	8	37						
		FL		6	9	11	5	6						
	4	F	2	31	54	2						1		
		R	1	40	13	11								
		FL		15	4	1								
Ronnie	1	F	2	15	6	2	3	6	1					
		R		4		2								
		FL		16	3									
	2	R*		3										
		FL		29	3	14								
Lee**	1	F		2										
	2	F			1			2						
	3	F		4	2	3				1				
Phelps	1	F		3	4	6								1
		FL			1					2				1
	10	F	1	4	8	5		18		5	1	3	8	
		R		1	3			6					1	
		FL		1	1			5				6	1	
	11	F		13	16	3						4	1	
		R		3	8	2								
		FL										1		
	12	F		2	7	6		2						
		FL		10	19	15								

Notes:

AU = Analytic Unit (FL = floor; R = roof; F = fill)

M2 = Style II Mimbres Black-on-white

M3 = Style III Mimbres Black-on-white

IM = Indeterminate Style Mimbres Black-on-white

CH = Chupadero Black-on-white
EPB = El Paso Bichrome
EPP = El Paso Polychrome
W   = Wingate Black-on-red
SJ   = St. Johns Polychrome
IW = Indeterminate White Mountain Redware
P   = Playas Red
T   = Tularosa Black-on-white
RT = Red-on-terracotta
*No separate fill above the roof in this room.
**No painted sherds or vessels in floor context in any room.

---

from questionable contexts. In addition, obsidian is scarce. The few radiocarbon and obsidian hydration dates from within the architectural portion of the site span a broad period from the A.D. 600s into the 1300s but are too few to interpret. On Lee Pueblo, not only were the structures apparently disassembled, but usable artifacts were removed either at abandonment or later. No reconstructible vessels were found, although two partial, broken bowls were recovered from mealing features. These are both Reserve and Tularosa textured-corrugated wares. The painted ceramics are too rare to carry any interpretive weight; they include one or a few sherds of Classic Mimbres Black-on-white, Chupadero Black-on-white, El Paso Polychrome, and St. Johns Polychrome (table 4.3).

Three of the seven rooms were excavated. All are from the center of the room block. Rooms 1 and 2 may have been among the earliest; their west wall appears to have extended continuously along the entire length of the pueblo and may have been the first wall constructed. All perpendicular walls abut it. These two rooms have substantially different obsidian hydration dates. Only one sample was dated from each room, however, and they are from different contexts; the one from Room 1 (sample number DL92428; A.D. 772–954, one-sigma range) was beneath the floor, while the one from Room 2 (sample number DL92429; A.D. 1289–1425, one-sigma range) was in the fill of the room. These dates bracket the probable range within which the actual occupation occurred; neither date range is consistent with the ceramics. Architectural data indicate that Room 3 may have been added later, but samples from the room yielded a wide range of chronometric dates, spanning the full range for the two dates reported above (tables 4.1 and 4.2).

Ronnie Pueblo

Within the six-room block on Ronnie Pueblo, two contiguous rooms were excavated (fig. 3.4). These are among the largest rooms of all those excavated on
the four sites, averaging more than 20 m² of floor area. The two rooms are in
the middle portion of a linear room block and may have formed the core of the
block. While it is impossible to determine from the surface whether all of the
rooms in the room block were constructed at one time, it is clear from excavation that Rooms 1 and 2 were constructed together. The east and west walls of
the two units are continuous, with a dividing wall that abuts the west wall and
forms a doorway between both rooms toward the east side. The north wall of
Room 1 and the south wall of Room 2 are bonded to at least one of the adjacent
east and west walls, suggesting further that Rooms 1 and 2 were constructed as
a unit.

All datable samples from the site were recovered from Room 2. This room
burned, burying an assemblage of floor artifacts and producing a plethora of
burned posts and beams. Room 1 burned to a limited extent but appears to
have been disassembled prior to burning; all usable artifacts were removed, and
the interior wall faces of collapsed walls rested directly on the floor, indicating
that the roof was removed at abandonment. Seven samples were dated by radiocarbon; six of the date ranges are similar, one is later. Their combined distribution is presented in figure 4.4. The mode for this distribution is 1060, which
has a calibrated date in the late A.D. 900s. Construction of Ronnie Pueblo may
have begun quite early, although the probability range at one sigma extends
into the early 1000s when calibrated. Only one of the radiocarbon samples
(number 6648) has an age range that extends after the mid-1000s (one sigma).
However, the ceramics in both rooms indicate occupation into the late 1100s
(table 4.3). In Room 2, two reconstructible Classic Mimbres Black-on-white
bowls and a Chupadero Black-on-white jar were found in close proximity near
the floor. These reconstructible vessels represent part of an abandonment assemblage that dates about A.D. 1150, early for Chupadero vessels and late for
Classic Mimbres. The one late radiocarbon date (sample number 6648) of A.D.
1193–1276 (calibrated, one-sigma range) on roof material suggests abandonment within the temporal range of Chupadero but well after the currently accepted period for production of Classic Mimbres.

Ronnie Pueblo was constructed early in the Classic Mimbres period, possibly earlier than the traditional dates for this period, and was used at least into
the twelfth century, perhaps as late as the late 1100s or into the early 1200s. It

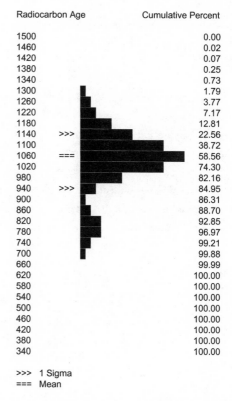

Radiocarbon Age		Cumulative Percent
1500		0.00
1460		0.02
1420		0.07
1380		0.25
1340		0.73
1300		1.79
1260		3.77
1220		7.17
1180		12.81
1140	>>>	22.56
1100		38.72
1060	===	58.56
1020		74.30
980		82.16
940	>>>	84.95
900		86.31
860		88.70
820		92.85
780		96.97
740		99.21
700		99.88
660		99.99
620		100.00
580		100.00
540		100.00
500		100.00
460		100.00
420		100.00
380		100.00
340		100.00

>>> 1 Sigma
=== Mean

Figure 4.4
The combined distribution of radiocarbon one-sigma probability ranges from Ronnie Pueblo; seven samples; mean radiocarbon age = 1041.

appears to have been abandoned before Buckaroo Site and Phelps Pueblo but was in use during the depopulation of the large Classic period villages in the region.

Phelps Pueblo

This small pueblo consists of two room blocks, one with two rooms and the other with from five to six rooms (fig. 3.5). One room in the small block and two rooms in the larger block have been excavated. These rooms are burned, and the two in the larger room block have sizable floor assemblages.

The site has a surface ceramic assemblage, indicating an occupation as early as A.D. 1000 and perhaps as late as the 1300s. An archaeomagnetic assessment of a burned hearth in Room 10 in the larger room block has a range of A.D. 1010 to A.D. 1275, with a mean paleopole location near A.D. 1125 (Klein 1992).

Three radiocarbon dates from the same floor have calibrated ranges in the late 1200s to 1300s (Table 4.1). Two additional radiocarbon dates from Room 11 in the same room block yield similar dates. One sample sealed between floors in Room 10 has a much earlier range of A.D. 800–1030 (calibrated). Thus, the site occupation could have begun during the period of occupation of large Classic period villages and continued through their abandonment and afterward. Obsidian hydration dates do not aid in sorting out the timing. Five hydration samples from two of the rooms were submitted for dating; four have ranges in the fifteenth through seventeenth centuries, far too late to be accurate for dating the site. These late dates may result from the intense burning of the contexts within which the samples were recovered.

The ceramics are consistent with an occupation during the eleventh through the thirteenth centuries. All of the rooms have a mixture of Classic Mimbres Black-on-white, Style III, and ceramics considered temporally later including Chupadero, St. Johns Polychrome, El Paso Polychrome, and Playas Red (tables 3.1 and 4.3). Two rooms, however, have early floor surfaces: the first floor of Room 1 in the small room block and the first floor of Room 10 in the larger room block. The only painted ceramic between the floors of Room 10 is one Classic Mimbres sherd. In Room 1, one Mimbres Black-on-white sherd is in a posthole constructed for this early structure. All of the reconstructible, temporally diagnostic vessels, which form the abandonment assemblages associated with the upper floors of these rooms and others added after the Classic period, are textured-corrugated wares similar to Tularosa textured wares.

The ceramics, radiocarbon dates and archaeomagnetic date indicate a range that includes the eleventh through the thirteenth centuries. The pueblo may have begun with two isolated rooms (1 and 10) that were expanded to form two room blocks.

Other Excavated Sites

Two other medium-sized pueblos on Palomas drainage are currently being studied. Both are similar in architectural form and ceramic assemblage composition to the four sites included in this study. Rooms are constructed of stone masonry, and ceramics include Classic Mimbres Black-on-white, Style III, along with Chupadero Black-on-white, El Paso Polychrome, White Mountain Redwares, Playas Red, and Reserve and Tularosa textured-corrugated wares (table 3.7). Lizard Terrace Pueblo has two terraces, each with a room block of approximately twelve rooms. Mountain Lion Hamlet has approximately four to six rooms in one block. Room sizes are similar to those at Phelps Pueblo and the

Buckaroo Site, although a few rooms are as large as those on Ronnie Pueblo. Eight rooms have been excavated on the two sites: three on the upper terrace of Lizard Terrace Pueblo, three on the lower terrace of the same site, and two on Mountain Lion Hamlet. Four rooms are particularly well dated because of the abundance of burned construction material or obsidian fragments, or both.

I include information on these sites because the patterns of occupation are similar to those at the sites included in the study, and I make reference to these supporting data in appropriate sections. Thus, it seems sensible to have a baseline of current information on the timing of their occupation; none of these data are yet published. In addition, the amount of datable material from these additional sites is more substantial than from the other four. They enrich the database for assessing the timing of occupation of Postclassic hamlets in the study area.

The combined probability distribution of radiocarbon ages from eight samples of construction material (wood and reeds) and maize (adjusted for C13) recovered from Lizard Terrace Pueblo form a wide range (fig. 4.5), but the mode is quite pronounced, centering on A.D. 1210 (uncalibrated). The twenty-six obsidian hydration dates from activity contexts (floor and roof) have a very flat distribution through the same three centuries (fig. 4.6). The obsidian includes dates with one-sigma ranges that extend as late as 1650. These may be the product of random error or may actually indicate Apache use of the site area.

The earliest surface architecture at Lizard Terrace Pueblo includes at least three rooms: Room 1, the earliest floor in Room 10, and possibly the earliest floor in Room 19. All are best dated by ceramic associations; the only painted sherds on or near the earliest floors in these rooms are Classic Mimbres, Style III. The fill above these floors is dominated by Mimbres Black-on-white but includes one to two sherds of El Paso Polychrome. Obsidian hydration dates from these rooms vary widely, probably representing the range of occupation of the site beginning before the time span of interest here. Rooms 19 and 10 were remodeled as the room block was expanded to include twelve rooms, as occurred at the Buckaroo Site and Phelps Pueblo.

All twelve radiocarbon dates from Mountain Lion Hamlet come from the only room that has been fully excavated. The combined distributions from all samples in this room (including many maize samples) produce a smooth normal distribution (fig. 4.7) around a mean of A.D. 1166 (uncalibrated). The one-sigma range of 1050 to 1290 (uncalibrated) is consistent with the range of painted ceramics on the site (not representative of the occupation length, which is probably considerably shorter) but does not provide much precision in dat-

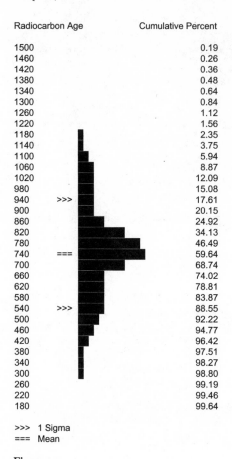

Radiocarbon Age		Cumulative Percent
1500		0.19
1460		0.26
1420		0.36
1380		0.48
1340		0.64
1300		0.84
1260		1.12
1220		1.56
1180		2.35
1140		3.75
1100		5.94
1060		8.87
1020		12.09
980		15.08
940	>>>	17.61
900		20.15
860		24.92
820		34.13
780		46.49
740	===	59.64
700		68.74
660		74.02
620		78.81
580		83.87
540	>>>	88.55
500		92.22
460		94.77
420		96.42
380		97.51
340		98.27
300		98.80
260		99.19
220		99.46
180		99.64

>>> 1 Sigma
=== Mean

Figure 4.5
The combined distribution of radiocarbon one-sigma probability ranges from Lizard Terrace Pueblo; eight samples; mean radiocarbon age = 751.

ing the occupation.[4] The structure had two floors; painted ceramics associated with the lower floor are Classic Mimbres, Style III, and an indeterminate White Mountain Redware; those on the later floor include Classic Mimbres, St. Johns Polychrome, El Paso Polychrome, and Playas Red. With the remodeling of Room 1, the hamlet was expanded; radiocarbon dates on the later remodeling, however, are within the range of the samples from earlier construction.

Early Surface Structure

Among the four sites excavated, the earliest surface structures are Classic Mimbres: most of these are early constructions, isolated or ephemeral struc-

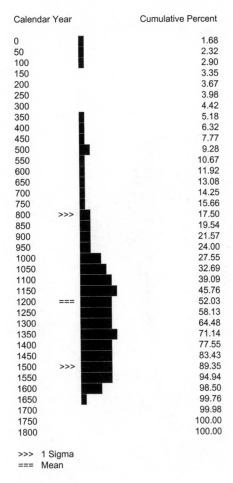

Calendar Year		Cumulative Percent
0		1.68
50		2.32
100		2.90
150		3.35
200		3.67
250		3.98
300		4.42
350		5.18
400		6.32
450		7.77
500		9.28
550		10.67
600		11.92
650		13.08
700		14.25
750		15.66
800	>>>	17.50
850		19.54
900		21.57
950		24.00
1000		27.55
1050		32.69
1100		39.09
1150		45.76
1200	===	52.03
1250		58.13
1300		64.48
1350		71.14
1400		77.55
1450		83.43
1500	>>>	89.35
1550		94.94
1600		98.50
1650		99.76
1700		99.98
1750		100.00
1800		100.00

>>> 1 Sigma
=== Mean

Figure 4.6

The combined distribution of one-sigma probability ranges for obsidian hydration dates from Lizard Terrace Pueblo; twenty-six samples.

tures that were later remodeled and incorporated into a pueblo room block. The early structures are identified by the presence of Classic Mimbres Black-on-white, Style III,[5] or similarly dated (pre–A.D. 1150), painted ceramic as the only painted types associated with the floor or fill directly above the floor.[6] In a few cases the early structures simply lack painted ceramics; their assignment to this period is based on their placement beneath other structural floors dated to the Postclassic (after A.D. 1150). Early surface structures include at least one room at the Buckaroo Site (early Room 1), at least one on Phelps Pueblo (early Room 1 and possibly early Room 10), and possibly the core rooms at Ronnie

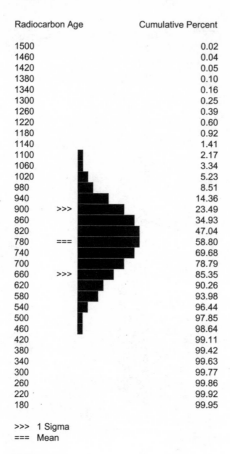

Radiocarbon Age		Cumulative Percent
1500		0.02
1460		0.04
1420		0.05
1380		0.10
1340		0.16
1300		0.25
1260		0.39
1220		0.60
1180		0.92
1140		1.41
1100		2.17
1060		3.34
1020		5.23
980		8.51
940		14.36
900	>>>	23.49
860		34.93
820		47.04
780	===	58.80
740		69.68
700		78.79
660	>>>	85.35
620		90.26
580		93.98
540		96.44
500		97.85
460		98.64
420		99.11
380		99.42
340		99.63
300		99.77
260		99.86
220		99.92
180		99.95

>>> 1 Sigma
=== Mean

Figure 4.7

The combined distribution of radiocarbon one-sigma probability ranges from Mountain Lion Hamlet; twelve samples; mean radiocarbon age = 784.

Pueblo (Rooms 1 and 2). Additional Classic Mimbres structures have been found on Lizard Terrace Pueblo (three structures) and Mountain Lion Hamlet (one structure). Some of the Classic period structures are lightly constructed, with no interior features; others are more substantial.

Ephemeral Structures

The early structures on Buckaroo Site (Room 1) and Phelps Pueblo (Room 1) illustrate the ephemeral structure forms.

Buckaroo, Early Room 1. A three-walled masonry room with a floor area of approximately 10 m² was the first surface masonry construction on the Buckaroo

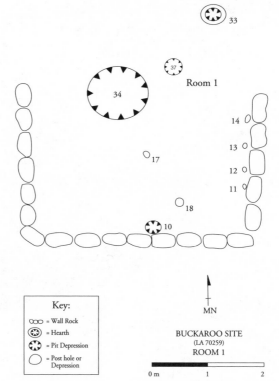

Figure 4.8
Early three-walled structure on the Buckaroo Site (early Room 1).

Site (fig. 4.8; see location on the site shown in figure 3.2). The few painted ceramics associated with the structure are entirely Classic Mimbres Black-on-white, Style III, and the radiocarbon date from the floor of the room places its use firmly in the Classic Mimbres period. The south and east walls were constructed of cobbles and mud. While the south wall was substantially constructed with several courses of flat cobbles resting on a base of upright cobbles cemented into footing trenches, the east wall had a mud base with cobbles and pebbles cemented into it. The west wall may initially have been half a meter in from the stone wall on the west side of the structure and may have been made with a mud base similar to the east wall. A block of puddled mud that may have been a wall remnant was noted in the southwest corner of the room. The north side of Room 1 was open to an outside activity area.

The floor of this structure was difficult to discern because it rested, in most places, on fill that covered a shallow pit structure. Segments of packed mud

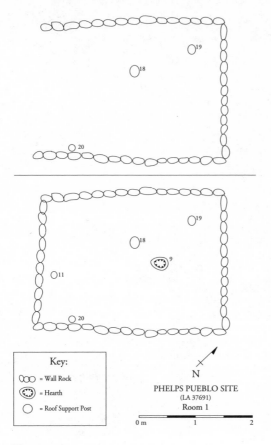

Figure 4.9
Early surface structure on Phelps Pueblo (early Room 1), and later, postclassic remodeling.

floor were identified most easily adjacent to the east wall; these were approximately 5 cm thick. As in later surface rooms on this site and on Ronnie Pueblo, the floor, although patchy, was quite level, varying only 5 cm from the walls to the center of the room.

The roof of Room 1 was not substantial. There is no center post to support the roof, which must have rested partially on the walls and been supported to some extent by thin posts along the walls and near the center of the room. Six postholes of uniform size (12–20 cm) and depth (12–14 cm) occur in the east half of the room. Four are fairly evenly spaced along the east wall; there were probably as many along the west wall. One postmold (17) appears near the center of the room, and another (18) is near the south wall. These are the size of secondary posts in other rooms; they would not have supported a substantial roof. No evidence of the roof remained; it may have been removed or incorporated into the new roof when the room was remodeled to a fully enclosed structure. The only floor features other than postholes are two shallow pits. The first is a large, shallow, oval, clay-lined pit (34) near the open side of the structure. The second is a shallow (8 cm deep), unlined pit (10) near the south wall, which contained a bit of charcoal and ash but was not burned. It may have held embers to warm the back of the structure.

The hearth (33) used by occupants of this structure is outside, to the north. It is a circular (diameter 50 cm), adobe-lined depression extending 14 cm into the gravel bedrock and filled with ash. Obsidian flakes were found next to this hearth. Adjacent to the hearth is a similarly large pit (37), filled with a variety of debris and covered at the top with ash and charcoal. This pit is more than twice as deep as the hearth. It may have served as a storage pit or warming oven and have been associated either with this surface structure or earlier pithouse occupation.[7]

Eighteen artifacts resting on the floor included chipped-stone cores and flakes, and plain and painted sherds (no reconstructible vessels). Fill was laid over this floor when the room was expanded and remodeled with the growth of the pueblo. All of the artifacts are small and may be either primary refuse of the room occupants or artifacts deposited in the fill. Whatever the source, they predate the remodeling. The few painted sherds on or near the floor of this tri-walled structure are all Classic Mimbres Black-on-white (A.D. 1000–1150).

Phelps, Early Room 1. In the small room block on Phelps Pueblo (fig. 3.5), the easternmost of the two rooms was excavated. It is the smallest room on the four sites, with a floor area of 4.9 m² (fig. 4.9). Room 1 was initially constructed with two rows of large, upright cobbles, placed in a mud base to form the north, east, and south walls. Above these are a few courses of horizontally laid cobbles with pebble and mud chinking and an adobe plastered wall face. No west wall is evident for the earliest construction and occupation of the room. Excavators commented on the lack of wall stones in the fill of the room. Abundant burned mud impressions of sticks and reeds suggest that portions of the walls were constructed of jacal. The roof was insubstantial, supported by three thin posts (18, 19, 20) ranging from 8 to 12 cm in depth and 5 to 6 cm in diameter, the size identified as secondary roof supports in other puebloan rooms (see next section). The post supports extend diagonally through the room from the northeast to southwest corner. The floor is packed mud, about 5 cm thick, and rests on a small amount of fill above gravel bedrock. In contrast to most other floor surfaces, this floor is well worn, varying 12 cm in elevation (33–45 cm below datum) from the corners to the worn center of the room. The only painted sherd associated with the floor is Mimbres Black-on-white (style indeterminate). There are no interior features in the structure other than posts. Unfortunately, we have not excavated to the west on Room 1 where we would probably find outdoor features associated with the use of this room.

Similarly ephemeral structures were found beneath later rooms on the two middle Palomas sites currently being studied: Lizard Terrace Pueblo and Mountain Lion Hamlet. These structures have jacal walls, or were tri-walled stone masonry, and lacked interior features. All but one was remodeled into a more substantial structure as the pueblo room blocks were expanded.

These ephemeral structures were probably not year-round residences. Absence of substantial walls, or fully enclosing walls coupled with light roof construction, indicated by the small size of the postholes, suggests use during mild seasons. The absence of hearths inside the rooms supports this inference. Whittlesey and Reid (1982) and Reid (1989) describe the common occurrence of three-walled stone structures on mountain Mogollon sites and conclude that they represent part-time habitation. In the Mountain Mogollon region, these occur on small sites along with large room blocks on large aggregated sites like Grasshopper Pueblo. Wilk (1991) describes field houses used by aggregated Kekchi Maya subsistence farmers in Belize. These structures are "simplified versions of houses, using less durable construction methods and materials . . . [which] may also serve as a secondary residence" (1991:94–95). Ramadas such as these were used in many areas of the Southwest. They are partially enclosed structures used as work areas adjacent to residential structures or as shelters at special-use sites. Farming was probably the special use made of these locales, as few resources other than arable land are available (see discussion in chap. 5).

Substantial Structures

Among the four sites examined in detail in this study, none have substantial rooms with ceramic assemblages that are exclusively types associated with the Classic Mimbres period. One room, Room 2 at Ronnie Pueblo, has radiocarbon dates that place construction most probably during the Classic Mimbres period (see table 4.1); although the "old wood effect" (Schiffer 1982) may be responsible for the early dates, six out of seven have one-sigma probability ranges consistent with assignment to the Classic Mimbres period or earlier. This room

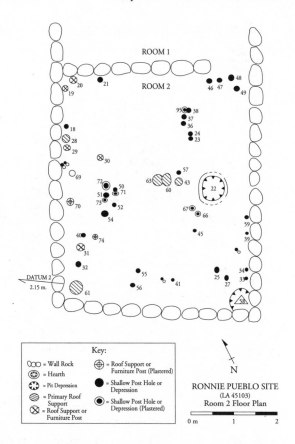

Figure 4.10
Classic to Postclassic Mimbres room on Ronnie Pueblo (Room 2).

and adjacent Room 1 form the core of Ronnie Pueblo. The ceramics from these rooms are a mixture of Classic Mimbres and later types, indicating abandonment after A.D. 1150. I briefly describe Room 2 as an example of possible Classic period construction on one of these hamlets that is more substantial than the ephemeral structures described above.[8] Another room, the earliest construction of Room 10 on Phelps Pueblo, has a partially preserved lower floor that may have been occupied during the Classic Mimbres period, based on the ceramic associations. I also describe this room, although separating the early from the later floor is difficult; it is quite similar to the rooms on Ronnie Pueblo.

Ronnie, Room 2. This room is quite large, with a floor area of 20 m² (fig. 4.10). A hearth (22) and a storage pit are the only features in the room other than

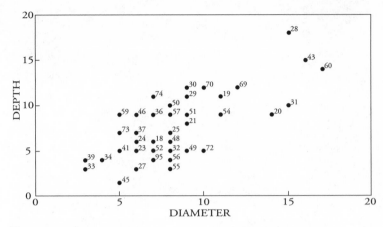

Figure 4.11

Dimensions of postholes and depressions in Room 2, Ronnie Pueblo. The two largest postholes from primary roof support posts were deleted because they are substantially larger than the others, compressing the distribution.

postholes and depressions. Room 2 was constructed by placing a course of adobe on the cleared bedrock surface of the terrace. Over the adobe were courses of river cobbles. The face of each wall was plastered with adobe, which extended across the surface of the floor. This construction is the same as in Room 1.

Roof fragments indicate a standard, thick, pueblo roof with large vegas (beams) covered by smaller sticks, then by reeds and finally by a thick (10–20 cm) adobe plaster on the rooftop (see Mindeleff 1989:fig. 37). Much roof debris was preserved in Room 2 because it burned. This substantial roof was supported primarily by the walls and a central post. Only one deep post (63) is noted, and this is in the center of the room. Many additional, smaller support posts are evident. A plot of post depth against diameter helps to sort out the myriad of depressions in the room. Those depressions near the upper right of figure 4.11 are large and deep and are interpreted as primary supports, while those in the lower left are small and shallow and are interpreted as furniture posts. Moving from upper right to lower left, the interpretation of postholes includes grades from primary roof support to secondary roof support to tertiary support or furniture posts.

The floor of Room 2 is strikingly level, varying by only 3 cm, with only two features present other than posts. The hearth (22) is a large shallow basin with an adobe collar located toward the east side of the center of the room.[9] The storage pit (58) is large, deep, and cylindrical in shape, located in the southeast corner of the room and filled with charcoal, ash, and bone. Three manos and a pestle rested near the top. It is possible that these were initially resting over the opening of the pit and were pushed down into it when the burning roof collapsed onto the floor. They may have been stored in the pit, however, which also held trash. All of the grinding stones are large and functional.

In figure 4.10 a cluster of small postholes and depressions (25, 27, 33, 34, 39, 59, and *a*) in the southeast corner of the room may be remnants of a kitchen worktable located between the hearth and the storage pit, which held four manos. Three other clusters of small postmolds are evident. The first (50, 51, 52, 54, 71, 72, 73), directly west of the central postholes, includes some posts that were covered with adobe plaster, presumably when the posts were removed and replaced. The number of other postholes located along the west wall indicates substantial construction, perhaps of storage cribs, racks, or bed platforms. No other evidence is available to support any specific inference about this construction. The second postmold cluster (23, 24, 36, 37, 38, 95) is north of the central posts and hearth. It was also modified slightly with post 38 replacing 95. Again, no evidence is available to indicate what these posts represent, but their proximity to the hearth may indicate a feature with a food processing function. The third cluster is in the northeast corner of the room, directly in front of the doorway. If these were in use with the doorway, they may have held a screen blocking view between the two rooms. However, they may have been in place before the doorway was created, the posts then being removed with the use of the doorway. Investment in furniture and its remodeling support the inference of extended use of Room 2. The remodeling, however, only modifies slightly the placement of furniture posts, not the organization of space use within the room.

The assemblage of artifacts on the floor of this room, which consists of a large number of whole, functional items, is discussed later in the section on the organization of these settlements. Here I discuss only the painted wares, which help to date the occupation. Among the five reconstructible vessels on or near the floor, the three painted wares include two Classic Mimbres Black-on-white bowls and one Chupadero Black-on-white seed jar. This association places the use of the room in the middle of the 1100s.

Phelps, Early Room 10. The earliest floor in this room may represent a Classic Mimbres period construction. The earliest floor surface was replaced with a full new plastering, with fill added between the floor in only one area; thus, no whole artifacts remain on the lower floor. It appears that the early floor articulated with the same walls associated with the later floor. If so, this room is a substantial cobble masonry construction that may have formed the initial room in the larger room block on the site (fig. 3.5). Room 10 has a floor area of 20 m², similar to the large rooms on Ronnie Pueblo.

The walls were constructed of two rows of upright stones with mud and pebbles forming the wall core. This formed the wall base. The upper portions had some stone construction judging from the enormous amount of stone piled around the room block and in the fill. Adobe plaster lines the inside face of each wall.

Burned pieces of roofing and roof support beams resting on the upper floor of the room are from a roof constructed much as in Ronnie Pueblo, Room 2. This was probably the same roof built for the earliest construction, as there is no evidence that the roof was changed substantially.

The upper floor and lower floors meld together throughout most of the room except near the center and toward the northwest of center. This is the location of a hearth (47) in the lower floor. The fill between the two floors in this area covers the hearth and levels the low areas around the hearth. This extensive floor replastering was done when a mealing feature was set in the northwest corner of the room. The upper floor hearth (17, 18) was constructed farther away from the area of the mealing feature, allowing more space to move around the mealing area. In fact, the hearth in the lower floor is too close to the mealing feature to have allowed grinding and cooking to have been performed at the same time. The only temporally diagnostic sherd from between these floors is from a Classic Mimbres bowl fragment; a single radiocarbon date on wood sealed between the floors has a range of A.D. 800–1030 (calibrated, one sigma) (Table 4.1). In the lower floor, a portion of a rectangular, possibly adobe-collared hearth is the only feature.

On Lizard Terrace Pueblo, there is a similar room, with a lower floor dating to the Classic Mimbres period. The walls and roof are substantial. The lower floor has only one feature, a hearth, and an associated sherd of Classic Mimbres Black-on-white Style III.

Summary. Among the four sites included in this study, three have evidence of early structures that were probably constructed during the Classic Mimbres period. The Buckaroo Site has a tri-walled structure with outside hearth and work areas. Ronnie Pueblo has two substantial cobble masonry rooms that may have been constructed during the Classic period; these have interior hearths but lack the mealing features added to most rooms after A.D. 1150 (see next section). Phelps Pueblo has a tri-walled, stone and jacal constructed room lacking interior features in one area and a possible stone masonry room with interior hearth in another. These form the basis for the room blocks that develop during the Postclassic occupation at the site. The room with the hearth also lacks a mealing facility. Examples of ephemeral structures and one substantial structure dating to the Classic period are found on two other hamlets on Palomas.

These Classic period structures are isolated markers on the landscape that contrast with the large Classic Mimbres villages of the same period. The ephemeral structures were only useful for seasonal occupation during fair weather, probably as field houses. The more substantially constructed rooms represent the initial shift toward greater residential use of these locales. In the next section, I discuss the remodeling of Classic period structures on these hamlets, documenting extensive change toward greater residential focus. The field houses were gradually transformed to more substantial residences. Figure 4.12 illustrates the early structures and their later remodeling into a substantial room block on the lower terrace at Lizard Terrace Pueblo. The transformation is associated with some continuity of Classic Mimbres styles but with a shift away from those styles toward considerable diversity of painted ceramic types.

Transformation

Two aspects of the transformation of the four sites are considered: continuity and reorganization. First, establishing that occupational continuity is a reasonable interpretation of regional settlement during the twelfth century is key to this study of reorganization. Evidence must point to a shift in settlement rather than the abandonment of the region by Classic period villagers. Architectural data document the continuity of structure use. The Classic period structures that marked field locales were not abandoned. Hamlet room blocks were constructed from the earlier structures. Further analysis of chronometric data supports this interpretation as does analysis of the composition of ceramic assemblages. Second, the changes that did accompany Classic village depopulation should be evident in those sites that continued to be occupied. Analysis of the remodeling of structures and expansion of room blocks at the hamlet sites in the study area provides perspective on the reorganization of land use. Shifts toward greater residential use are evident in the changes in architectural form and artifact composition. In addition, the history of occupation of the structures suggests that although they were continuously maintained, occupation may have been intermittent.

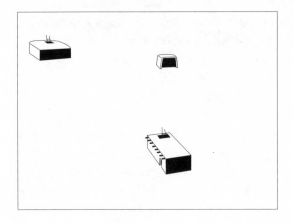

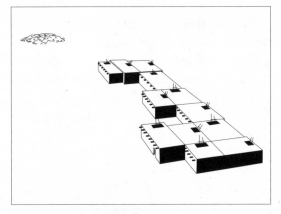

Figure 4.12
Artist's reconstruction of the transformation of a Classic Mimbres field camp into a Postclassic residential hamlet.

Evidence for Continuity

Most of the Classic period structures on the four hamlets were remodeled. In each case, the existing structure was modified while standing. Walls were extended and sometimes made more substantial; roofs were heavier and supported by more substantial posts; additional domestic facilities were added, including formally constructed hearths and often mealing facilities. Even the fairly substantial Classic period room that was remodeled (Room 10 on Phelps Pueblo) had a grinding facility added in addition to a new hearth, which was repositioned and expanded to include a warming pit.

The remodeling of Classic structures could have occurred anytime in the twelfth century; the exact timing of the transformation cannot be determined with the chronometric data available. However, the important aspect of timing is that the initial structures were built during the Classic period and were transformed to serve a more residential focus that extended beyond the middle of the 1100s when Classic period villages were depopulated. The strongest evidence for timing of the occupation of the modified structures are the ceramics associated with their roofs and floors. As discussed above, these include a variety of types that span the twelfth century, some types that were made before the twelfth century and other types that extend well after the twelfth century. Thus, structures that were constructed by people making Classic Mimbres ceramics were remodeled and continuously maintained by people who used Classic and a variety of other ceramics. By the end of the occupation of most of the four sites, Classic Mimbres was no longer used; later types, common during the mid to late thirteenth century comprise most abandonment assemblages in the rooms.

The following descriptions of the remodeling of the one of the ephemeral structures (Buckaroo Site, Room 1) and one substantial structure (Phelps Pueblo, Room 10), described in the previous section, illustrate the architectural and ceramic evidence for continuity. In addition, I include information in the description of each room in order to contextualize the data and to establish the nature of structure maintenance, wear to the floors, and assemblage composition, all of which aid in interpreting the organization of site occupation and land use.

Remodeling an Ephemeral Structure: Buckaroo Rooms 1 and 2. The initial remodeling of the Classic Mimbres structure, which was the earliest form of Room 1, involved substantial changes in room use, with the extension of the walls, modification toward a more substantial roof, and addition of new, interior features. These changes were accomplished by modifying the Classic Mimbres structure that forms the framework for the room, not by replacing it. Later repair and remodeling of the room indicate only minor change in the organization of space, as in other rooms in the pueblo. Room 2 was added when Room 1 was remodeled from its ephemeral form; therefore, I discuss the two rooms together.

Room 1 was remodeled and Room 2 constructed when the western wall of the Classic Mimbres structure was extended north. Both are masonry structures with full-height stone walls. Room 1 has approximately 17.5 m² of floor

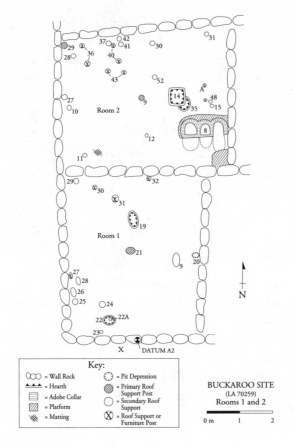

Figure 4.13

Postclassic Mimbres rooms on the Buckaroo Site (Rooms 1 and 2). Room 1 is remodeled from an earlier ephemeral structure.

area (fig. 4.13). When the walls of the three-walled structure were extended north, a new floor was laid and a stone wall added to delimit the north end on Room 1. The north wall was constructed in the same way as were the south and west walls, with large, upright cobbles as a base, but these were set in adobe rather than in a footing trench. A vent was cut into the east wall and later filled in and plastered over. This vent is not adjacent to either of the hearths. Room 2 shares the north wall of Room 1 (fig. 4.13) but is oriented perpendicular to the latter room. The floor area is similar, approximately 18 m². No vents or doorways were identified.

In each room, the adobe plaster floor was well preserved. In Room 1 the northern half of the floor rested on the gravel bedrock of the terrace; any artifact accumulation from earlier occupations was removed before the floor was laid (perhaps tossed into one of the pithouses, which are filled with Classic Mimbres period trash). In the southern half the floor rested on fill covering the floor of the field house, which was depressed a few centimeters into the bedrock gravel. The floor in Room 1 had not been replastered, yet it remained relatively unworn, sloping only slightly (3–5 cm) from the edges to the center of the room. Similarly, the floor in Room 2 was extraordinarily level, varying only 4 cm from walls to center, even though most of the floor rested on the fill of a pithouse (Nelson 1993b). This floor was thinly replastered late in the occupation in only the north half of the room, where a hearth, several postholes, and furniture posts were covered with a thin coat of adobe.

The roof in both rooms burned, leaving sections intact and resting on the room floor. In Room 1 the remodeled roof was supported by one large post in the center of the room (21) and at least eight secondary posts (9, 22A, 23, 24, 25, 26, 28, 29).[10] Feature 20 may also be a roof support posthole, although it is very shallow; no other post supports were evident along the east wall. Most of the secondary posts are located in the southwest corner of the room near one of the hearths. The roof in Room 2 was also supported by a deeply set central post (9) with one additional primary support post (29) in the northwest corner (fig. 4.13). Secondary posts are found north (30) and south (12) of the central post, in pairs toward the middle of the west (10, 27) and east (15, 48) walls (although 48 was plastered over, possibly replaced by 15), and clustered in the northwest corner. This substantial roof support contrasts sharply with the construction of the Classic period structure from which these later rooms were made.

Once Buckaroo Site had been remodeled into a small pueblo room block, minor changes were made to the architecture over the time during which it was occupied. Although these changes are not relevant to the argument for continuity from Classic to Postclassic occupation, they show continued use of the remodeled and expanded pueblo room block. The rooms appear to have been occupied long enough time for the structure to deteriorate and be repaired. These later repairs do not represent a major change in occupation focus, as occurred with the transformation from Classic to Postclassic, but a shift in the layout of space that appears to result from the need to shore up sagging portions of the roofs. In both rooms some secondary posts were thinly plastered over and replaced. For example, in Room 1, one post (22A) actually extends through hearth feature 22; it was added to this part of the room when the hearth was plastered over and replaced by hearth feature 19. Over the history of use of hearth feature 22, the roof became weakened (possibly because of a chimney or ceiling vent) and required considerable bolstering with posts, which are represented by the many postholes in this corner, so much so that working around the hearth would have been difficult. Finally, the hearth was abandoned and a new hearth (19) constructed in the north half of the room. The east wall vent may have been added at this time. The southwest corner of the room was so weak that nearly the entire corner had collapsed outward after abandonment, when the roof finally fell. Throughout the rest of the room, three or four courses of wall stone, standing about 60 cm high, remained intact. In Room 2 the primary post support in the northwest corner (29) may have been added late in the occupation of the room to shore a sagging roof in this corner. Three secondary posts in the same corner (37, 41, 42) were removed and plastered over sometime during the occupation of the structure, perhaps replaced with the more substantial corner post. Additional evidence of roof modification in Room 2 is seen in the changed location of the ladder to the roof. Initially, the ladder to the roof exit was placed adjacent to the north wall in the west half of the room. This is the corner that was deteriorating. Not only were roof supports changed, as noted above, but the depressions from the placement of the ladder were thinly plastered over. The later placement of the ladder was further east (A1 and A2). As in Room 1, the position and shape of the hearth was changed. Initially, the room had an oval hearth (35), which was partially plastered over and replaced by a square hearth (14). The latter was placed slightly to the west, farther from the new ladder placement.

In both rooms formal hearths were built when the ephemeral Classic structure was remodeled. All of the hearths in these two rooms are oval or square and lined with adobe plaster. In remodeled Room 1 the first hearth (22) is the smallest on the site, 30 cm in diameter, but is quite deep (13 cm). This depth may be from many repeated uses. Eventually, it was thinly covered with floor plaster and replaced by Hearth 19. The newer hearth is only 4 cm deep but quite large, 35 cm by 50 cm. Southeast of this hearth, near the wall vent is a large ashy lens, a possible ephemeral hearth for warming food or people. The formal and ephemeral hearths probably had different uses. Adjacent to Hearth 19 is a whole metate and a ceramic vessel, while adjacent to the ashy lens are many obsidian micro flakes. These were also recovered from the level directly above the ashy lens. Tool finishing and retouch may have been occurring in this area, the ashy lens a product of a warming hearth. Obsidian knapping would not be suitable in a kitchen area around hearth 19, not only because of the space needed for knapping activities (Newcomer and Sieveking 1980), but because the by products are extremely sharp. In Room 2 there were also two hearths, which are superimposed. The first hearth (35) was a small, deep, oval as was the first formal hearth in Room 1. It was altered by construction of a larger, shallower, square hearth (14).

In addition to the construction of formal hearths in both rooms, Room 1 may have had a wooden table and Room 2 a built-in mealing station (fig. 4.13). Wooden furnishings are suggested by clusters of small, shallow postholes and are found in nearly all of the Postclassic rooms. In Room 1, toward the west end of the north wall, are three small, shallow postholes (30, 31, 32) that form a pattern that could have supported a table or other furnishing. In the Guatemalan village of San Mateo Ixtatan, Maya kitchen areas in traditional wood and mud houses have corner worktables with one post standing outside and extending slightly above the edge of the table surface. The metate rests on this post and on the table to elevate one end when grinding (personal observation, 1979). In the room on Buckaroo Site, no formal grinding features were constructed, but a variety of grinding tools were found in roof and floor contexts. If this was a table, it represents fixed commitment of space to household food processing. In Room 2 a substantial mealing station (8) was built into the southeast corner. This feature has three adobe-lined basins surrounded by a thick adobe collar, and a roughened, depressed area to the south of each basin where the metates rested. In form this facility is much like the mealing stations found in Tularosa phase rooms in the Pine Lawn area (Martin et al. 1956:38–39; Martin et al. 1957:31–32). Additional mealing features were found in Postclassic rooms on the Buckaroo Site; Room 4 has a double-basin feature, and Room 3 has two, single-basin features. The changes toward investment in fixed, interior facilities that support domestic activities, including formal hearths, grinding facilities, and other interior wooden furnishings, contrast with the lack of domestic features in the Classic period structure at this site (table 4.4).

The floor assemblages in Rooms 1 and 2 indicate a range of domestic activities. In Room 1 most items of value had been removed, while in Room 2 the household assemblage was reasonably intact, and many items appear in their use locations. In Room 1 some usable items were resting on the floor, including hammerstones, chipped-stone flakes, a pigment-grinding slab, and two (possibly three) reconstructible, ceramic vessels. The vessels are a large Tularosa fillet-rimlike bowl with interior smudging and polishing, a Chupadero jar, and a few large sherds from an indented corrugated bowl, burnished on the interior. The Tularosa bowl was resting upright on the floor, but the jar was top down on the floor, with bits of its body found up to .25 m above the floor. Although nearly all of the sherds were recovered, the base is missing, and around the open bot-

Table 4.4

Characteristics of the architecture of Classic Mimbres and Postclassic period excavated structures on the Palomas hamlet sites

Site	Room	Time Period	Structure Construction	Formal Hearths	Mealing Stations	Other Furnishings*
Buckaroo	1	C	TS	0	0	Ash patch
Phelps	1	C	TSJ	0	0	0
	10	C	S	1	0	0
Ronnie	1	C/PC	S	1	0	Storage pit, rack or tripod
	2	C/PC	S	1	0	Storage pit, rack or tripod
Buckaroo	1	PC	S	2	0	Possible table, ashy patch
	2	PC	S	2	1	0
	3	PC	S	1	2	Storage pit
	4	PC	S	1	1	Possible storage pit
Lee	1	PC	S	1	1	0
	2	PC	S	0	1	Possible wooden rack or crib
	3	PC	S	1	1	0
Phelps	1	PC	SJ	1	0	0
	10	PC	S	1	2	Possible wooden tripod
	11	PC	S	1	1	Wood rack or screen, possible table

Notes:

* wooden features all listed as possible

TS   = Tri-wall structure of stone

TSJ   = Tri-wall structure of stone and jacal

S   = Rectangular stone construction, full height stone walls

SJ   = Rectangular stone and jacal construction, full height stone and jacal walls

C   = Classic Mimbres

C/PC = Classic or Postclassic Mimbres

PC   = Postclassic Mimbres

tom the edge had been neatly pecked. Mindeleff (1989:figs. 43, 74) shows the use of bottomless jars as chimneys and roof drains in the Zuni area, which might explain the intentional modification of this vessel. The vessel may have fallen from a collapsing roof; however, its rim was resting on the floor, which may indicate use for some other purpose within the room. Whatever the case, the vessel was not usable as a ceramic container, although the open base may have had an attached fabric cover. The archaeological assemblage of intact ceramic vessels in Room 1 is limited to no more than two bowls. Reconstructible cooking and storage jars are absent. A whole metate was located on the floor, face down, with pigment on that face. On the floor of Room 2, whole and reconstructible artifacts were abundant. Nine reconstructible, or nearly recon-structible, vessels were resting on the floor; one or two more may have been on the roof (tables 4.5 and 4.6). All are textured and/or corrugated, most with indented and patterned bands, a common feature of Reserve- and Tularosa-phase plainwares. All six or seven bowls are smudged and burnished in the interior (as is the bowl in Room 1), also a common feature of Reserve and Tularosa textured-corrugated wares and rare among Mimbres corrugated wares (Rinaldo and Bluhm 1956; Anyon and LeBlanc 1984).

The assemblage of reconstructible vessels on the floor includes four large bowls, two medium-sized bowls, two large jars, and a medium-sized jar (tables 4.5 and 4.6). Any of the jars could have served as cooking or storage vessels; all have exterior sooting. The burnished bowls would have functioned well as con-tainers or serving dishes; they also have sooting on the exterior. One large jar, and possibly a bowl, were in the roof debris. Sherds of Classic Mimbres Black-on-white, Chupadero Black-on-white, St. Johns Polychrome, El Paso Bichrome and El Paso Plain, and Tularosa Fillet rim were also found in roof and floor context, indicating a wide range of ceramic types used by occupants of Room 2. Sooting on ceramic vessels may be from their use for cooking but may also result from the fire that burned so extensively at the time of abandonment.

A range of other domestic activities produced materials that remained on the floor of Room 2, many of which are whole and usable. In the vicinity of the hearth and mealing feature in the eastern half of the room were two rectangular basalt manos, a circular rhyolitic tuff mano, and two shaft straighteners. A whole stone mortar and slab metate rested just above the floor in the vicinity of the cooking hearth and manos. In this same area were three bifaces, four cores, three unifaces, and a variety of chipped-stone flakes. The cores are of varied forms (single platform, multiple platform, and bifacial), perhaps for making a variety of flake forms useful for a range of domestic activities.

In the western half of the room, away from the food preparation area, were several obsidian flakes and a hammerstone. Two whole obsidian projectile points also were recovered from the floor of this room. Obsidian knapping may have been done indoors but away from food preparation. In close proximity to the obsidian were nine small smoothing stones, perhaps used for burnishing the interiors of the bowls found in this and other rooms.

Thus, varied core forms of local materials associated with grinding stones

Table 4.5

Posctclassic Mimbres floor assemblages at the Palomas hamlet sites

SITE	ROOM	B	J	M	P	MO	ME	SS	HS	C	ST	A	FL	O	AC
Buckaroo	1	2	1	—	—	—	—	1	—	1	—	—	many	1JW, 1BN, 1W	T
	2	7	4	1	—	3	1	2	1	4	8	—	many	9PS	OC
	3	7	6	—	—	15	2	—	1	—	—	1	few	2JW, 3BN	OC
	4	1	2	—	—	1	—	—	—	—	2	—	few	1W	OC
Ronnie	1	—	—	—	—	—	1	—	—	7	—	—	few	—	D
	2	2	3	—	1	8	—	—	few	few	1	—	many	—	OC
Lee	1	—	—	—	—	—	1	—	—	—	—	—	1	—	D
	2	—	—	—	—	—	—	—	—	1	—	—	—	—	D
	3	2	—	—	—	—	—	—	—	—	—	—	many	—	D
Phelps	1	—	—	—	—	—	—	—	—	—	—	—	1	—	D
	10	8	2	—	—	2	1	—	—	—	—	—	few	2Q	OC
	11	3	4	—	—	2	1	—	—	—	—	—	many	1JW, 1PS, 1OH	T

Notes:

B = Ceramic Bowl

J = Ceramic Jar

M = Ground stone mortar

P = Ground stone pestle

MO = Mano

ME = Metate

SS = Shaft straightener

HS = Hammerstone

C = Core

ST = Chipped stone tool (biface, uniface)

A = Ground stone axe

FL = Chipped stone flakes

O = Other (JW = shell, bone, and stone jewelry; Q = quartz crystal; BN = bone tool;
      PS = polishing stone; OH = ochre; W = worked sherd)

AC = Interpretation of abandonment status of room (T = temporarily abandoned; OC = in
      use when burned; D = disassembled, unoccupied)

and ceramic vessels were found in the east portion of the room adjacent to hearth and mealing station, while obsidian flakes and tools and polishing stones were clustered on the east side of the room. The spatial separation of these clustered objects indicates task separation or a division of space within the room. Those with ready access to exotic materials were making shaped tools in an area

Table 4.6

Vessel assemblage composition of the roof and floor assemblages within Postclassic Mimbres hamlets

	JAR			BOWL		
SITES/Rooms	L	M	S	L	M	S
RONNIE						
Room 2F	1	1*	1		2*	
BUCKAROO						
Room 3F	2*	1		3	1	1
Room 3R	1*	2				
Room 4F		2			1	
Room 1F	1*			1	1	
Room 2F	2	1		4	2	
Room 2R	1				1	
PHELPS						
Room 1F	1					
Room 10F		2		1	4	
Room 11F	2	1	1	1		1

Notes:

Only portable vessels are included in this table; those embedded in the mealing stations are excluded.

L = large; M = medium; S = small.

There were no reconstructible vessels in Room 1 on Ronnie Pueblo or in any of the rooms on Lee Pueblo.

An asterisk indicates painted vessels. In Room 3 on the Buckaroo Site, only one of the large jars on the floor is painted. The painted vessels include three Chupadero Black-on-white jars (Ronnie and Buckaroo), two Classic Mimbres Black-on-white bowls (Ronnie), and an El Paso Polychrome jar (Buckaroo).

"F" refers to the floor assemblage; "R" refers to roof assemblage.

also used for a polishing activity, probably burnishing the interiors of vessels. Food preparation was limited to a separate area. This division could represent a gendered division of household space; if women prepared food for the household, their activity domain may have been primarily in the eastern half of the room. The diversity of core forms in the food preparation area suggests varied core reduction techniques, perhaps used by women. Men may have worked in the western half. The association of knapping and burnishing is interesting and

may indicate male participation in an aspect of ceramic production. This conclusion assumes that the tool production and burnishing were done by men
and food preparation by women; while food preparation by women is a common pattern, it is equally possible that all of the work within the residence,
including the knapping, was by women and that task separation was for other
reasons (see Gero 1991). In either case the division of household space is consistent with lengthy or regular reuse.

Because this richness of abandonment assemblage was not found in Room 1,
the fragments on and near the floor were examined to evaluate the range of
items used in the room. The inventory of small items on the floor and embedded in it is diverse. Joyce and Johannessen (1993:149–50) argue that small
items embedded in the floor as primary refuse may be one of the few indicators
of activities of occupants under conditions of gradual abandonment, when portable items would be moved to other places. Portable items may also be rare in
rooms that are temporarily abandoned, that is, those to which people intend to
return. The residents may move some items with them, while storing other
items. The assemblage in this and other rooms appears more consistent with
the move-some–store-some interpretation in that some portable items remain
(table 4.5). In either case, in a room with a limited assemblage of whole items,
the small embedded artifacts are remnants, deposited through loss or breakage,
of activities conducted in the room. As such, they are excellent indicators of
room function and the organization of activities. In this room the artifacts on
and near the floor were not deposited on the floor as postoccupational trash.
Artifact densities in the fill are too low to support such an inference.

Small sherds from a range of vessel types and forms, shell fragments, a bone
awl, a polished stone, a bone bead, a worked sherd, and a variety of small chipped-
stone flakes were found in, on, and slightly above the floor. These indicate the
same range of activities represented by the fuller in situ assemblage in other
rooms at the site. The vessels include cooking and noncooking plainwares and
painted bowls and jars. A range of domestic activities are indicated by these and
the other fragmentary bone and stone artifacts. Grinding tools, however, are
noticeably lacking on the floor; there are no fragments of manos or metates,
although one whole metate rested on the floor.

The construction and occupation of these two rooms serve as examples of
the continuity and change that occurred in the Eastern Mimbres area during
the twelfth century. An ephemeral Classic period structure was remade to serve
a more residential focus, and the residential area was expanded. These changes
were accomplished by modifying a standing structure, not by building over the

remains of an earlier, collapsed structure. With initial remodeling, the structure was made more substantial, and greater commitment was made to building domestic facilities into rooms. The artifact assemblages of reconstructible and fragmentary pieces on floors and roofs indicate a diverse domestic assemblage. One interesting difference between the two rooms is the status of their use when burning occurred. Room 1 appears to have been temporarily abandoned. This inference is based on the overturned metate and jar and on the lack of portable items in the room. As Schlanger and Wilshusen (1993:90) suggest, temporarily abandoned rooms may have been scavenged by others, which may also account for the small inventory in Room 1. It is also possible that the overturned metate with pigment on its grinding face marks final abandonment or closure of the room occupation. If so, that closure occurred at abandonment of the site, because there is no trash fill in the room.

Two other abandonment assemblages on this site contrast with that from Room 1. In Rooms 2 and 3 the abandonment assemblages are rich. Not only are there more than a dozen vessels in each room, but rare items such as shaft straighteners, an axe, bone tools, and jewelry are on the floors. The placement of these items away from walls and adjacent to facilities is indicative of active use of the rooms. Abandonment appears to have been rapid or to have involved sanctions against removing any items. In either case the rich complement of household items left behind provides information about the domestic activities in these residences. These assemblages and the differences among them are discussed below in the section on change. Although the abandonment process was different between these rooms, their use as residences appears similar.

Other ephemeral Classic period structures were modified in the same ways. Room 1 on the Phelps site was changed through addition of a fourth enclosing wall and a formal, interior hearth. On Lizard Terrace Pueblo one early tri-wall structure was remodeled by the addition of a fourth enclosing wall. At Mountain Lion Hamlet an ephemeral jacal structure was changed to a more substantial room; the walls were reinforced, the roof was made thicker, and a formal hearth and mealing facility were added to the interior. In each of these cases, the modifications were made to existing, standing structures.

Remodeling a Substantial Structure: Phelps, Room 10. Room 10 (fig. 4.14) has two floors, each with an associated hearth. Architectural detail indicates remodeling rather than reoccupation. Room function did not change from one floor occupation to the next as it did in Room 1 on this site, at Room 1 on the Buckaroo Site, and at other excavated Postclassic sites in the Eastern Mimbres

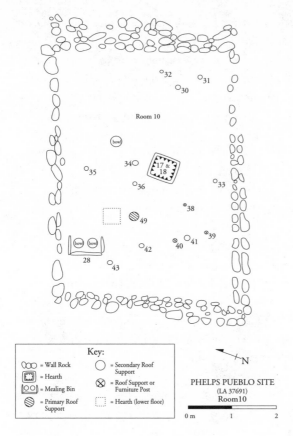

Figure 4.14

Postclassic Mimbres room on Phelps Pueblo (Room 10), remodeled from an earlier structure.

area (Hegmon and Nelson 1994; Nelson and Hegmon 1995, 1996). However, the organization of space and commitment to grinding facilities increased with remodeling. The upper floor yielded an extensive floor assemblage similar to those in Rooms 2 and 3 on the Buckaroo Site.

Throughout Room 10 the walls were full-height masonry, and the roof was substantial. Although supported by somewhat shallow posts, there were many posts (fig. 4.15), and two are wide enough to have been substantial supports (30, 49). One alignment of small posts (33, 34, 35, 36) extended north to south, through the center of the room; another (41, 42, 43) followed the same orientation on the west side of the room. Three additional posts (30, 31, 32)

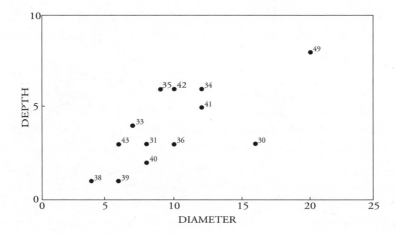

Figure 4.15

Dimensions of postholes and depressions in Room 10, Phelps Pueblo.

were clustered in the southeast corner, perhaps a weak spot in the roof. This corner is on the edge of the room block, with no additional support from rooms to the south or east.

The upper floor merges in places with the lower floor. Remodeling of the earlier, possibly Classic period structure was accomplished through extensive replastering of the floor to add a mealing station (28) to the northwest corner of the room. The upper floor hearth (17, 18) was placed toward the center of the room, farther from the area of the mealing feature than was the earlier hearth, which was used before the mealing station was built. This change allowed adequate space to move around the mealing area; in fact, the hearth in the lower floor is too close to the new mealing feature to have allowed grinding and cooking to have been performed at the same time. The upper hearth is rectangular, with an adobe collar and lining. It is among the larger hearths in the area, 54–63 cm in diameter and 11 cm deep but comparable to the hearth features in Ronnie Pueblo. The dated archaeomagnetic sample came from this upper hearth, as discussed earlier in the chapter. The mealing feature (28) is substantial; it was added to the room by building up the floor of the earlier room to create a slight platform. Large, upright slabs form a partial bin around the platform, with one open side. On the open side were set two bowls, embedded in the raised portion of the floor and each surrounded by an adobe collar. Inside one of the bowls rested a two-handed mano. The embedded bowls have indented corrugated bands near the rim and smudged, polished interiors. These vessel forms and the form of the grinding station resemble vessels and features in Tularosa phase rooms in the Pine Lawn area (Rinaldo and Bluhm 1956), northwest of the Mimbres region (fig. 1.1).

Two other features that supported domestic activities were built into the upper floor. Northeast of the hearth, a bowl (16) was embedded in the floor as a second mealing station. The indented, corrugated design is similar to Reserve and Tularosa textured wares found in other mealing facilities. Although its use as a grinding station was clear, its location near the center of the room was unusual. Southwest of the hearth were three small, shallow, oblong post depressions (38, 39, 40) that formed a triangle, perhaps the remains of a wooden tripod. Within the space formed by the triangle was a broken jar. The patterned, corrugated design near the rim of this vessel is similar to Tularosa Patterned Corrugated (Rinaldo and Bluhm 1956). The jar, if resting on a tripod, would have been placed adjacent to a roof support post (41), which would have stabilized it.

Whole artifacts were abundant on the floor of this room. Ten reconstructible vessels, four whole grinding tools, and a variety of orphan sherds and flakes rested on the floor. In addition to the three bowls set in the mealing features, seven vessels were in the vicinity of the hearth and grinding area. Clustered around the hearth were six vessels. The broad, squat jar with patterned, corrugated design that may have rested on a tripod was adjacent to a large plain bowl, which held an indented, corrugated jar. Both jars have charring at the base, but the bowl does not. Also part of this cluster is a bowl with patterned, corrugated design near the rim. It is not burned at the base. Two bowls were found northeast of the hearth: one is indented corrugated, the other clapboard corrugated. The latter design gave way to the former during the late twelfth century. Their association as whole vessels is unusual. No record was made regarding charring on these vessels. Thus, the vessel assemblage from around the hearth has at least two cooking vessels (charred at the base); both are jars. The four other vessels are bowls of different sizes (table 4.6). Within this cluster of vessels was a stone pestle and several whole flakes, probably used in food preparation.

Adjacent to the large mealing station that held two bowls was a third bowl with indented, corrugated design similar to the two embedded in the feature. The excavators noted that the bowls seemed loose in their collared depressions, thus removable. The third bowl may have rested near the others to replace a full bowl removed from the feature.

Although a mano rested in the mealing area, the only metate in the room was an unshaped, sandstone slab near the center of the east wall. Although it remains functional, other metates must have been removed at abandonment or before the room burned. None was found in the roof debris. A second mano rested along the north wall in the vicinity of the embedded bowl that served as a secondary mealing facility; that mano is also functional. The manos are both of basalt; either all grinding was medium or coarse-textured or additional manos of finer texture were removed from the room. Again, no manos were found in roof debris.

No small items other than the few chipped-stone flakes and a variety of orphan sherds rested on the floor. Directly above the floor were two quartz crystals, which may have been left on the floor at abandonment or have been lost prior to abandonment and have shifted slightly through various postdepositional processes.

The floor assemblage in this room is rich in vessels but has a paucity of grinding tools and small household items (table 4.5). The under representation of grinding tools cannot be explained by their use in outdoor facilities; two such facilities are built into the room. Their low frequency indicates that they were removed either by people who temporarily abandoned the room, with intention to reoccupy (as is indicated for Room 1 on Buckaroo Site), by others scavenging from temporarily abandoned rooms, or as part of the permanent abandonment process. Temporary abandonment is a less reasonable interpretation than gradual abandonment because the items left in the room are in use areas, associated with facilities, rather than in storage areas. In either case, burning eliminated the option of removing any more items and sealed the partial assemblage of domestic tools. The other excavated room in this block (Room 11) has similar features (fig. 4.16) and assemblage composition (table 4.5). It also has a limited assemblage of floor artifacts other than ceramic vessels. The ceramic vessels, except one, are lined against the wall in the northeast corner, beneath a possible table, perhaps in temporary storage. Together, the placement of vessels and paucity of other portable items support the conclusion that the Room 11 was temporarily abandoned. The one vessel not in apparent storage, however, was a jar that was resting on the hearth, which contradicts the evidence for temporary abandonment. This room was intensely burned, to the point that part of the adobe became vitrified.

Remodeling of the early structure forming Room 10 is similar to only one other room in the study area. At Lizard Terrace Pueblo (LA37726) a substantially constructed Classic period room was remodeled by adding a new floor, changing the form of the hearth, and building a fixed mealing station. The early floor in this structure had only a single painted sherd on the floor, which is

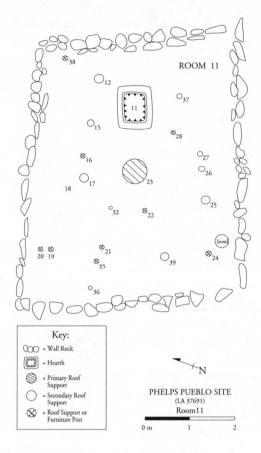

Figure 4.16
Postclassic Mimbres room on Phelps Pueblo (Room 11).

Classic Mimbres Black-on-white, Style III; the later floor has ceramics that included Classic Mimbres Black-on-white and a variety of later types (table 4.3). In both the room on Lizard Terrace and Phelps Pueblos, the early structure was modified while standing; all changes were toward greater investment in domestic activities within rooms.

Ceramics. Further evidence for continuity is found in the ceramic assemblages in these rooms. Classic Mimbres Black-on-white, Style III, is present in the ceramic assemblages in association with a variety of types that are assumed not to have been made until after the Classic Mimbres period (tables 3.1 and 4.3). These associations are not in fill contexts alone. Roof and floor contexts in nearly every excavated room have Classic Mimbres sherds associated with other types (table 4.3). In Room 2 on Ronnie Pueblo, two Classic Mimbres, Style III, Black-on-white bowls are found in association with a Chupadero Black-on-white jar (table 4.6). In all other rooms, however, Classic Mimbres is found only as sherds, while other ceramic types (El Paso Polychrome and Chupadero Black-on-white) are found as individual sherds and reconstructible vessels. The vessel assemblages from rooms comprise abandonment assemblages, which should be the last vessels used before a site or room was abandoned. Chronometric and ceramic data indicate that many of the rooms could have been occupied into the mid to late 1200s and possibly later. By that time, Classic Mimbres was no longer used. What is the process by which the Classic sherds are deposited in these floor contexts, in rooms with in situ assemblages? The sherds are quite small and must be the remnants of vessels used and broken in the rooms. Sweeping or clearing would be expected in these domestic spaces, but small sherds become embedded in activity surfaces or lost in corners and along walls. During the early decades of the Postclassic (post A.D. 1150) after remodeling and expansion of the residential space on the hamlet sites, the domestic assemblages included Classic Mimbres Black-on-white; unfortunately, only one room, Room 2 on Ronnie Pueblo, preserved this association because of the intense burning of that room.

Chronometric Date Distributions. Chronometric dates also support occupational continuity. Although the age ranges are quite broad, the summed probability distributions of the uncalibrated radiocarbon ages for all samples from a site can be examined for evidence of breaks or modes in the distribution. Analysis of continuity is based on contrasting models of date distribution for continuous as opposed to interrupted site use. If the occupants of a site used it continuously, constructing, remodeling, and repairing their homes, the true ages of construction materials should have a fairly flat, unimodal distribution. The distribution would appear flatter the longer the site was continuously used. This distribution might have its mode to the left if more construction activity occurred early in the occupation span or to the right if most construction immediately preceded abandonment. It might look like a flattened, normal distribution if the site grew and was abandoned gradually. Similarly, the dates on maize from a variety of contexts should have a flat, unimodal distribution as maize was grown and consumed over the occupation span of the site. A bimodal distribution would be produced by true dates from two occupations or use episodes separated by time.

There are at least two problems with these models and expectations. First, the time span of an occupational hiatus might be too short to be evident in dates that have standard errors of the size found in these samples. Second, very small samples of dates for fairly long periods of occupation or use produce multiple modes (Kintigh, personal communication, 1996). Multiple modes were evident for samples of three to five, depending on the probable length of occupation. Thus, this method for evaluating continuity could not be applied to specific rooms but was applicable at the level of sites.

Figures 4.2, 4.4, 4.5, and 4.7, discussed earlier, show the summed probability distributions around all radiocarbon mean ages from four of the sites (using Kintigh 1994).[11] All are unimodal, although the sample from Buckaroo Site has a minor mode in the range of radiocarbon age 840 to 880, which calibrates to the late A.D. 1100s or early 1200s. The distributions are also quite flat, with the exception of the distribution from Ronnie Pueblo.[12] The pattern for radiocarbon dates contrasts with the obsidian hydration probability distributions. The distribution for samples from the Buckaroo Site (fig. 4.3) illustrates this point. The combined sample distribution has multiple modes. The difference between radiocarbon age distribution and that from obsidian can be explained in terms of occupation histories and the difference in the behaviors represented by the different kinds of samples, but not by sample size. (The samples are of equivalent size.) Radiocarbon samples were carefully selected from surface rooms to represent their construction, firewood from hearths, and maize on activity surfaces. They should represent surface structure occupation only, except where construction wood was salvaged from earlier pithouse structures. The obsidian, by contrast, comes from a range of contexts. Obsidian is exotic to the region but extremely valuable for producing sharp cutting edges. Obsidian can be scavenged from discards of earlier site occupations. We know that most, if not all, of the sites have pithouses. Thus, the distribution of obsidian dates would more closely represent the entire range of time during which obsidian was acquired and brought to the sites, with more dates toward the time of abandonment, after which obsidian was not scavenged from deposits. The distributions of obsidian hydration dates from Buckaroo Site are consistent with the model of discontinuity; there is a possible hiatus in acquisition of obsidian in the late pithouse to early Classic Mimbres periods (late 900s to 1000s). This is the time during which I have argued for limited use of the sites as secondary agricultural camps. Obsidian may not have been needed to the extent that people were willing to make long trips to acquire it or trade for it. If users of the field houses during the Classic period only scavenged local trash for obsidian, there would have been no dates from that period of site use.

Evidence for Change

Descriptions of the remodeling of the rooms points to the changes that occurred on the four sites—and by implication in the Eastern Mimbres area during the twelfth century. Occupation at the field houses shifted from limited to more residential use, which was expanded. While the exact number of structures that constituted the Classic period portion of the sites cannot be determined without excavating each of the four sites completely, lack of Classic components in many of the Postclassic rooms indicates an expansion of the residential aspect of the four sites with the remodeling of Classic period structures. The size of the Postclassic occupation at each site is estimated in the site maps provided in figures 3.2–3.5, ranging from approximately six to twelve rooms. The increased residential focus at locales that had previously served as small field houses and the depopulation of villages were also associated with a reorganization of land use. Paleoethnobotanical and faunal indices of these changes are discussed in the next chapter, but the architectural and artifactual indices of increased residential mobility are examined in the sections that follow.

Increased Residential Focus. Change toward increased residential focus is indicated in the addition of built-in domestic facilities to the rooms. A few examples of this change are described in the previous section. The facilities in all structures are summarized in table 4.4. Postclassic rooms consistently have formal hearths and mealing stations; hearths occur in some of the Classic period floors, but mealing stations are absent. A variety of other domestic furnishings were constructed in rooms, including storage pits and wooden furniture. The form of furnishings is speculative because the wooden facilities were not preserved; I have indicated my tentative interpretations in table 4.4, based on the arrangements of small, shallow postholes that would not have served as roof support. While my interpretations of the distributions of furniture posts may be challenged, the presence of wooden furnishings in the Postclassic rooms and their absence in Classic period structures are of interest. The addition of furnishings is further evidence for the domestic focus of occupation of the sites and the designation of space to specific tasks.

The consistency with which hearths and mealing stations occur in Postclassic rooms indicates similar use of the rooms. Few appear to have been linked to others by doorways, all (except Room 2 at Lee Pueblo) have substantial hearths, and most have mealing stations. The room suites so common on large Classic villages (see chap. 2) are not found in these Postclassic hamlets. Two rooms are exceptions. On Lee Pueblo, Room 2 may be a specialized mealing room; it has no hearth but has evidence of wooden racks or cribs and a mealing station. Phelps Pueblo has a partially enclosed work area to the west of Room 11 that lacks built-in features. Such work enclosures may be fairly common; one other was found in recent excavations at Mountain Lion Hamlet.

Unfortunately, abandonment assemblages from the Classic and Postclassic floors cannot be compared. Classic structures were remade into Postclassic rooms, leaving no usable artifacts in place.[13] Looking at the abandonment assemblages in Postclassic rooms, however, provides information about the range of activities performed or prepared for in the rooms; their composition is consistent with a residential focus. Table 4.5 summarizes the abandonment assemblages from the twelve excavated Postclassic rooms. Some had been cleared of artifacts during or after abandonment, especially the rooms on Lee Pueblo and Room 1 on Ronnie Pueblo, which appear also to have had the roof beams and support posts removed. Five of the rooms provide information on the domestic assemblage possibly used in all rooms. Room 3 on Buckaroo Site has the richest assemblage. Its distribution is indicative of active use of the room at the time it burned and was abandoned. Description of the assemblage and its distribution follow; figure 4.17 is a map of the floor features.

Buckaroo Site, Room 3, abandonment assemblage: The artifact assemblage on the floor of Room 3 includes ten reconstructible vessels, fifteen manos, two metates, and a variety of other whole artifacts found on the floor. Additional vessels and whole artifacts were in use on the roof. From the forms and distribution of these items, the organization of household space is evident.

The ceramic vessels include two large jars, a smaller jar, and seven bowls. Two of the bowls were embedded in the mealing stations at opposite corners of the room (13 and 14). Both bowls have indented, corrugated design near the rim and black, burnished interior similar to bowls made in the Pine Lawn area to the northwest of the Mimbres region (Rinaldo and Bluhm 1956:158–71). Adjacent to one mealing feature (13) were two vessels: a large El Paso Polychrome jar and a large bowl with wide, indented bands of corrugation near the rim and a smudged-polished interior. A similar bowl rested near the other mealing feature (14). The El Paso jar was probably for storage of water or grain. It is far too large for cooking and is not sooted. The bowls may have been used to hold meal after it was ground. The remainder of the vessels were clustered to the

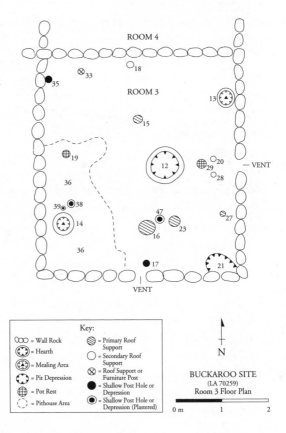

Figure 4.17
Postclassic Mimbres room on Buckaroo Site (Room 3).

southeast side of the hearth, between the hearth (12) and storage pit (21). These included a large, patterned, corrugated jar, a slightly smaller incised redware jar, two indented, corrugated bowls (one large, one small), and a plain bowl. All are heavily charred, indicating their use as cooking vessels. Why large, open bowls would have been used in this way is unclear; food may have been warmed in bowls. The charring may be from the burning of the roof, although the jars and one of the bowls are clearly charred on the base only. Further assessments of their composition is necessary to determine if they could have served as cooking vessels (Mills 1984; Wilson, Skibo, and Schiffer 1996).

In addition to the assemblage of two jars and three bowls, the clustering of artifacts southeast of the hearth includes two metates and a mano. One is a large, thick, trough metate, with considerable use-life remaining; a rectangular, two-handed mano would have been used with it. The other metate is a slab that may have been used with the oval mano. These grinding tools must have been used expediently in food preparation within the hearth area and perhaps moved to the mealing features for more extensive grinding periods. To the west of the hearth was a whole, ground-stone axe.

Each of the mealing stations had an associated clustering of artifacts. In the northeast corner of the room the El Paso Jar was on the south side of the feature, and four rectangular, two-handed manos were piled on the north side. These are all extremely worn or broken and may be in a state of provisional discard, piled for eventual removal or set aside of a possible secondary use (Nelson and Nelson 1986). In the southwest corner, east of the grinding feature, were stacked four, whole, rectangular, two-handed manos with a hammerstone and turquoise pendant beneath. Adjacent were three bone awls and the large, indented, corrugated bowl. These may have been the personal property of one of the principal room occupants, perhaps an adult female, if women were primarily responsible for grinding. Six more manos (whole, rectangular, and two-handed) were found toward the center of the room in the north half. They were scattered linearly on their sides from the north wall into the room; they may have been stacked against the north wall and have fallen when the roof collapsed. These may have been a mano cache of the user of the grinding feature in the northeast corner of the room.

In contrast to Rooms 1 and 2 in this room block, chipped-stone artifacts were rare on the floor of Room 3. The hammerstone found with the manos may have been for rejuvenating grinding tools. No cores were found on the floor. A few, late-stage, cryptocrystalline flakes were left on the floor, and several were embedded in it, products of stone working in the room, most of which had been swept up and deposited elsewhere. Nearly all are cryptocrystalline, and most were embedded in the floor in the southwest quadrant of the room, between the hearth and the grinding area; these large flakes may have been produced to aid in food processing. A bone bead was also embedded in the floor.

Three jars appear to have fallen, along with several more manos, from the roof when it collapsed. The jars are all fairly large and are of varied decoration. One is Chupadero Black-on-white; the mouth and neck are heavily calcified, suggesting that the top of the vessel was embedded in the adobe of the roof or had an attachment that is now missing. The other two jars are indented, corrugated forms similar to those made in the Pine Lawn area. One of these has a Tularosa patterned, corrugated design on the neck and extending down to the maximum circumference at the shoulder. The other has a simple, indented, corrugated design on the neck. No other whole or reconstructible artifacts were clearly associated with the roof debris.

This room has a rich floor and roof assemblage, with a range of utilitarian items indicative of a household assemblage. Thirteen reconstructible vessels (two or three fixed in the structure), two usable metates, more than a dozen whole manos, three bone awls, an axe, a hammerstone, and flakes provide the necessary items for food preparation and maintenance activities. This assemblage provides a picture of the domestic tools used within rooms at these hamlets and a baseline to which abandonment assemblages in other rooms can be compared to assess what items are lacking in other rooms. In addition, the distribution of items provides information about the organization of the household. Grinding features in the northeast and southwest corners appear to have been the loci of food processing for individuals, each with a cache of personal items. The southeast quadrant of the room was devoted to food preparation, perhaps the domain of women. The northwest quadrant, by contrast, was devoid of features and artifacts except for a spilled stack of manos. This may have been a general-use area kept clear for varied activities, or it may have been a sleeping or storage area. Spatial segregation of tasks was described above for Room 2 on Buckaroo Site. The commitment of space to a limited range of tasks, indicated by both these artifact distributions and the construction of fixed facilities, correlates with extended periods of regular use or occupation (Graham 1993).

Residential Mobility. The shift toward increased residential occupation and expanded room blocks at Postclassic hamlets occurred when people were depopulating the large villages. The architectural and artifactual data are consistent with a shift in residence from aggregated villages to these small, hamlet settlements, at least for some portion of the population. Details of the architecture also suggest that this shift in residence was associated with a shift in residential stability. A number of aspects of the hamlet architecture and assemblage composition are inconsistent with a model of continuous occupation of each room. Although the sites may have been continuously occupied or maintained, each household may have engaged in a fair amount of residential movement. Thus, the occupation of each room was intermittent. This contrasts with the current view of a residentially stable occupation of the villages during the preceding Classic period. Data discussed below are merely suggestive of a pattern of continuous site occupation by intermittently moving households.

Residential mobility in the form of regular, intermittent occupation of rooms is indicated in details of the architecture and artifact assemblages in Postclassic hamlet rooms. Continuous use of structures over an extended period of time should be evident either in replastering and repair of walls, roofs, and floors or in their deteriorated condition (if not repaired). In the Postclassic hamlet rooms nearly every roof was substantially repaired to the extent that fixed features were sometimes rebuilt and remodeled to shift the roofed entryway away from sagging areas. The description of Room 2 at Buckaroo Site in the previous section provides an example of such structure maintenance. In contrast, the floor of this room and nearly every other Postclassic room was barely worn and rarely replastered. Episodes of replastering were found only as small, thin patches covering the holes of replaced posts or other features (e.g., hearths). Lack of wear to the floors can be seen in the slight variation in floor elevation from walls to the center; among the nine rooms with preserved floors, eight vary 10 cm or less in elevation from wall edge to center of the room.[14] This amount of depression is minimal for such large rooms. The possibility of complete floor replacement was considered by examining the articulation between walls and floors; there were no cases of this kind of repair in Postclassic rooms. Rooms that were occupied extensively should have had portions of their floor worn down around high traffic areas and commonly used activity areas. Creel (personal communication, 1997) has recovered matting from floor surfaces in Mimbres Valley sites, which he suggests might limit wear but not in high traffic areas. With the cooking area in the middle of this room, the floor should acquire a dish shape if used extensively. This effect was observed in Maya houses in San Mateo Ixtatan, Guatemala, where some floors were worn down as much as half of a meter in high-use area; only the newest houses had fairly level floors (personal observation, 1979, Brian Hayden's Coxoh Ethnoarchaeological Project). Yet, Postclassic rooms, with their extensive roof repair, had little wear to floor surfaces.

Incongruity between the evidence for deterioration and repair between the superstructure of buildings and the floors could be explained in various ways. The occupants of these rooms could have conducted most of their activities outside. The presence of fixed cooking and mealing facilities inside, however, suggests that food preparation was conducted in the rooms. Other activities are also indicated by the floor assemblages, examples of which are described earlier for Rooms 2 (in the section "Evidence for Continuity") and 3 ("Evidence for Change") on Buckaroo Site. The lack of depression of room floors in the center and adjacent to frequently used facilities might also result from placement of floors on an unyielding bedrock surface. However, many of the floors of

Postclassic rooms are placed over fill. They should have worn and become depressed fairly easily. A third possibility, derived from the expectation about occupational continuity stated at the outset, is that the slightly worn floors, and therefore the rooms, were not occupied continuously, but the superstructures were maintained to allow regular, intermittent reuse, which others have referred to as anticipated, intentional, or planned reoccupation (Horne 1993; Kent 1992; Tomka 1993).

Two aspects of the artifact assemblage are consistent with the suggestion of intermittent residential occupation of rooms. First, some rooms appear to have been temporarily unoccupied when they burned. This inference is based on the presence of usable items in storage contexts and the lack of a full domestic assemblage. The absence of a domestic assemblage could be explained by removal at final abandonment, but these rooms differ from others with limited assemblages in that the remaining items appear to have been placed in storage. Four rooms had a limited assemblage of usable items on the floors; two of these appear to have been temporarily abandoned (table 4.5). In Postclassic Room 1 on Buckaroo Site, described above, a metate was overturned on the floor, and one jar was placed upside down on the floor, although this jar had the base removed. Most of the domestic assemblage is absent from this room. Also described above is Room 11 on Phelps Pueblo, in which most artifacts are placed along the walls; possibly, most vessels are beneath a table. By contrast, in two of the rooms with limited domestic assemblages, the usable items are adjacent to features and in other open space. For example, in Room 2 on Ronnie Pueblo, the vessels, at least half of the manos, and the stone working tools are distributed in open space in the south half of the room, south of the hearth. Only one pile of three manos and a pestle are in a corner, at the top of a storage pit. In a second room, not fully described in this text, artifacts are similarly distributed in activity areas. Room 4 on Buckaroo Site has a limited abandonment assemblage of one ceramic bowl, two ceramic jars, one mano, two unifaces, a shaped ceramic sherd, and a few chipped-stone flakes. Most of these are clustered around the hearth and mealing station.

Second, the vessel assemblages are minimal in those few rooms with fairly full domestic assemblages, although they include a range of forms. (For discussion of minimum household-assemblage size, see Reid et al. 1989:810–11, Schiffer 1985:21, and Smith 1983:307.) Year-round occupation ought to be supported with a vessel assemblage that includes replacements for those items that break frequently or are important to the operation of a household (Reid et al. 1989:811; Smith 1983:277). Breakage of cooking, serving, or water-storage vessels would have been problematic, because replacements are not in evidence. Among residentially mobile households, however, those in residence may have relied on the inventory of those absent as a backup (Schlanger and Wilshusen 1993:90). In addition, if people moved among local residences, they may have been able to return to their temporarily abandoned residences where stored vessels could have been acquired for replacement. (Graham 1993 discusses vessel transport among residences of a single household.) These strategies require less ceramic production for mobile households than manufacture of a full inventory of domestic items and replacements for each residence.

Table 4.6 summarizes the portable-vessel assemblage in each room. The vessels are not categorized by function because I have not evaluated their performance characteristics; except in the most general way, too few are reconstructible to provide the functional redundancy necessary for evaluating variation. I have chosen to use size as a general index of function, along with information about the conditions of the vessel wall, that is, sooting and calcification. All of the jars have relatively narrow orifices. To serve the needs of each residence, medium and large bowls and jars are minimally required. The large jars appear to have been for storage of water, based on the calcification of their walls. The medium, unpainted jars and the medium and large bowls were used for warming and serving food, based on the presence of sooting on their base and sides. Some medium and large bowls that are not sooted must also have been used to mix food and hold ground meal.

The largest vessel assemblages, those in Rooms 2 and 3 on the Buckaroo Site, which I have argued may represent active use at the time of burning, have a few vessels in most size and form classes. The third room that appeared occupied, Room 10 on Phelps Pueblo, has fewer vessels; notably missing is any large jar. Those rooms that I argued were temporarily abandoned when they burned, Room 1 on Buckaroo Site and Room 11 on Phelps Pueblo, have little redundancy in size or form classes and are absent some key forms: large jars in the room on Buckaroo Site and medium bowls in the room on Phelps Pueblo. At both of these pueblos, however, some rooms appeared actively in use and others temporarily abandoned when the structures burned. If the assemblages are combined, that is, if the temporarily abandoned rooms at each pueblo served as a backup to the "in-use" assemblages, then a functional domestic vessel assemblage and sufficient replacements are available. The vessel assemblage for each of the two "in-use" residences at Buckaroo Site and the one at Phelps would be about thirteen vessels. Others have estimated the domestic assemblages from "in-use" rooms in Southwestern sites in this range (Lightfoot 1994:81; Nelson and LeBlanc 1986). At Chodistaas Pueblo in the Grasshopper region to the west, houses had more than five times as many vessels (Montgomery 1993).

A structural feature of the hamlet sites may also be understood in light of a model of entrenched residential mobility. The majority of the sites lack storage features. Only one possible storage room (Room 2 on Lee Pueblo) and three small storage pits (two at Ronnie Pueblo and one at Buckaroo Site) across all four pueblos were found. If a household moved among several hamlets, however, the rooms themselves could have been used for storage. This pattern was observed among the Highland Maya in Guatemala (personal observation 1979). Some families with more than one house stored the food grown at one residence by stacking it within their house at that locale.

These characteristics of architecture and artifact assemblage are only suggestive of a pattern of residential mobility that deserves further attention. If this argument regarding residential mobility is correct, the pattern for the study area is similar to that observed among the Tarahumara, who are cultivators and pastoralists in northern Mexico. They move residence within an annual cycle; some members of small villages are in residence when others are absent. From season to season and year to year the same people do not reside in a village. On both the Buckaroo Site and Phelps Pueblo some occupants were in residence while others had temporarily moved elsewhere at the time the pueblos burned. Horne (1993) refers to the pattern of regular reuse as locational stability in contrast to occupational stability. Locational stability is the repeated occupation of areas rather than the continuous occupation of specific places, a pattern that she believes is important in arid environments.

Conclusion

The Classic Mimbres settlement pattern of occupation primarily in villages with outlying farmsteads changed in the Eastern Mimbres region to a Postclassic pattern of settlement in small residential hamlets. Architectural, ceramic, and dating evidence support a model of continuity in the occupation and use of farmsteads as they were remodeled and expanded to become the residential base during the Postclassic Mimbres period. This continuity and change provide for regional stability through reorganization of the local population on the landscape.

Classic period farmsteads were isolated structures, many of which were constructed from light material or were open on one side. Most lacked interior domestic features. These were excavated at Buckaroo Site and Phelps Pueblo, and possibly on Ronnie Pueblo. While standing, these structures were extensively modified: walls and roofs were made more substantial, and domestic features were constructed within structures. This extensive remodeling occurred at Buckaroo Site and Phelps Pueblo, and at two other sites recently excavated in the study area, Mountain Lion Hamlet and Lizard Terrace Pueblo. The best estimate of the timing of this substantial change was during the middle of the twelfth century. Ronnie Pueblo was constructed during the Classic period and occupied for a short time through the middle of the twelfth century. Lee Pueblo is difficult to place except as a Classic to Postclassic site.

With extensive remodeling, the residential area of the sites was expanded. By the end of their use, perhaps in the mid-thirteenth century, Buckaroo Site had about twelve rooms, and Ronnie, Phelps, and Lee Pueblos each had about six rooms. During the Postclassic use of the sites, the superstructures of rooms were repaired and maintained through adding posts, replacing posts, shifting the roof entryway, shifting the hearths, replastering hearths, and shifting other furnishings. Floors, however, do not appear to have needed replastering in most cases. Few are worn. This incongruity may be accounted for by regular, intermittent occupation of the rooms at these hamlets. Analysis of the artifact assemblages is consistent with this interpretation. Some rooms appear to have been temporarily abandoned at the time they burned, while others were actively in use. Other rooms on the sites were disassembled when they were abandoned. Disassembled rooms include all of those at Lee Pueblo and Room 1 on Ronnie Pueblo.

The assemblages in the rooms vary in ways that are consistent with household autonomy and variability of practice among those residing in a hamlet. At Buckaroo Site one room appears temporarily abandoned (Room 1), two were in use when the site burned (Rooms 2 and 3), and a third may have been more gradually abandoned (Room 4). At Ronnie Pueblo one room was disassembled when abandoned (Room 1), while the other may have been in use when burning occurred, with some material removed at abandonment or scavenged after the fire. At Phelps, one room was cleared of material and possibly disassembled (Room 1), one appears to have been temporarily unoccupied (Room 11), and one was in use when the site burned (Room 10). Clearly, the residents of each room were not acting in concert.

The twelfth-century reorganization in the Eastern Mimbres area contrasts with current understanding of the twelfth century as seen from the Mimbres Valley. Most archaeologists argue that villagers left the region, moving south to participate in the emerging Casas Grandes polity (see chap. 2). The assumption is made that the region was unoccupied. More importantly, the assumption is made that moving away was more attractive than staying. In this book I have documented regional occupational continuity for the Eastern Mimbres area. Continuity was achieved by settlement reorganization involving a shift in the structure, location, and organization of settlements. Thus, staying in the region was important, at least for some people in part of the Mimbres region. Very recently, Creel (1998) has argued that Classic villages in the Mimbres Valley were not entirely abandoned, although they were depopulated. It will be interesting in the future to compare his findings to those from the Eastern Mimbres area.

The changes in settlement pattern were accompanied by changes in economic and social patterns. In the following chapters, I examine economic and social changes. I assess whether resource selection changed with population dispersion, and I examine the possibility of residential mobility. Both of these latter subjects are aspects of the analysis of ethnobotanical and faunal data in chapter 5. The subject of chapter 6 is the changes in the social relationships at the scale of settlement, community, and region, and I provide a closer look at the composition of Postclassic ceramic assemblages and domestic architecture.

Since burning signals the final abandonment of the small pueblos, it would be useful to understand why the rooms were burned. The burning does coincide with the growth of new, large aggregated villages in the Eastern Mimbres region (chap. 6). The Eastern Mimbres region may have become the frontier for several expanding groups in the late thirteenth and early fourteenth centuries, who were drawn to their area by their contacts with Postclassic hamlet residents. Residents of the small hamlets may have been forced to shift back to an aggregated settlement pose. The nature of the burning suggests such a forced change. Sites appear to have been burned while still in use in a way that allowed little removal of personal items by those present. Regional dynamics are discussed in greater detail in chapter 6.

FORAGING AND FARMING ⑤

Margaret C. Nelson and Michael W. Diehl

The transition from aggregated settlement in large villages to dispersed settlement in small, residential hamlets involves reorganization of economic and social patterns. During the eleventh and twelfth centuries in the Eastern Mimbres area, people resided in large villages with small satellite settlements or field houses in secondary farming locales. During the latter half of the twelfth century, the large communities dispersed across the region. This shift in land use was accomplished through transformation of field houses from special to residential use. In this chapter we evaluate the question of whether this dispersion was accompanied by a shift toward a hunting-and-gathering economy as well as the influence of different environments on resource selection. We further explore the residential mobility of Postclassic hamlet dwellers and their impact on the environment immediately surrounding their residences.

We describe and analyze ethnobotanical and faunal data from six excavated hamlet sites on Palomas drainage. The four sites described in detail in chapter 4 are supplemented by two sites with similar occupational histories at which research is still in progress. These are the same two, Lizard Terrace Pueblo and Mountain Lion Hamlet, to which reference was made in chapter 4. These data indicate that cultivation was an important subsistence focus from the earliest Classic Mimbres use of these sites in the eleventh century through to the final thirteenth- or fourteenth-century occupation. Wild foods were almost exclusively limited to the plant and animal species that were available in the immediate vicinity of the sites. Little use was made of the upland resources or of the potentially productive Rio Grande Valley. Seed and wood data further support an argument for low-intensity use of sites and adjacent farmland, consistent with the pattern of residential mobility.

Resource Use and Residential Mobility

The correlation of cultivation with increased sedentism applies at a broad temporal scale of human history, although sedentism precedes cultivation in some areas of the world, and cultivation does not increase sedentism to any great degree in other areas. Unfortunately, this broad-scale generalization has led to the equation of cultivation with sedentism and of foraging with mobility (Rocek 1996). Various discussions of long-term change in the Southwest assume that mobility is exclusively a strategy of hunter-gatherers and that sedentism is directly correlated with cultivation. Upham (1984), Stuart and Gauthier (1984), and Carmichael (1990) argue that periods of sedentary farming were interspersed with periods of mobile hunting and gathering, a contrast they refer to as the "power" and "efficiency" modes of organization. In the power mode people concentrate their subsistence efforts on high-yield resources such as crops and a few very productive wild resources. In the efficiency mode, groups focus their subsistence efforts on a wide array of resources, none intensively.

"Sedentism," defined as sustained, continuous occupation at a location, is difficult without cultivation or some other high-yield wild resource (Fish, Fish, and Madsen 1990; Renouf 1991). Cultivators, however, can exercise considerable mobility (Eder 1984; Graham 1993; Hard and Merrill 1992; Lekson 1988; Minnis 1985b; Powell 1983, 1990; Wills 1985). Some attention has been directed at examining the potential for mobility among prehistoric cultivators, addressing mobility on multiyear scales of analysis (Nelson and LeBlanc 1986), although less attention is paid to seasonal or more frequent residential moves (but see Diehl 1994; Gilman 1987; Lekson 1988; Minnis 1985b; Powell 1983, 1990). This topic is especially important in the Southwest, because the potential for long-term sedentary cultivation in such an arid climate is limited by the periodic occurrences of local, long-term droughts (Cordell and Gumerman 1989; Gumerman and Dean 1989).

Minnis (1985b) and Lekson (1988) discussed mobility among cultivators in the North American Southwest, both of them drawing on an Apache model. Minnis uses Apache land-use strategies as an analog to land-use organization among early cultivators during the late Archaic Period. Lekson uses the same analogy to explain the distribution of Classic Mimbres ceramics, arguing that eleventh-century villagers in the southern Southwest had an extensive seasonal round. Both characterize mobility by cultivators as a broad-ranging, seasonal cycle in which cultivation is a small part of the year-long economic cycle of exploiting diverse resources in the uplands and lowlands.

We evaluate the hypothesis that dispersed populations rely heavily on hunted and gathered resources. If this hypothesis is correct, wild resources rather than cultigens should be ubiquitous in the Postclassic deposits on the hamlets. We found the opposite to be true, indicating that hamlet dwellers in the Eastern Mimbres invested considerably in cultivation. Sites in two different environments had the same pattern of emphasis on cultivation and local resources. Hamlet dwellers in the less xeric, middle portion of Palomas drainage hunted large game more than those in more xeric settings or those from the earlier Classic Mimbres period.

Although investment in cultivation and need for storing cultigens might have kept people confined within the Eastern Mimbres area, permanent, year-round occupation by all households at each site may not have been necessary. People may have shifted between agricultural locales within the region. If shifting did occur, we should find evidence that field areas were not intensively cultivated. Natural flora from the floodplain does not appear to have been depleted, indicating the presence of low-intensity farming. Similarly, houses may not have been continuously occupied, though they were continuously maintained as is indicated by the architectural analysis in chapter 4. Analysis of charred seeds suggests that seed rain on room floors was light, supporting the suggestion that room use was not intensive or continuous.

The Data

Charred plant remains and animal bones have been recovered from six sites in two areal clusters, Middle Palomas and Lower Palomas (fig. 1.2). Unfortunately, not all samples from all sites have been analyzed, but some data are available from each site. Analysis tables reflect the uneven coverage of ongoing analyses. All of the samples are from excavated contexts within room features and fill deposits.

Macrobotanical Data: Sources, Handling and Analytical Methods

The macrobotanical samples used in this research were excavated during four field seasons. The depositional contexts of the samples discussed in this section include formal hearths, ash pits, and postholes. Macrobotanical specimens were separated from soil samples by means of water flotation. Specimens were recovered with a set of disposable dip nets made of a polymer fabric with a mesh size of approximately .3 mm. Processed flotation samples were sealed within their nets and allowed to dry. Dried samples were stored in tyvek soil sample bags.

Flotation samples were subjected to two kinds of macrobotanical analyses. Charred seed and nonwood tissue identifications from macrobotanical samples were observed and counted under a variable magnification (10–30x) stereoscopic microscope and separated into plastic storage vials and gelatin capsules. This research assumes that uncharred seeds may be modern contaminants, since only charred tissues are likely to preserve well in open-air archaeological sites (Miksicek 1987; Minnis 1981; Popper 1988). Identifications were accomplished by comparing the charred tissues with a large collection of modern Southwestern seeds of known taxa and using a set of reference texts—Martin and Barkley 1961; Montgomery 1977; Parker 1990; USDA 1974. Identifications were made to the genus level for most plants and to the species level for a few highly diagnostic seeds such as maize (*Zea mays*).

Charred woods were identified using a variable magnification (30–160x) stereoscopic microscope, a comparative collection of charred Southwestern woods of known taxa, and texts, specifically Minnis 1987 and Saul 1955. Samples containing charred wood fragments were passed through a set of nested geological sieves, and up to forty pieces of charred wood (larger than 1 mm^2) were identified to the genus level of specificity. After identification, the fragments of charred wood were weighed by species and sealed in foil bags for indefinite curation.

Faunal Data: Handling and Analytical Methods

The faunal remains used in this study were excavated from the fill deposits in rooms, intramural floor features, and from trash deposits used to level areas prior to room construction. The total number of bones from each site is so low that the analysis of faunal remains is limited to generalized site data, with limited information from the earliest Classic Mimbres occupation for comparison. The minimum number of individuals was not calculated because of the low volume of animal bone. All analyses are frequencies of bones (NISP) comprising each sample. Identification was to the most specific level possible. Most bones were small fragments that could be identified only as far as class, with some differentiation by animal size within class. For mammals, "small" includes rodents of various sorts. "Medium" refers to rabbits (*Sylvilagus* sp. and *Lepus* sp.). "Large" includes ungulates, cervids, bear (*Ursus* sp.) and mountain lions (*Felis concolor*). Skeletal elements were identifiable for less than half of the bone, but these data are not discussed.

Ethnobotanical Analyses

Three lines of evidence were used to evaluate the relative importance of cultivated and wild plants and the intensity of site use. These included the proportions of maize and other agricultural domesticates in the flotation samples from
hearths, the ubiquity of weedy perennials, and the kind of wood used for construction and fires.

Quantitative Measures of Plant Importance

There are many ways to quantify paleobotanical data, and this research makes
use of species ubiquity. The ubiquity of a plant taxon is the proportion of samples
that contain that taxon relative to the total number of analyzed samples. For
example, if maize (*Zea mays*) is present in seven out of ten analyzed samples,
and goosefoot/amaranth (*Chenopodium/Amaranthus* sp.) is present in four of
ten samples, then maize is said to have a ubiquity of 70 percent and goosefoot/
amaranth, a ubiquity of 40 percent. To assess the nature of plant use, the
ubiquities of charred plant taxa from different hearth features are compared.
Minnis (1985b) argues that charring of prehistoric seeds is essentially a minor
accident or spill that occurred when seeds were processed near heat sources.
The ubiquity of a taxon is therefore proportional to the frequency of these
accidents in their normal contexts of use, and the frequency of accidents is itself
proportional to the frequency of plant processing events. Thus, taxon ubiquity
is here assumed to be an appropriate measure of the importance of each plant.

As a quantitative measure of the importance of plants, ubiquity offers some
advantages over the ratios or proportions of raw frequency counts. Seeds of
different species deteriorate at different rates. Furthermore, seeds may be processed in different ways; thus species that were consumed in roughly equal proportions may be deposited at different rates, or in different states of destruction
(Miksicek 1987; Pearsall 1989; Popper 1988). Accordingly, comparisons of the
raw frequencies of different taxa may produce ratios of different species that are
largely a consequence of differential preservation. In contrast, ubiquity is a fairly
resilient measure in the face of differential deposition or preservation, because
one plant's ubiquity score does not affect the score for other species. Ubiquity is
best used to track changes in the importance of a single species. It also is mod-
erately useful for assessing changes in the relative importance of different species.

Table 5.1 presents the composition of charred plant species (wood, seeds,
and other reproductive tissues) for hearths listed by site and occupation period.
The first noteworthy feature is the presence of maize in nearly every sample that

Table 5.1

Charred macroplant remains from hearths in Palomas hamlet sites

PERIOD	SITE	ROOM	FEATURE	cottonwood	juniper (wood)	oak	mesquite	saltbush	walnut	maize	beans	squash	juniper (seed)	goosefoot	dropseed	purslane	barrel cactus	prickly pear	t. mustard	piñon	grasses
				Hearth Woods						Seeds and Other Plant Parts											
1	Buckaroo	1	33	X			X	X		X			X								
2	Buckaroo	1	22	X			X	X		X			X								
2	Buckaroo	2	14	X			X				X			X		X	X	X		X	
2	Buckaroo	3	12	X			X			X	X	X		X		X	X	X		X	
2	Buckaroo	4	11	X			X			X				X		X			X		
2	Ronnie	1	14	X		X	X	X		X											
2	Ronnie	2	22	X			X					X			X	X					X
2	Lizard T	10	17	X	X	X	X			X	X	X			X						
2	Lizard T	30	14	X	X	X	X			X	X	X		X		X			X		X
2	Lizard T	31	12	X	X	X	X		X	no seeds in sample											
1	Mt. Lion	1	41	X			X			no seeds in sample											
1	Phelps	10	47	X	X	X	X			no seeds in sample											
2	Phelps	11	11	X	X		X			X		X									

Notes:

1 = Classic Mimbres

2 = Postclassic Mimbres

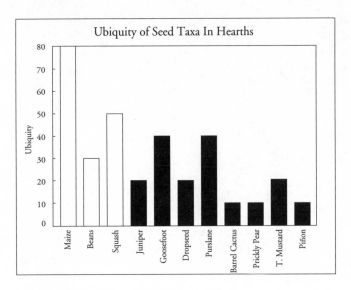

Figure 5.1
Ubiquity values of seed taxa in hearth flotation samples from Postclassic rooms. White bars indicate cultigens; black bars indicate wild plants.

yielded charred seeds. Those few Postclassic samples that lack maize have other cultigens (beans or squash). These data are converted to ubiquity values (fig. 5.1). These results indicate that cultivation of maize was important as a food resource. No wild plant is especially ubiquitous, though the range of wild plants used is fairly broad for such a small sample.

Among the wild species in table 5.1, plants that could have been obtained locally predominate. These include edible weedy horticultural parasites (goosefoot, dropseed, purslane, tansey mustard, and grass) and wild plants that produce large edible fruits (mesquite, prickly pear, juniper, barrel cactus, and piñon). These kinds of plants grow well on or near riparian floodplains and in disturbed areas on the margins of human settlements (Brown 1994; Parker 1990), with the exception of piñon, for which only one cone scale was recovered. All except piñon have been observed growing in the immediate vicinity of the sites. Regardless of the frequency of residential or logistical moves, it is clear that occupants of the Palomas drainage concentrated their subsistence efforts on plants that could be planted in the floodplain or that were otherwise locally available.

Potentially Useful Wild Plants

Economically important nonagricultural seeds in the samples are limited to goosefoot/amaranth, mesquite (*Prosopis* sp.), and cactus fruit (*Opuntia* sp., *Echinocactus* sp.). Mesquite pods are edible late-fall foods that could have produced high yields (Minnis 1991). Their chief dietary drawback is their extraordinarily high fiber content (Ensminger et al. 1994). Consumption of unprocessed mesquite has been known to cause intestinal blockage in cattle (Parker 1990). The occurrence of cactus seeds (*Opuntia* sp. and *Echinocactus* sp.) in these samples indicates that the occupants made use of cactus fruits, which are available in the early summer on rocky slopes. Goosefoot would be abundant in agricultural fields. All of these potentially useful plants are rare in the analyzed samples. Either they were not economically important in prehistoric Palomas Creek diets, their seeds did not preserve well, or they were processed and consumed in locations away from residences. Despite their low representation, these species may have made important contributions to the diet. Ethnoarchaeological studies of Seri cactus-fruit processing have shown that these seeds are extremely unlikely to be preserved in any context, even when cactus fruit are a significant item in the economy (Miksicek 1987). The importance of cactus fruit to the prehistoric occupants of Palomas Creek cannot be easily assessed. It seems likely that this fruit was used whenever it was available. Large patches of prickly pear (*Opuntia* sp.) were observed growing in the vicinity of these sites, so the costs of obtaining and transporting the fruits would have been minimal. Goosefoot and amaranth would have grown well in and around field areas, which were adjacent to the residential sites. Mesquite thrives in disturbed soils, as is evident by its prevalence on archaeological sites. Thus, all would have been easy to procure.

Many of these plants may have been included in the diet as pot herbs, flavor additives, or as "famine foods." Minnis (1991) examined ethnographic instances of the use of Southwestern plants as famine foods and noted that acorns, juniper seeds, goosefoot seeds and greens, amaranth seeds and greens, and the seeds of other weedy perennials were popular dietary supplements in years that produced poor agricultural yields.

Seed Rain and the Intensity of Household Use

In addition to their possible inclusion in the diet, many of the low-ubiquity seeds listed in tables 5.1 and figure 5.1 may have found their way into prehistoric contexts as a consequence of seed rain and accidental transportation. Many of these weedy perennials flourish in disturbed contexts, and their success is attributable to heightened activity of humans. If we view accidental transportation as a process that randomly selects seeds from plants growing in the vicinity of archaeological sites, then the frequency of transportation events should be proportional to the intensity of activity in and around households. In other words, changes in the proportions of weedy-plant species may be used as an index for changes in the intensity of site use. This suggestion is used to assess changes in the intensity of site use. Such a measure must be used with caution, controlling for the environmental context of sites, as we have done in this study.

Goosefoot and amaranth are prolific disturbance plants that grow on the margins of agricultural fields and in disturbed floodplains (Parker 1990). Although both plants produce edible seeds, Minnis (1981) pointed out that it is easy to overestimate their economic importance since their tiny, gritty seeds are produced abundantly as "seed rain." Goosefoot and amaranth were by far the most abundant *noncharred* seeds represented in these samples (approaching 100 percent ubiquity). Furthermore, these species have tough husks that could have become easily snagged on clothing or gear, permitting them to "piggy back" their way onto household contexts. Once inside the household, these tiny seeds might have been unnoticed and simply brushed into the fire. Other small-seeded species listed in tables 5.1 have characteristics that would promote their accidental transportation into household contexts as well. Plants of the mustard family (*Cruciferae* and *Descurainia* sp.) often produce seeds in spikelike pods that could easily have become stuck to clothing (Parker 1990). Saltbush (*Atriplex* sp.) produces wedge-shaped glabrous (hairy) seeds that also stick to clothes. All of the preceding species except the buckwheats were observed on the floors of cleaned structures after two months of use by archaeologists (Minnis 1981).

Current data on charred wild seeds suggest that they are rare on the floors and in the floor features of rooms. This impression requires further detailed analysis of flotation samples from all floor features and from the floor surfaces. Low ubiquities of seeds (fig. 5.1) may be a useful index of the intensity of structure occupation; if future data are consistent with the information in figure 5.1, the intensity of the room use at Palomas Creek sites was generally low. Architectural evidence of lengthy occupation span (indicated by extensive remodeling) but limited wear on floors (lack of replastering) are consistent with the impression from the seed data.

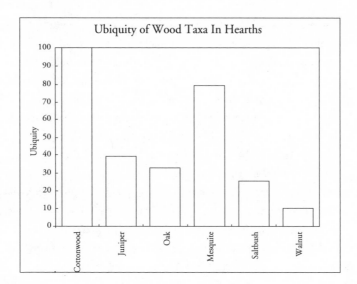

Figure 5.2

Ubiquity values of wood taxa in hearth samples from Postclassic rooms.

The Use of Floodplain Woods and Agricultural Land Clearing

Proportions of riparian and nonriparian wood in hearths and major roof support posts may be an index of the intensity of land clearance for cultivation. Along Palomas Creek the prime agricultural land in the vicinity of sites is located in the floodplain. Numerous wild plants with deep taproots grow well in floodplain contexts. These plants would have been cleared to make space for crops and to eliminate competition from these water hoarders. Minnis (1985a:88–90) argued that the proportion of phreatophitic versus xeric plants may therefore be used as an index of the intensity of floodplain land clearing for farming. In comparing the proportions of riparian plants to xeric plants, Minnis found evidence for increased land clearance along floodplain contexts during the Classic Mimbres phase in the Mimbres Valley.

In charred wood samples from hearths (table 5.1 and fig. 5.2) and posts (table 5.2) from the Palomas Creek sites, the dominant riparian plant is a cottonwood (*Populus* sp.), also the dominant riparian tree in the area today. The post wood in table 5.2 represents wood available when the rooms were constructed and remodeled; as such, it is a less sensitive index of impact on the riparian species. The high proportion of cottonwood in Postclassic construction and remodeling that followed the initial Classic Mimbres construction, however, indicates that riparian species were available at least into the Postclassic period. The hearth wood listed in table 5.1 includes all wood types found in each hearth. These are presumably from the last few cooking or heating events before abandonment; they represent the wood available at the end of occupations. All have cottonwood (fig. 5.2).

Honey mesquite (*Prosopis juliflora*) is common in the hearths. It grows well as shrubs in the drainage bottoms, on hillsides around archaeological sites, and in areas that have been heavily grazed by cattle. Of the plant species found in the Palomas Creek charcoal samples, only oak (probably *Quercus emoryii*) and juniper (*Juniperus monospermum*) are xeric plants that grow primarily away from the floodplain. Both occur infrequently in the study area, with juniper the more prevalent tree. In archaeological contexts xeric species are found in 54 percent of the hearth samples, while riparian species occur in 100 percent of the same samples, both Classic and Postclassic. Among the twenty-three post samples, xeric woods are dominant or codominant in 22 percent; riparian woods are dominant or codominant in 87 percent. Among the Postclassic samples alone, xeric species are even more rare, comprising only 13 percent of the post samples.

These observations support the conclusion that cultivation by hamlet dwellers, while important to their subsistence, did not significantly modify the natural riparian vegetation. This may have been accomplished by cyclical use of plots along the entire floodplain or may have involved intensive use of small, widely spaced plots between which was undisturbed riparian habitat. Either strategy preserves the riparian habitat. At no time did the intensity of land-clearing activities for farming or fuel wood approach levels where the supply of riparian woods was exhausted. If denuding of riparian vegetation is an index of agricultural intensification, the absence of evidence for overcutting riparian plants indicates that agricultural land use was extensive in nature, rather than intensive. The absence of any evidence for overcutting is consistent with the hypothesis that the occupants of the Lower Palomas hamlets employed a land-use strategy that incorporated multiple residential locations near agricultural fields. Dependence on numerous small fields rather than intensive production at one primary locale would have produced the observed pattern.

Intersite variation in the use of different woods deserves comment. Phelps Pueblo, Lizard Terrace Pueblo, and Mountain Lion Hamlet are all in the middle section of Palomas Creek, which is within a piñon-, juniper-, and oak-dominated environment. The other three sites in the Lower Palomas Creek cluster are in a mesquite and creosote area. Among the hearth and post samples nearly

Table 5.2

Charred wood in postholes from primary roof supports in rooms on Palomas hamlet sites

PERIOD	SITE	ROOM	FEATURE	DOMINANT WOOD AS PRIMARY POSTS					
--------	------	------	---------	cottonwood	juniper	oak	mesquite	walnut	none
1	Lizard T.	1	10		X				
1	Lizard T.	1	12	X					
1	Lizard T.	1	17						X
2	Lizard T.	10	15		X				
1	Lizard T.	10	34	X					
1	Lizard T.	10	36	X		X			
1	Lizard T.	10	38	X	X				
1	Lizard T.	10	41	X					
1	Lizard T.	10	45						X
1	Lizard T.	10	46						X
1	Lizard T.	10	55						X
2	Lizard T.	30	15	X					
1	Mt. Lion	1	45					X	
2	Mt. Lion	1	18	X					
2	Mt. Lion	1	31	X					
2	Mt. Lion	1	34	X					
2	Mt. Lion	1	36	X					
2	Phelps	10	36	X					
2	Phelps	10	30		X				
2	Phelps	11	25	X					
2	Phelps	11	12	X					
2	Buckaroo	4	25	X					
2	Buckaroo	4	24	X					
2	Ronnie	1	21	X					
2	Ronnie	1	19	X					
2	Ronnie	1	20	X					
2	Ronnie	2	63	X					

Note:

1 = Classic Mimbres

2 = Postclassic Mimbres

all with juniper and oak are from the middle cluster. Thus, the presence of these xeric species reflects their immediate availability in the vicinity of sites.

Faunal Analyses

The primary research questions addressed through faunal analysis are whether hunting played a large part in the subsistence base of Palomas Postclassic hamlet dwellers and whether hunting varied across the two environments represented by the two site clusters (Lower and Middle Palomas). These questions are addressed by using data on the frequencies of animal bone of different classes, sizes within classes, and species within classes. The Postclassic data are the focus of analysis, with two samples from Classic Mimbres contexts included for comparison. These are a small sample from the Buckaroo Site, representing the special use of the site during the Classic period, and a sample from a large Classic Mimbres village on an adjacent drainage in the Eastern Mimbres area (Hegmon and Nelson 1994; Nelson and Hegmon 1993, 1995). The Classic Mimbres village is in a setting much like that of the Lower Palomas hamlets.

Table 5.3 presents the current summaries of faunal data for those fragments that could be identified at least to class, and to size for the mammals. Relative to the total area of excavation on each site, animal bone is not abundant. No middens have been found on any sites, either outside or inside room fills. These low densities may result from off-site processing or dumping of animal bone, processing that consumes the bone (e.g., grinding), or a lack of emphasis on hunting.

A second feature of table 5.3 is the predominance of local resources. In all of the samples at least 98 percent of the bone is from animals that could have been captured in the immediate vicinity of the sites. Deer, cottontail, and jackrabbits are all attracted to the riparian vegetation and cultivated fields. Antelope move in more open areas on adjacent mesa tops. The only animals not common in the Lower and Middle Palomas are mountain sheep and bison. These comprise no more than 1.5 percent of any sample. The faunal samples lack evidence for hunting in the mountains to the west. Similarly, hunting and fishing along the marshy Rio Grande are not indicated. Fish remains are rare in the faunal collections, as are bird bones. If these zones were exploited, the occupants of the hamlets did not transport resources back to their homes along Palomas drainage.

Location along the drainage accounts for similarities and differences among the samples. Figure 5.3 illustrates the composition of samples according to the

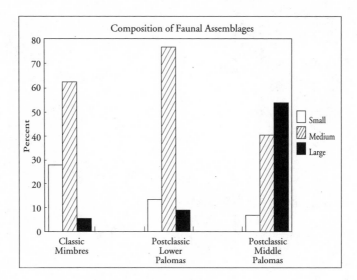

Figure 5.3

The composition of samples of mammal bones from Classic and Postclassic Mimbres contexts in the study area, expressed as percent of all mammal bone.

body size of the mammals. The artiodactyls are classified as large, the lagomorphs as medium, and the rodents as small. The three sites in the lower segment of Palomas drainage (Buckaroo, Lee, and Ronnie) have similar faunal assemblages; lagomorphs dominate these assemblages, as is expected in their more xeric setting. The Middle Palomas samples (Phelps Pueblo, Mountain Lion Hamlet, and Lizard Terrace Pueblo) several miles upstream have more large game including deer and antelope, which are more abundant in this portion of the study area. The difference implies more emphasis on animal protein and fat by occupants of the Middle Palomas sites, where large game are more abundant, but no increase in total amount of bone or range over which hunting was conducted.

In the Lower Palomas Postclassic assemblages, 68–81 percent of the bone is from medium-sized mammals (table 5.3), probably all rabbits. Cottontail (*Sylvilagus* sp.) predominate (fig. 5.4), comprising more than 60 percent of the bone from medium-sized mammals identifiable to genus. This proportion is similar to that for the samples from earlier Classic Mimbres contexts. The proportion of identifiable rabbits is lower in the Middle Palomas Postclassic samples, although cottontail still comprise 21–32 percent of all bone in the analyzed samples from two of the three Middle Palomas sites, compared with 35–37

Table 5.3

Composition of animal bone samples from Classic and Postclassic Mimbres sites in the study area. Values are percentages of total number of bones

CLASS	SIZE	ORDER	GENUS	COMMON NAME	POSTCLASSIC LOWER PALOMAS			POSTCLASSIC MIDDLE PALOMAS			ALL CLASSIC MIMBRES	
					Buckaroo	Lee	Ronnie	Phelps	Lizard T.	Mt. Lion	Buckaroo	Animas
Mammalia	Large	Artiodactyl	*Ocodoileus*	Deer	1	1	1	2	<1	1	1	
			Antilocapra	Antelope				4	<1			
			Cervus	Elk								
			Ovis	Mt Sheep	<1			1				<1
			Bison	Bison				<1				
			Unknown			1		7	5	3		3
		Unknown			4	11	4	53	29	55	<1	3
				SUBTOTAL	6	13	5	67	34	59	1	6
Mammalia	Medium	Lagomorph	*Lepus*	Jackrabbit	19	17	23	3	2	4	15	9
			Sylvilagus	Cottontail	37	35	35	5	32	21	26	11
		Unknown			12	27	23	22	20	10	6	57
				SUBTOTAL	68	79	81	30	54	35	47	77

					POSTCLASSIC LOWER PALOMAS			POSTCLASSIC MIDDLE PALOMAS			ALL CLASSIC MIMBRES	
CLASS	SIZE	ORDER	GENUS	COMMON NAME	Buckaroo	Lee	Ronnie	Phelps	Lizard T.	Mt. Lion	Buckaroo	Animas
Mammalia	Small	Rodentia			4	3	8	2	7	5	13	5
		Unknown			20	1	3	1	3	1	33	4
		SUBTOTAL			24	4	11	3	10	6	46	9
Amphibia			Anura			3						
Reptilia					<1	<1	3	<1	<1		2	2
Aves					2	<1	<1	<1	1		3	
Osteichthyes					<1							
Total number of Bones					2230	289	1058	615	734	184	497	324
Number of rms excavated					4	3	2	3	3	2	1	4

percent from Lower Palomas Postclassic samples and 11–26 percent in the samples from Classic period sites. Cottontail prefer habitats with dense vegetation (Bailey 1932; Szuter 1991); the riparian zone, which was prime farmland, was the only locale with the thick vegetation that is attractive to them. Continued hunting of cottontail indicates that dense stands of riparian wood existed throughout the Classic and Postclassic occupations along Palomas Creek. This observation is independent of, yet consistent with, the presence of charred riparian wood in all flotation samples from hearths on these sites. Occupants of the Palomas Creek sites apparently did not denude the natural vegetation of the floodplain as part of their cultivation practice, as they had in the Mimbres Valley (Minnis 1985b); it may have been that their cultivation strategy was spatially extensive, involving either several small patches of farmland or intermittent use of fields. A spatially extensive agricultural strategy is consistent with the thesis that prehistoric land-use strategies incorporated multiple agricultural locations and residences.

Within the three Lower Palomas samples, jackrabbits (*Lepus* sp.) are the second most-common fauna identifiable to genus, comprising 17 to 23 percent of the samples (table 5.3). Jackrabbits would have been attracted to agricultural fields by their openness and the increased availability of food and water (Bailey 1932). The constant, yet relatively lower, proportion of jackrabbits relative to cottontails in the faunal samples is further evidence for the absence of severe denuding of riparian vegetation (fig. 5.4). In the Middle Palomas samples, jackrabbit bones are relatively rare.

In contrast to the argument that the relative frequencies of rabbit taxa in faunal assemblages are sensitive to farming practices, Sanchez (1996) discusses the effect of elevation on the relative frequencies of jackrabbits and cottontails. She reanalyzes faunal assemblages from the Mimbres Valley, including sites from the Late Pithouse and Classic periods. The proportion of cottontails is consistently higher in the faunal samples from the upper valley sites where natural vegetation is more dense. In these samples the decline in cottontails and increase in jackrabbits expected due to field clearing is evident. However, in the middle and lower Mimbres Valley, cottontails are less abundant naturally. Shifts in their abundance relative to jackrabbits in the faunal samples from Late Pithouse and Classic period sites are inconsistent and variable. Thus, where cottontails are naturally an infrequent rabbit taxon, variation in their relative abundance is not the best index of environmental impacts. The interesting difference between Sanchez's data and ours is that cottontails are most abundant in the samples

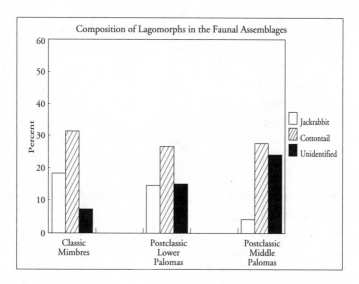

Figure 5.4

The percentage of jackrabbits and cottontail rabbits in samples from Classic and Postclassic Mimbres contexts in the study area. These are percentages of total bone identified as medium mammal, all of which is probably lagomorph.

from the more xeric areas, along Lower Palomas Creek. For cottontail to be such a relatively high proportion of the faunal assemblage, preservation of the fragile riparian zone in this area must have been occurring. Thus, Sanchez's analysis bolsters our interpretation of the rabbit data.

How were rabbits incorporated into a diet composed primarily of carbohydrate-rich cultigens? According to Shaffer (1991), both genera could be passively hunted with traps and snares, perhaps as a strategy for keeping animals out of the fields (Shaffer 1991; Szuter 1991) as well as for supplementing the diet of cultigens. If rabbits comprised a substantial portion of the meat consumed, they may have been processed in a way that maximized the fat and protein value of each animal. Boiling the entire body would extract more fat than would roasting (Speth and Spielmann 1983; Szuter 1991). Consistent with this expectation, the skeletal elements of rabbits in these samples included all parts of the animals, with no segment favored. Boiling causes the bones to fracture in an angular pattern different from that of fresh bone broken during preparation (Kardaman 1993; Shaffer 1991). The rabbit bones in these sites had angular fracture (Kardaman 1993).

Other small animals include rodents, reptiles, birds, fish, and toads or frogs (table 5.3). All are extremely rare except for the rodents. Assuming that all bones from small mammals are rodent bones, the proportion of rodents is 4 to 24 percent from Lower Palomas Postclassic sites and 3 to 10 percent for Middle Palomas Postclassic sites. The rarity of other small animal bones cannot be accounted for by collection error, since all deposits were screened through one-sixteenth-inch window screen, and a considerable amount of soil was collected for flotation, insuring recovery of extremely small bones. In addition, many bird, toad, and fish bones are equivalent in size to the bones of small rabbits and rodents. Since rodents and small rabbits were recovered, it follows that the absence of other small genera was not a consequence of sampling bias. Small animals may have been processed in such a way that their bones were destroyed or deposited off-site, but there is no positive evidence for more than fortuitous contribution to the diet.

The presence of rodents in samples may or may not be indicative of their contribution to the diet. Rodent burrowing is common in the fill of the pueblo rooms. Many of the rodents may have died in these burrows. Charring on the bone could indicate prehistoric consumption of rodents (Szuter 1991); though charred bones are infrequent, a few rodent bones in the sample are charred, indicating some contribution of rodents to the diet.

Large animals identifiable to genus are all artiodactyls (table 5.3). Bones from large mammals comprise a smaller proportion of the total faunal sample from the Lower Palomas Postclassic sites (5–13 percent) than from Postclassic sites on the Middle Palomas (34–67 percent). In this regard the Postclassic samples from Lower Palomas are similar to those from Classic period sites (1–9 percent large mammals; see fig. 5.3).

In the Lower Palomas samples, bone identified as artiodactyl comprises from 1 percent to nearly 12 percent of all bone identifiable, at least to class. Although the family of artiodactyls includes deer, antelope, elk, mountain sheep, peccaries, and bison, all artiodactyl bones identifiable to genus were deer (*Odocoileus*) except four Mountain sheep bones from the Buckaroo Site. Deer are attracted to cultivated fields and the riparian zone along the floodplains, and they occur naturally in riparian zones throughout the Eastern Mimbres area.

The Middle Palomas Postclassic sites have relatively more large-mammal bones than do other Classic or Postclassic sites. Deer and antelope are the most common animals identifiable in these samples of large-mammal bone. The sample from Phelps Pueblo is unusual. Not only does large-mammal bone comprise 67 percent of the sample, which is three to five times the amount on Lower Palomas sites, but rare nonlocal types occur as well. Mountain sheep (*Ovis*) are more frequent on Phelps Pueblo than on any other site, although they comprise only 1 percent. A few possible bison foot bones were also recovered. In contrast to the localized pattern of faunal acquisition indicated by most of the bone, the presence of a few bison foot bones may indicate distant contact. Although occasional bison may have roamed into the Eastern Mimbres area, Frederick (1993, personal communication) suggests that local conditions would have prevented herds of bison from becoming successfully established in the area. The bones found in Rooms 10 and 11 on the Phelps Pueblo are from a bison foot (tentative identification by H. Savage, personal communication 1994). These few bones may be products of exchange or of acquisition of hides rather than indicators of a dietary supplement to maize. Given the broad-ranging, distant social interactions indicated from ceramic evidence (chap. 6), contact with bison hunters in the open plains areas to the north and east is not surprising.

The data from faunal samples support a model of locally focused resource exploitation consistent with results from the ethnobotanical analysis. The population dispersion following the Classic period and the accompanying reorganization of land use by dispersed Postclassic hamlet dwellers involved varied strategies focused on local resources. In the drier Lower Palomas where rabbits are more abundant than large mammals, hunting focused on small- and medium-sized mammals more than on large mammals. In the wetter habitats of Middle Palomas where more artiodactyls could be supported, hunting involved greater emphasis on these large mammals. However, the relatively low density of bone on the sites supports the conclusion that there was not a general shift toward more hunting. It is possible that hunters residing in the Lower Palomas hamlets processed their large game differently from those at Middle Palomas sites and brought back only selected parts. An elemental analysis will be needed to evaluate this possibility.

Although hunting apparently did not increase from Classic to Postclassic, animal protein and fat certainly always were important in the Eastern Mimbres. We have noted the tremendously fragmented condition of rabbit bones. The large-mammal bones are often in the same condition, which is why so many are unidentifiable. Occupants of the Eastern Mimbres area may have processed whatever game they captured as fully as possible, including boiling and grinding, to derive the benefit of animal protein and fat from even the smallest bones. However, they did not invest heavily in hunting.

The faunal data also support our interpretation of the "light" use of farmland. Ethnobotanical data show that the natural vegetation of the riparian areas continued to be present throughout Classic and Postclassic occupation on Palomas Creek; cultivation did not denude the riparian woods. The representation of cottontails in the faunal assemblages is consistent with this interpretation.

Locational Evidence

Locational information supports the inference that cultivation was a primary subsistence activity of dispersed, Postclassic groups. Three kinds of data are relevant: the setting and distribution of architectural sites, the nature of sites and their assemblages in the uplands, and the nature of sites along the Rio Grande.

Architectural Sites

Excavation data from the six Palomas hamlets demonstrate that they were residential locales. Assuming their location was at least partially conditioned by land use (see chap. 6), information on setting and distribution is important to understanding resource selection. All of the Classic Mimbres and immediately Postclassic architectural sites in Palomas drainage system are located adjacent to floodplains or alluvial fans. Floodplains are the most common location. This pattern has been established by systematic intensive and sample surveys of the entire drainage system and is discussed at length in chapter 3 of this volume and by Lekson (1984) and Nelson (1993a). Laumbach and Kirkpatrick's sample survey of New Mexico State land in the Eastern Mimbres region (1983) found the same pattern. Furthermore, no architectural sites are evident above the segment of Palomas that offers arable land. The small hamlets occur along Palomas beginning several kilometers up from the Rio Grande, where water flows in the channel and from springs. They extend up the drainage to the last sizable patch of arable floodplain at about 6,200 feet elevation, where the growing season is sufficiently long to permit cultivation during most years.

The Uplands

Along the west side of the study area, Palomas drainage has headwaters in the Black Range. The slopes and peaks reach to above 11,000 feet and offer the flora and fauna of Upper Chihuahuan and Transitional zones (see chap. 1). The Black Range, however, was not regularly an economically important resource area for the occupants of the Palomas agricultural hamlets. Evidence of residence is absent. Although this area does have many artifact scatters, deposits in rock shelters and open sites are ephemeral. They are dominated by chipped stone, lacking the range of domestic artifacts common on residential sites (Nelson 1989; Nelson and Lippmeier 1993).

The combination of ephemeral and opportunistic use of places in the Black Range and the absence of upland resources in Lower Palomas Creek macrobotanical samples obviates the importance of the Black Range as a critical resource area for the prehistoric occupants of Palomas drainage. Rock shelters in the mountains could have served as seasonal residences, as they do for the Tarahumara in northern Mexico (Hard and Merrill 1992). However, based on analyses of the materials within rock shelters in the Black Range, Nelson (1989; Nelson and Lippmeier 1993) argues that these locales were used opportunistically rather than incorporated into a system of anticipated land use. The use of low-quality raw materials, a lack of standardization of tool form, ephemeral tool use-wear, and infrequent modification through reuse in the stone-tool assemblages from rock shelters are consistent with infrequent and unplanned uses of locations.

The River

To the east, the Rio Grande Valley might have offered a diversity of resources, including birds, fish, and wild plants. Contour maps of the topography of the floodplain indicate that it was a slow, meandering river prior to damming in the 1920s. A wide, slow river would have attracted a variety of animals and could have been a major flyway for waterfowl (see Brown 1994:248–73). Large villages were once located along the Rio Grande at the mouths of side drainages flowing from the Black Range (Lekson 1989). We know little about these villages because they were destroyed by construction and looting earlier in this century. Based on analysis of existing data from one of these large sites, the Garfield or Rio Vista site (LA1082), Mayo (1994) believes that the occupation extended only until A.D. 1130, when other large Mimbres villages in the Mimbres Valley were abandoned. Lekson (1989:62) suggests the same for other large sites on the Rio Grande. If Mayo and Lekson are correct, the large sites on the Rio Grande are contemporary with the early field houses beneath the residential occupation of small hamlets on Palomas. The Rio Grande may not have been the focus of settlement immediately after A.D. 1130. We have little evidence for the Postclassic; one site with twenty-five rooms may be the only sizable settlement contemporary with the Postclassic hamlets on Palomas (chap. 6), although large sites appear in the area sometime during the 1200s, possibly late in that century.

Indirect evidence for use of the resources of the Rio Grande Valley come from the faunal assemblages within the small hamlets. As reported, fish and bird bones are rare. These resources were either not used frequently, were processed in ways that undermined their preservation, or were processed and consumed at locales away from the hamlets. Further evidence is needed from sites along the Rio Grande that have occupations after A.D. 1130. Lekson's survey (1989) provides reconnaissance information from which such a study could develop, but sites are so extensively disturbed by development and looting that considerable time and patience would be needed.

Land Use and Mobility

Three patterns are consistently evident in the ethnobotanical, faunal, and locational data. First, maize cultivation was a primary subsistence focus at the small hamlets along Palomas drainage. Second, resources were selected from those in the immediate vicinity of sites. Third, use of the floodplains for farming was not so intensive that natural flora and fauna were eliminated. The ethnobotanical data also support an argument from architectural data for short episodes of occupation at the hamlets over a long period of time.

Analyses of the ubiquities of maize in flotation samples from hearths indicate that agricultural plants were an extremely important component of the diet during all occupation periods at all excavated Palomas Creek sites. (All other seeds from edible plants have low ubiquity values.) Furthermore, the charred wild seeds recovered from the sites are nearly all available within a very short distance of each site. These observations indicate that prehistoric land use in the region concentrated on cultivation and easily accessible wild resources. Long-duration logistical forays into other areas are not indicated.

Nearly all bones on these sites are from animals that inhabited terrain in and around the field areas adjacent to the hamlets. Deer, rabbits, and rodents would have been attracted to cultivated fields and could have been captured with relative ease. The primary animal component of the diets of the occupants of Lower Palomas Creek was rabbits. Cottontail was the predominant genus in all samples of rabbit bone. These and jackrabbit were processed in a manner that supported the maximum extraction of fat and protein. Artiodactyls comprise more of the faunal sample from the Middle Palomas, with deer and antelope dominating the large-mammal sample. Clearly, animal carcasses were an important supplement to the carbohydrate rich, primarily agricultural diet.

Settlement data also indicate that logistical forays and residential moves to the nearby mountains and the Rio Grande Valley did not occur with any regularity, or at least are not evident. If Postclassic groups had used these areas regularly, we should have found evidence for transport of seeds, wood, or animal taxa from these areas as well as substantial sites at prime locales in the mountains and along the Rio Grande. If land use involved seasonal movement between zones for hunting and wild-plant procurement, such moves must have been to areas outside the Eastern Mimbres but too distant to have involved transport of those resources back to the Palomas hamlets. We suggest, alternatively, that people moved within the region through a series of hamlets, each adjacent to a small patch of farmland.

Two independent lines of evidence indicate lack of full clearing of the floodplain vegetation for creation of cultivated fields. First, the ratio of cottontail to jackrabbit is consistently high across samples from all sites, with cottontail comprising an especially high proportion of rabbits in all samples. Cottontail depend on riparian cover; thus, their relatively high frequency, especially in the more xeric lower parts of Palomas Creek, indicates that field clearing was limited. Agricultural activity never intensified to the point where cottontails were unavailable. Second, riparian wood charcoal is ubiquitous in postholes, roof fall, and hearths. This proportion does not vary significantly over time. Riparian species were not eliminated from the Palomas floodplain as they were in the Mimbres Valley. Cultivation may have been organized extensively, possibly including several field areas for each household or long periods of fallow of fields rather than intensive focus on plots in a primary farming area. Each household might have cultivated several small parcels of land located in different settings along the drainage. Analyses of the ubiquities of weedy perennials is consistent with the argument for intra-annual residential mobility. Weedy seed rain is low within structures, which we argue is evidence for low occupational intensity.

No single class of data provides enough information for understanding the organization of land use among the Postclassic dispersed population in the Eastern Mimbres area. Taken as a whole, however, the data support a model of extensive cultivation, dependence on resources local to each site, and low impact on the riparian farmland. In addition, these data are consistent with a model of residential mobility at the household level. The combined analysis of architectural, artifactual, ethnobotanical, faunal, and settlement data point to a need for evaluation of the role of mobility in the dispersed land use of the

Postclassic farmers of the Eastern Mimbres area. Assessment of the agricultural productivity of field areas (Brady 1997) and the nutritional requirements of hamlet dwellers, along with closer attention to the variety of mobility strategies that could have been employed (Nelson and Hegmon 1998), will enrich our knowledge of land use by small-scale farmers.

SOCIAL CONTEXTS
OF THE POSTCLASSIC

Margaret C. Nelson
and Michelle Hegmon

The small residential groups of the Postclassic period in the Eastern Mimbres faced new social contexts in their villages, local area, and region. Having moved from village centers, these farmers had to reestablish social networks in order at least to hedge against shortages and meet social obligations. Although mobility was apparently an option and scalar stress was minimal in these small settlements (Johnson 1982), new social relations would have developed at various scales. This chapter is an exploration of the intrasite, intraregional, and panregional social relations that emerged during the Postclassic period. The intrasite patterns are different from those at earlier Classic Mimbres village centers. The stylistic conformity that was apparent at Classic Mimbres villages is lacking at the Postclassic hamlets, where variation and diversity best describe ceramic and architectural forms. Among the Postclassic sites along the Palomas drainage in the Eastern Mimbres, site spacing may reflect earlier relations among households (see Adler 1993) and earlier ownership patterns of secondary farmland (see Kohler 1992), although, in contrast to the Classic pattern, no site is substantially larger than others. Panregional interactions were considerably broader in the Postclassic period than in the Classic. The importation and adoption of ceramic wares from areas to the northwest, east, and south indicate a wider range of relations. These are regions where the population was growing and new village centers were developing after A.D. 1150.

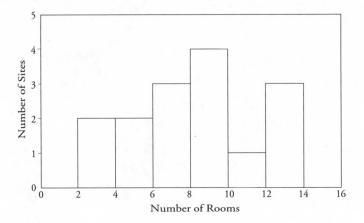

Figure 6.1

Size distribution of recorded Postclassic Mimbres sites in the Palomas Creek drainage.

Intrasite Social Patterns

None of the small Postclassic hamlets has been fully excavated. Inferences about the relations among residential units are derived from analysis of surface data and a sample of excavated structures. Surface data are problematic for two reasons: first, at all sites, surface artifacts have been removed by others, and at some, looting has disturbed the architecture; second, some sites are not assignable to any period or are not assignable to the correct period without excavation data. We discuss intrasite structure within these limitations.

The distribution of sites by size is presented in figure 6.1. These are small residential sites. The largest of all Postclassic sites with Mimbres ceramics on the surveyed portion of Palomas drainage has no more than twelve rooms in one block; these are the Buckaroo Site and the upper portion of Lizard Terrace Pueblo. The Lizard Terrace site also has a lower terrace with an additional ten to twelve rooms. Whether these form a single occupation or two hamlets is unclear. We have treated them as separate hamlets. Among the excavated sites, each room has a similar complement of features and artifacts, indicating that each was similarly used, most likely as a residence (except one room on Lee Pueblo). Thus, the largest room blocks may have housed a dozen households.

Six of the fifteen Postclassic Mimbres sites have multiple room blocks, with a maximum of four, although most multi-room-block sites have two. Among the surveyed sites with two blocks, one block has only one or two rooms, while the other has five or more. Excavation at two of these sites indicates that the smaller room block is earlier, constructed during the Classic Mimbres period and either not remodeled or occupied for a brief time after remodeling in the Postclassic period. Thus, the room blocks may not be contemporary. At one site, however, there are four small room blocks, three with one or two rooms, the fourth with six. The site may be a cluster of households that is less well integrated than the larger room-block sites. These separate blocks might be indicative of social divisions within the hamlets, either kin-based or cooperative, as has been argued for larger sites (e.g., Reid 1989:87), although not at all large settlements (e.g., Cameron 1991). Surface data are insufficient for making comparisons based on ceramic styles, as few diagnostic sherds remain on the surface. Excavation data suggest, however, a temporal distinction between room blocks in most cases.

Two kinds of architectural features are consistently found in Postclassic rooms in the Eastern Mimbres area: hearths and mealing facilities. Architectural features from the excavated sites may vary, depending on the ways in which villages formed and were integrated (Hegmon, Nelson, and Ruth 1998; Lowell 1991, 1995). While behavioral conformity may be evident in formal standardization, social division and different regional identities may be indicated by patterned variation within the villages and by the appearance of new forms. For this analysis, excavated rooms from six Postclassic sites on Palomas Creek are included: the four reported in this text and two others that are currently being studied and were referred to in chapter 4. Six hearth forms and six mealing facility forms were distinguished on the basis of characteristics that would have been visible when these features were in use (table 6.1). Hearth and mealing facilities are quite varied in form at each hamlet and within the Palomas area as a whole (table 6.2). In contrast, those in the large villages that precede the Postclassic (Classic Mimbres villages) and in large villages from the period following the Postclassic (Tularosa phase villages)[1] have a high degree of stylistic conformity in the forms of hearths and, in the Tularosa phase, in the form of mealing facilities (fig. 6.2). In the large Classic Mimbres and Tularosa villages, integration may have depended in part on behavioral conformity. Lack of conformity in the forms of architectural features within the Postclassic hamlets may be the result of the absence of social cohesion at the site level or the absence of the *need* to represent participation in a larger group through architectural style. The hamlets may have been occupied by such small groups that daily face-to-face interaction sufficed to integrate the group; it is also possible that integration was simply not an issue. In either case, community integration is not indicated in architectural style.

Table 6.1

Hearth and mealing facility forms in Classic Mimbres, Postclassic Mimbres, and Tularosa phase rooms

CODE	FORM
Hearth A	ephemeral fired area
Hearth B	shallow circle or oval, sometimes clay-lined
Hearth C	shallow circle or oval with rock rim
Hearth D	rectangle or square with slab lining and rim
Hearth E	rectangle or square with clay lining, sometimes with slab base
Hearth F	any shape with adobe collar
Mealing A	no built-in mealing facility
Mealing B	single bowl or depression only
Mealing C	single bowl or depression with adobe collar
Mealing D	2 bowls or depressions with collars and/or platforms
Mealing E	3 bowls or depressions with collars and/or platforms
Mealing F	slab bins with multiple depressions or bowls without collars
Mealing G	slab bins with multiple depressions or bowls with adobe collars

Table 6.2

Hearth and mealing features in Postclassic Mimbres rooms within the study area

	HEARTH FORMS					MEALING STATION FORMS					
SITE	A	B	D	E	F	A	B	C	D	E	G
Buckaroo Site		3		1	2	2		2	1	2	
Ronnie Pueblo					2	2					
Lee Pueblo		1			1	1		1			
Phelps Pueblo		1		1	2	2	1				1
Mt. Lion Hamlet			1	1	3			1			
Lizard Terrace Pueblo	1	1				2		3			

We found no association between hearth form and mealing feature form (table 6.3). (The sample is too small to evaluate statistically.) Hearth form F, the collared hearth, occurs with nearly all mealing facility forms, including the absence of a formal mealing feature. Similarly, rooms that lack mealing facilities, Mealing Form A (the most frequent of the cases of this variable), have all hearth

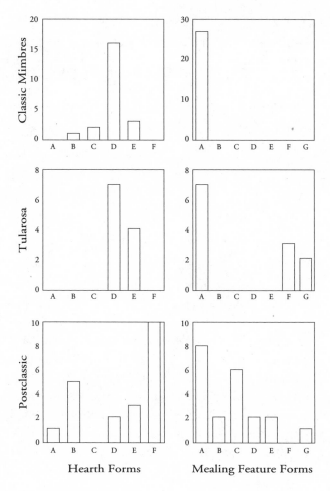

Figure 6.2
The forms of hearths and mealing facilities for different regions and time periods of occupation in southwestern New Mexico.

forms. The only site with apparently standardized architectural features is the Ronnie site; within the two excavated rooms there, we found collared hearths but no formal grinding facilities. Thus, the stylistic variation in architectural features within the Postclassic hamlets does not indicate discrete social divisions for occupants of different sites or rooms within a hamlet. The features are not associated as would be expected for an immigrant household or enclave. (See Hegmon, Nelson, and Ruth 1998 for a detailed discussion of this argument.)

Table 6.3

Analysis of association between hearth and mealing facility forms within rooms

Mealing Facility Form	Hearth A	Hearth B	Hearth D	Hearth E	Hearth F	Total
A	1	3	1	1	3	9
B	0	1	0	0	1	2
C	0	0	1	1	3	5
D	0	0	0	0	2	2
E	0	1	0	1	0	2
G	0	0	0	0	1	1
Total	1	5	2	3	10	21

Thus, the Postclassic hamlets of the Eastern Mimbres are comprised of a block of rooms, each room serving as a residence. (One site might have up to four contemporaneous blocks, while another might have two.) Within most sites, styles of architecture vary, but not in a pattern that indicates either social divisions within the hamlet or the presence of separate immigrant groups. The variation may result from a lack of social cohesion at the site level (Hegmon, Nelson, and Ruth 1998). As discussed in chapter 4, other architectural data and the lack of trash on the sites are indices of residential mobility. If the timing of occupation of rooms was not the same for every room in a hamlet, as has been reported for the residential mobile Tarahumara farmers (Graham 1993; Hard and Merrill 1992), the hamlet may not have been a locus of community cohesion.

Intersite Spatial Patterns

Spatial clusters of residential sites can be recognized, and intragroup social ties are assumed to have been closest among those groups living in closest proximity (Rocek 1995). Within Palomas Creek drainage fifteen sites are recognized as Postclassic; they have Classic Mimbres ceramics and some other later ceramics on the surface. Analysis of intersite patterning relies on surface information derived from survey, with the same limitations as applied to analysis of intrasite relations; some Postclassic sites are not recognized or may be misclassified as Classic Mimbres for lack of surface artifacts, and some have been destroyed. The Rio Grande data have been so compromised by development and looting that they cannot be used for this analysis. Also, as discussed in the next section, the case may be that only one substantial site in the Rio Grande Valley is part of the initial Postclassic Mimbres occupation of the area.

In an earlier analysis of site distribution along Palomas drainage, Nelson delineated five clusters of architectural sites with Classic Mimbres ceramics (Nelson 1986, 1989), not recognizing the current distinction between Classic Mimbres and Postclassic Mimbres periods. For this analysis, we use the ceramic distinctions discussed in chapter 3 to analyze a Classic Mimbres as compared to a Postclassic Mimbres sample. The Postclassic sites began as very small Classic Mimbres sites; therefore, some consideration of the Classic occupation on them must be included with analysis of the more purely Classic Mimbres sites. We review the Classic Mimbres pattern, first, for comparison to the Postclassic. Sites can, however, be misclassified more easily as Classic Mimbres than as Postclassic because Classic Mimbres sherds are more common on the surfaces of most sites than are any later forms, and all painted sherds are rare. Resolving this classification problem would involve excavating at all fifty sites, which is not desirable or feasible.

Architectural sites with Classic Mimbres Black-on-white (Style III) form four large clusters and one or two small clusters along Palomas drainage (fig. 6.3). All seem to have been placed to make use of the best arable land. Two of the large clusters are located at the western (upstream) end of the drainage, one (A) just below a narrow constriction of the floodplain where water flows continuously and one (B) on a side drainage with rich alluvial fans. About 5 km downstream from these clusters is another large cluster (C) at the upper end of a second narrow constriction of the drainage, extending into the narrows. Here water flows continuously. At the downstream end of this group of sites, in the narrows, are two groups of small sites that may form a very small site cluster (Y). The last large cluster (D), at the downstream end of the drainage, is centered on a group of springs in an area of perennial water flow. Five sites tail off the lower end of this cluster in a more xeric portion of the drainage; these may form a second, very small cluster (Z).

The spatial clusters may represent cooperating social units within the drainage area, but they also may simply represent the clustering of sites in the vicinity of the best farm land. These explanations are not mutually exclusive; proximity among residential settlements would require and make possible some degree of interaction. Alternatively, each cluster may represent a single settlement surrounded by special-use sites. In three out of four large clusters, one site is substantially larger than the others. In Cluster A, one site has twenty-nine rooms, the next largest has seven; in Cluster B, one site has nineteen rooms, the next

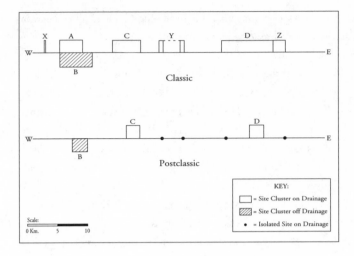

Figure 6.3

The distribution of site clusters for Classic and Postclassic Mimbres periods along Palomas Creek drainage.

largest has four; in Cluster C one site has twenty-one rooms, the next largest has five (although recall that we cannot be certain that all the rooms are Classic period occupations). This pattern appears to be the same in the Rio Grande to the east (Lekson 1989:57, 63) and on Las Animas Creek, another of the Eastern Mimbres drainages (Mayo, Hegmon, and Nelson 1993), although the village centers there are much larger (fifty to more than one hundred rooms). The small Classic Mimbres components on excavated Postclassic sites (the only small Classic Mimbres sites yet excavated) are special-use farming locales (see chaps. 4 and 5). The only cluster that does not follow this pattern is D, in which the largest site has only ten rooms. Patterning in Cluster D may be obscured by a large, late site in the area (Nelson 1993a). Its ceramic assemblage is dominated by types that date to the mid-1200s or later, though Classic Mimbres ceramics are present. There may have been a village of the Classic Mimbres period at this locus, which was abandoned and later covered by the late village. Unfortunately, the site is not accessible for research or even basic surface investigation. Another large, late village on nearby Las Animas Creek has a substantial Classic Mimbres village, which was abandoned in the mid-1100s and reoccupied about 1300 (Hegmon and Nelson 1994; Nelson and Hegmon 1993, 1995, 1996). Lekson observes for the Rio Grande portion of the Eastern Mimbres that "almost all large Mimbres phase room blocks were part of a larger complex of sites which included from two to twelve small room blocks and isolated rooms" (1989:57).

Classic Mimbres site clusters are larger and more spatially extensive than those of the Postclassic. Three of the large clusters have ten or eleven sites and the fourth has six; Postclassic clusters have from two to five sites (fig. 6.3). The number of Classic rooms in each cluster is difficult to estimate. Some of the sites are Classic and Postclassic occupations, at which excavation has revealed a very small Classic occupation. Assuming that each Postclassic site began as a Classic site with two structures, the large clusters dating to the Classic period have approximately thirty-six to forty-eight rooms, although rooms on the small sites may have been only seasonally used (Nelson 1993b). Ignoring the small sites, assuming they are special-use loci, and counting only the rooms in the large sites in each cluster, there are from nineteen to twenty-nine rooms per cluster. (We did not include cluster D for which there is no large site recorded.) Interestingly, there are approximately the same number of rooms at the small, special-use sites as there are in the large sites in each cluster. Each household may have had a secondary field house; if so, all occupants of the Classic Mimbres villages might have had the option of remaining in the region.

The Classic Mimbres land-use pattern along most of Palomas and the adjacent Rio Grande includes a village center surrounded by smaller, possibly special-use sites, among which we have discussed only those with architecture and diagnostic ceramics. The Postclassic pattern developed from shifting occupation to the secondary field sites. Small Classic Mimbres field-house sites on Palomas were enlarged to form small Postclassic pueblo hamlets. Large Classic Mimbres villages were abandoned.

Among the fifteen Postclassic sites, eleven form three spatial groups at the downstream ends of three of the Classic site clusters (fig. 6.3). The first, within Cluster B, is located on the eastern (lower) edge of the piñon-juniper zone in an area of juniper and grassland, south of the main channel of Palomas Creek on a side drainage with a deep alluvial fan. This Postclassic group includes only two sites, spaced 2.6 km apart, although we expect that some of the sites in this area are misclassified as Classic Mimbres. The two sites have a total of fourteen rooms: one has nine, the other, five. The second spatial cluster is in a juniper and mesquite environment within Classic Cluster C. Four sites at the upstream end of the lower narrows on the first and second terraces above the floodplain have Postclassic Mimbres ceramic assemblages. They cluster within a 2.1 km segment of the drainage. Among the four sites, two have approximately seven rooms and two have twelve, for a total of thirty-eight rooms. The third spatially distinct group is in the mesquite-creosote zone toward the eastern (downstream) end of the drainage in an area with a concentration of large springs. Five sites occur along the first terraces within a 2.15 km segment of Palomas Creek at the downstream end of Cluster D from the Classic Mimbres period. Among the five sites are two with two rooms, one with four, one with eleven, and one with twelve, for a combined total of thirty-one rooms. Four other Postclassic sites are more isolated; they developed from the spatially more-isolated Classic Mimbres sites.

The number of rooms and spacing within the last two Postclassic site clusters are strikingly similar. These two could represent small multihousehold social groupings of about thirty to forty residential units (households?), less aggregated than the Classic Mimbres sites but similar in size to the villages in the Classic Mimbres clusters. Even if the Postclassic spatial groups functioned at times as integrated social units, the architectural evidence, discussed in the previous section, suggests that they were not integrated in the same way as were the Classic Mimbres villages. Future research should focus on the occurrence of integrative community features such as kivas and plazas within these spatial groupings (see Lipe and Hegmon 1989).

Spatial clustering may result instead from the differential distribution of resources used by independent small social units. The richer farmland in the area of the three clusters may have supported more people than did land between the clusters. Additional sites are scattered over drier portions of the main channel, downstream from, between, and upstream from the site clusters. These four isolated sites have from seven to nine rooms, which may represent the group size that can be supported in these drier areas during the Postclassic period. None of the very small hamlets (two to five rooms) occur as isolates. Lekson (1989:62–63) notes that the distribution of sites on the adjacent Rio Grande during the period A.D. 1150 to 1300 was less clustered than earlier.

Unfortunately, ceramic data from the surfaces of the sites are insufficient (owing to looting) to evaluate the spatial clusters further. While there is clear spatial grouping within Palomas drainage, it is unclear whether these groups are a reflection of independent entities concentrating their land use in particularly productive areas or are the result of integrated social units cooperating in the use of segments of land along the drainage. As noted for the Classic Mimbres clusters, the proximity of people at the clustered sites would have promoted interaction among them. The residential mobility posited for Postclassic cultivators, however, may have created a context in which local community was not as important as a broader regional community.

Regional Interaction

Regional networks provide support in the form of goods, mates, and ritual practice, among many other valued materials and activities (Braun and Plog 1982; Hegmon 1998; Rautman 1993; Wobst 1977). With the abandonment of village centers at the end of the Classic Mimbres period, new networks of regional relations would have been necessary. Classic Mimbres regional networks appear to have been most developed *within* the Mimbres region, at least for the Eastern Mimbres villagers (Hegmon, Nelson, and Ruth 1998). But the Postclassic pattern is quite different. Expansive regional networks are evident for the hamlet dwellers.

The Postclassic reorganization is associated with a dramatic increase in ceramic diversity. Although surface and subsurface ceramic assemblages are small, the number of different wares is substantially greater than for Classic Mimbres villages, which have larger assemblages. Nonlocal wares are also more abundant in the Postclassic assemblages. According to Hegmon, Nelson, and Ruth (1998:152, table 1), the percentages of decorated, nonlocal ceramics as a portion of the total decorated assemblage in excavated Classic Mimbres villages in the Eastern Mimbres is no higher than 1.3 percent as compared with 17.4 percent, 24.6 percent, and 35.9 percent for decorated wares from three excavated Postclassic hamlets.

The ceramics on Postclassic hamlets are from various regions surrounding the Eastern Mimbres. Many of these nonlocal types are macroscopically indistinguishable from typical examples in other areas. Thus, it is likely that these types were imported into the Eastern Mimbres area, an assumption supported by related compositional analyses (Creel et al. 1995; Hegmon, Nelson, and Ruth 1998), although it is also possible that some of the apparently nonlocal types were locally manufactured copies of foreign wares (Hegmon, Ennes, and Nelson 1996). Chupadero Black-on-white is made primarily to the east, on the eastern side of the Rio Grande (Wiseman 1986). El Paso painted wares (e.g., El Paso Polychrome) are made to the south, especially in the Jornada area (Stallings 1931; Whalen 1981). The White Mountain Redwares [e.g., St. Johns Polychrome (Carlson 1970)] are from the northwest, as are the Cibola Whitewares (e.g., Tularosa Black-on-white) and textured corrugated wares (Rinaldo and Bluhm 1956). Playas Redwares are from the south and west. Table 3.8 lists all of the Postclassic sites identified through survey on Palomas Creek, in order of location from west to east along the drainage. Excavation data that add to information from the surface assemblages are indicated in parentheses. While sur-

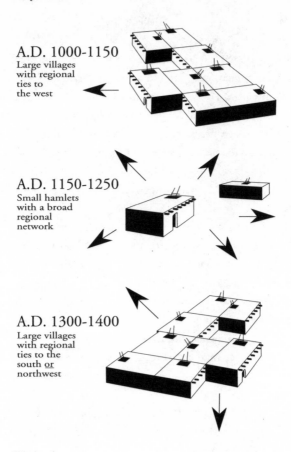

A.D. 1000-1150
Large villages
with regional
ties to
the west

A.D. 1150-1250
Small hamlets
with a broad
regional
network

A.D. 1300-1400
Large villages
with regional
ties to the
south or
northwest

Figure 6.4
Regional interaction for the Classic Mimbres, Postclassic Mimbres, and subsequent period of occupation in the Eastern Mimbres area.

face assemblages are sparse, the excavation data show a consistent pattern of
similar ceramic assemblages across all Postclassic hamlets. The diversity seen for
the whole Postclassic sample is not the result of summing sites with different
ceramic assemblages. This diversity is represented in figure 6.4, in contrast to
the Classic Mimbres pattern in the Eastern Mimbres area.

Ceramic diversity may result from regional trade or travel, or from people
moving into the area (Hegmon, Nelson, and Ruth 1998:5; Hegmon, Ennes,
and Nelson 1996). If people in the Eastern Mimbres were fairly mobile, they
may have traveled widely in an annual or multiannual round. Alternatively,
they may have remained primarily in the Eastern Mimbres area, exchanging
goods with people at distant village centers as part of the process of becoming

reestablished with aggregated social groups. To evaluate various ideas about regional interaction, it is useful to know the "layout" of the regional social environment (fig. 1.1). Creel (1998) has argued that understanding the Postclassic period requires attention to developments in other regions. We focus on the middle-to-late 1100s, early in the Postclassic period.

The Rio Grande Valley

Closest to the Palomas sites is the Rio Grande Valley to the east. Lekson (1989) conducted a reconnaissance survey of the segment of the river valley that defines the eastern edge of the Mimbres region. He recorded a pattern of site size and distribution for the Classic Mimbres period similar to that on Palomas drainage: large villages surrounded by very small sites (1989:57). A few of these large villages have at least a hundred rooms (Lekson 1989:76–77; Mayo 1994) and are comparable in size to large Mimbres Valley villages (Lekson 1989:59–61). Most of the largest sites have a few late ceramics on the surface, which Lekson (1989:62) assumes represent small-scale, late reuse. While a similar assumption proved to be incorrect at small sites on Palomas drainage, Lekson's assumption may be correct for the large villages in the region. Excavation data from large villages at which dominant ceramics are Mimbres on Palomas Creek (Nelson 1984), Las Animas Creek (Hegmon and Nelson 1994; Nelson and Hegmon 1995), and on the Rio Grande (Mayo 1994) reveal that these settlements were abandoned in the mid-1100s and later reoccupied or reused.

Lekson's data on sites contemporary with Postclassic sites on Palomas Creek are less clear. All sites with ceramics dating to the period A.D. 1150 to 1300 were grouped together as Early El Paso phase because they all have early El Paso Polychrome (Lekson 1989:59–64). One group of these sites has ceramics that include Chupadero Black-on-white, El Paso Polychrome, Three Rivers Red-on-terra-cotta, and Classic Mimbres. This group is comprised of two sites, one with one or two rooms and the other with about twenty-five rooms in four blocks. These room blocks are the only ones made from stone masonry among the Early El Paso phase sites on the Rio Grande (Lekson 1989:62). They are similar in architectural form and size to the Postclassic hamlets on Palomas Creek and may be an extension of that settlement system. The ceramic assemblage on this site of twenty-five rooms is also similar to ceramics from Postclassic sites on Palomas Creek. The second group of Early El Paso phase sites has the same ceramic assemblage except that it lacks Classic Mimbres. All of the sites in this group have adobe architecture, more characteristic of the El Paso phase to the south. Four have from twenty to thirty rooms, which is slightly larger than

the Postclassic sites on Palomas Creek but similar in form, with one large room
block or a few small ones. Both groups of Early El Paso phase sites are much
smaller than the largest Classic Mimbres villages on the Rio Grande. The latter
group, which lacks Classic Mimbres ceramics, may date slightly later than the
first site group and represent movement from the southern desert up the Rio
Grande after A.D. 1150, when the only occupation on the major river was a
single Postclassic, twenty-five-room settlement.

North and West

The portion of the Cibola area most directly relevant to the Postclassic in the
Eastern Mimbres area is the Pine Lawn branch (Accola 1981; Berman 1989;
Bluhm 1957; Martin et al. 1956; Martin and Rinaldo 1950b; Martin, Rinaldo,
and Barter 1957; Neely n.d.; Peterson 1988), also referred to as Alpine branch
(Danson 1957) and Cibola branch (Martin 1979), although Berman (1979:59)
notes that demographic trends are similar throughout the area north and west
of the Eastern Mimbres, the study area for her Socorro cultural resources overview. By the 1100s, population was gradually aggregating from a previously
dispersed pattern (Berman 1989:58–59; Danson 1957; Wendorf 1956). During the Reserve phase, population was increasing, and sites were distributed
over a wide range of areas, including major and minor drainages, parklands,
upland meadows, and cienegas (Berman 1989:104). The largest Reserve phase
sites had from fifteen to twenty rooms (Accola 1981:163–164; Berman
1989:105; Bluhm 1960:541). During the Tularosa phase that followed, large
settlements developed along substantial streams.

The Tularosa phase villages have up to a hundred rooms, with some possibly
larger (Berman 1989:119; Danson 1957). Rinaldo and Bluhm (1956) placed
this phase in the 1100s, but reevaluation of the dating of Tularosa ceramics
places the beginning of this phase in the 1200s (Tuggle and Reid 1982). The
process of aggregation may have begun with the formation of medium-sized
pueblos (Lekson 1992b:21; Martin, Rinaldo, and Barter 1957; Peckham,
Wendorf, and Ferdon 1956) and culminated with the "Classic" large pueblo
villages (Hough 1907, 1914; Lekson 1992b:21). Berman (1989) argues that
the late concentration into a few large villages, some in defensive locations, was
a response to food stress. Lekson reports that by the mid- to late-1200s, near
the end of the Tularosa phase, droughts plagued the area (Lekson 1992b:27–
28).

Ceramics on the Tularosa phase sites are similar to wares found on the

Postclassic hamlets in the Eastern Mimbres area. Tularosa Black-on-white, St. Johns Polychrome, and textured corrugated wares with black polished interiors are common. These textured corrugated wares replaced the obliterated corrugated Classic Mimbres plainwares in the Eastern Mimbres area and appear to have been locally made (Hegmon, Ennes, and Nelson 1996).

Thus, during the reorganization period in the Eastern Mimbres, sometime in the late 1100s or early 1200s, large Tularosa phase villages were forming in the Pine Lawn area. The possible shortfalls in food, indicated by Berman and Lekson, may have prompted people in the Pine Lawn area to look to other regions for resources and trading relations. Large Tularosa phase sites have been documented in the Eastern Mimbres area on upper Alamosa drainage (Laumbach 1992) and upper Cuchillo Negro drainage (Enloe et al. 1981).

South

Village size and settlement density in the Jornada area increased substantially after the Formative period, by the mid-1100s (Carmichael 1990; LeBlanc and Whalen 1980; Lehmer 1948; Whalen 1994). Large adobe pueblos of the El Paso phase (A.D. 1150 to 1300) replaced the small settlements of the Formative period. A few large "winter base camps" date to the Formative, and these were occupied more intensively and continuously by the Late Formative or Transitional periods in the early A.D. 1100s (Hard 1983; Whalen 1994). Land use may have involved a high degree of mobility and only seasonal use of the southern Jornada area throughout the Formative, with only short periods of residential stability during the Transitional (Dona Ana) and Pueblo (El Paso) phases (Carmichael 1981, 1983, 1990). The large El Paso pueblos are located adjacent to the prime agricultural land where water is most abundant or easily captured (Carmichael 1990:129; Whalen 1994:22–25). Investment in cultivation increased during this late period but wild resource use was extensive, involving considerable mobility (Whalen 1994:25).

Dona Ana phase sites, described in some studies within the southern Jornada area, have ceramic assemblages similar to the Postclassic sites in the Eastern Mimbres. The basic assemblage includes Classic Mimbres Black-on-white, El Paso painted wares, Chupadero Black-on-white, and a red-on-terra-cotta ware. A carbon-painted white-slipped ware (Seaman and Mills 1988:171), Playas Red (Hard et al. 1992:1), and St. John's Polychrome (Carmichael 1986:68) have also been noted with this group. Hard et al. (1992:1) have a radiocarbon date on excavated deposits with this assemblage of A.D. 1150+50. Whalen dates a similar assemblage between A.D. 1100 and 1200 (LeBlanc and Whalen 1980:392; Whalen 1981:80). The occupation of Dona Ana phase sites may be closely linked to the Postclassic occupations in the Eastern Mimbres area.

Large adobe pueblos are also found in southern Hidalgo and Grant counties and western Luna county, in the southwest corner of New Mexico dating from the end of the 1100s. In recent work these are referred to as Black Mountain phase sites (Kidder, Cosgrove, and Cosgrove 1949; LeBlanc 1977; LeBlanc and Whalen 1980). LeBlanc (1977:11–16) suggests that they resemble the architectural styles at Casas Grandes in northern Mexico and argues for a direct connection.

Ceramics on the El Paso phase sites are Mimbres Black-on-white, El Paso painted wares (bichrome and polychrome), Chupadero Black-on-white, Three Rivers Red-on-terra-cotta, and some Chihuahuan wares (Lekson 1992b:22). The Black Mountain phase sites have similar assemblages that also include White Mountain Redwares (St. John's and Wingate) and various Reserve- and Tularosa-style textured corrugated wares (LeBlanc 1977:13–14; Nelson and LeBlanc 1986). Postclassic hamlets in the Eastern Mimbres have ceramic wares such as these, with the exception of the Chihuahuan types.

The appearance of large pueblos in the deserts of southwestern New Mexico and western Texas coincides with the regional reorganization of the Postclassic in the Eastern Mimbres. Researchers do not agree about whether there was a transition to aggregation and sedentism in the southern desert areas or short episodes of aggregation and dispersion (Nelson and Anyon 1996), with the largest and longest aggregations in the late periods. Similarly, there is disagreement about whether large settlements were formed by local groups or by immigrants. The presence of large villages, however, provided a locus of interaction to the south for the Eastern Mimbres Postclassic groups. The architectural form of the large adobe pueblos and Chihuahuan ceramics appears later (A.D. 1300s) in the Eastern Mimbres area (Hegmon and Nelson 1994; Nelson and Hegmon 1993, 1995).

East

In the northern Jornada, pithouse occupation with ephemeral jacal surface structures in small clusters continued until about A.D. 1200, the end of the Corona and Glencoe phases in the Sierra Blanca region (Kelley 1966, 1984; Rautman 1995; Rocek 1991). If Gilman's model (1987) of seasonal occupation at pithouse villages is correct, residential mobility dominated the land-use pattern in the northern Jornada at least until the 1200s, which is somewhat later than the pattern for the southern Jornada area. Kelley (1966, 1984) argues that hunting was important during the Glencoe and Corona phases. By A.D. 1200, large sites with surface pueblos were constructed, some with linear arrangements and others around plazas.

Late Glencoe phase sites are contemporary with Postclassic hamlets in the Eastern Mimbres; their ceramics are as diverse as those on Postclassic sites. Painted wares include Chupadero Black-on-white, El Paso Polychrome, Three Rivers Red-on-terracotta, White Mountain Redwares, Lincoln Black-on-red, Gila Polychrome, Ramos Polychrome, and Rio Grande Glaze I (Kelley 1966). The first four wares are also found on Postclassic sites in the Eastern Mimbres.

In the Rio Grande Valley, around Socorro, settlement was sparse during the period A.D. 1100 to 1300 (Stuart and Gauthier 1984:139–41; Wimberly and Eidenbach 1980:227). Wimberly and Eidenbach report no sites of the Pueblo III period (A.D. 1100–1300) identifiable from surface data in the Rio Salado and lower Puerco areas along the Rio Grande. Tainter and Levine (1987:38–39) report increasing village size and movement to defensible locations from the Early to Late Elmendorf phases (A.D. 950–1300). The ceramics on these sites are not similar to those in the Eastern Mimbres area.

During the Postclassic period of reorganization in the Eastern Mimbres, the pattern in the north and east appears to have been seasonal residential mobility among pithouse villagers living in relatively small settlements. Although pithouses were occupied east of the Rio Grande at the time when Postclassic settlements in the Eastern Mimbres were stone masonry room blocks, the kinds and diversity of ceramics are similar. Although little is known about sites in the Rio Grande Valley to the north, the sites appear to have ceramic assemblages different from those of the Postclassic hamlets in the Eastern Mimbres area.

The dispersion of population and probable emigration from the Eastern Mimbres area occurred at a time of population growth and aggregation in the deserts to the south and in the mountains to the northwest. Ceramic affinities with these areas are most strong in the Eastern Mimbres Postclassic: El Paso Polychrome, Playas Red, and Chupadero Black-on-white similar to southern sites; Tularosa Black-on-white, St. John's Polychrome, and Tularosa textured corrugated wares similar to those from the northwest. Hamlet dwellers may have sought new networks in these areas because of the growth that was occurring there. The aggregated villages in those regions may have provided loci for information, support, and new social arrangements with which to align. In return, groups from these adjacent regions may have viewed the Eastern Mimbres as more open to new settlement than it was during the previous Classic Mimbres period. Settlement data from upper Alamosa and Cuchillo Negro drainages in the Eastern Mimbres may represent immigration in the 1200s. With the reorganization of the hamlet sites, a new plainware ceramic technology was adopted from the northwest. Limited evidence from analysis of these Tularosa style textured corrugated wares from the hamlets reveals local production of extremely well-executed forms. Hegmon et al. (1996) have argued that the introduction of the new plainware technology may indicate that pottery makers from the northwest married into local Eastern Mimbres groups. Settlement data from the Rio Grande Valley (discussed earlier) suggests immigration from the south as well.

To the north and northeast, population remained dispersed in the 1100s, similar to the Postclassic pattern. Many of the ceramic wares found on sites to the east are similar to those on Postclassic sites, which may indicate similar networks or direct social contacts between the areas. The diversity of ceramics at small sites in the Eastern Mimbres and the Sierra Blanca areas could represent a common strategy of maintaining broad regional networks when local community integration might not have been as strong as during periods of settlement aggregation.

Conclusion

The small hamlets of the Postclassic Mimbres period in the Eastern Mimbres area grew as Classic Mimbres farming camps were transformed into the residential settlements of local farmers. Social reorganization during the Postclassic Mimbres period in the Eastern Mimbres area was accompanied by a shift toward greater interaction with people in other regions (or perhaps the delineation of boundaries changed). Community may have been defined at a broad spatial scale. Analysis of intrasite patterns, although limited, shows a pattern of stylistic diversity that may be interpreted as representing a lack of cohesion within each settlement. The diversity does not pattern among the rooms in a way that would indicate social groupings within each hamlet. At the local level, sites are clustered. These clusters of people probably interacted frequently, owing to spatial proximity and wide spacing between clusters, but it is not clear whether the clusters are the product of social grouping or concentration of population around the best remaining farmland, or both. At the regional level, ceramic diversity shows a broad range of interactions by people at each of the hamlets, especially with areas to the northwest and south where population was increasing and aggregating. At some time in the 1200s, large settlements similar to those in the Pine Lawn and southern Jornada areas formed in the Eastern Mimbres area.

The residential mobility postulated for these hamlet dwellers may explain the apparent lack of local community cohesion and the range of regional networks. If hamlet dwellers moved frequently, either within the local area (as we currently think) or over a broad area of the southern Southwest, the hamlets in the Eastern Mimbres area, and possibly the local area, may not have been inhabited by the same complement of people from one season or one year to the next. Security, information, and social needs might not have been met locally. The broad regional ties that are indicated by the ceramic assemblages provided contact with more residentially stable groups to the northwest and south and possibly with other mobile cultivators to the east. These new networks appear to have encouraged immigration into the Eastern Mimbres area and to have stimulated the formation of new large villages by the late 1200s and early 1300s, some of which look very much like southern desert settlements (Hegmon and Nelson 1994; Nelson and Hegmon 1993, 1995) and others that look like Tularosa villages. These later developments are only beginning to be studied.

RETHINKING
ABANDONMENT

7

The archaeological record appears to be full of failures. People left places; their structures collapsed and were buried. The obvious question: What went wrong? But this question is only obvious if we perceive leaving and abandonment as failure. People move because their situations change; sometimes others force them to move. The changed situation can be perceived as a failure, and reasonably so for some times and places; but such characterization may not be productive for other times and places. This study of the twelfth century in the Eastern Mimbres area serves as an example of the importance of considering abandonment as a dimension of land use, part of a strategy for continuity. By viewing abandonment in this way, our models for explaining abandonments are broadened to include not only what may have "failed" but how movement away from one place to another serves the needs of people. Abandonments are reconceptualized as aspects of strategies for addressing ever-changing relationships among people and between people and their landscape.

Rethinking abandonment as an aspect of land-use strategies changes the way the past is viewed. "Leaving" is understood by examining the situations or contexts within which people were making decisions. Context can be described in a number of different ways. For this study, I have focused on landscape and population distribution. I argue that in arid landscapes, of which the North American Southwest is one example, various kinds of movement can provide for continuity. While hunting and gathering over much of the Southwest required intra-annual movement, cultivating along with hunting and gathering could be achieved through a number of different approaches, all requiring some degree of residential movement. Intra-annual residential movement among small field plots or less frequent movement of settlements within regions and between regions were all practiced in the Southwest. Understanding the organization of movement at any one time and the changes in organization over time aids in understanding abandonment in relation to landscapes.

What is the strategy? is too narrow a question. In all communities, people or households have different roles that are evident in the ways they gain their subsistence, interact with one another, and contribute to the community or take from it. This variability should be recognized by asking What are the strategies? The varied roles of individuals and household groups create different options for each. Change within a community follows different pathways; any overall pattern that we see in the archaeological record, such as the abandonment of a site, is a product of the cumulative pathways taken by individuals. For any individual, the decision to leave a place (not considering the forced removal of people) is influenced by their perception of the advantages and disadvantages of staying in relation to those of leaving (similar to the notion of push-and-pull factors [Lipe 1995]). Since roles are varied, so will be the perception of advantages and disadvantages. What are people giving up? To which places do they have the option of moving?

In this book I have examined one of the strategies of movement taken by some villagers during the twelfth century in the Mimbres region. Their strategy was to move from aggregated village settlements to smaller hamlet settlements while continuing to live and farm within the region. Repositioning themselves within their landscape, people changed the way they farmed and the ways they related to one another within settlements, within the local community, and within the region. Archaeologically, we see this as population dispersion; rather than describe it as a failed attempt at aggregation, I have examined dispersion as an approach by cultivators to maintaining regional occupational continuity in an arid landscape. Prehistorically, people have taken other approaches to insure their continued occupation within a region; agricultural intensification is one example from the Hohokam region. In the case of the Mimbres, the strategies were different.

The Mimbres Case

Traditionally, Mimbres archaeology has been dominated by the enumeration of aspects of village life during the eleventh and twelfth centuries and by the mystery of what happened to the Mimbres people. The Classic Mimbres period villages are among the largest in the region, and the black-on-white pottery of the Mimbres is spectacular. Why would it come to an end? The key here is to be clear about what came to an end. During the twelfth century, Mimbres Black-on-white pottery eventually ceased to be made, and the large, stone masonry villages were depopulated. But occupation of the region continued. This study of continuity alters current understanding of Mimbres prehistory and of the relationship between village abandonment and regional abandonment.

The dominant settlements of the eleventh through mid-twelfth centuries were large, stone-masonry villages. Many smaller field houses and secondary settlements were established in the Mimbres region, but the majority of people lived in large communities. Their domestic architecture was fairly standardized. Their painted pottery was of a single type throughout the region, with little trade in painted wares with people in other regions. The social networks of these people were primarily internal. Styles of pottery and domestic architecture are partially determined by the rules or behaviors that integrate groups. Thus, standardization may reinforce for village dwellers their inwardly focused, regional community. Internal regional hierarchy, if present, is not evident in the archaeological remains from villages, although a few stand out as having more exotic goods. Internal village hierarchy, although necessary for villages of this size, is not evident in the accumulation of materials or construction of special structures for some individuals or households. The presence of ritual structures within many room blocks within any village suggests that even ritual knowledge was not concentrated in a single individual or residential group.

In the middle of the twelfth century, the beginning of the Postclassic Mimbres period, many of these patterns changed. The villages were depopulated, many completely abandoned as residences. This study of the Eastern Mimbres provides information on the other kinds of changes that accompany the abandonment of Mimbres village rooms: small settlements or field houses grew, new painted and plain ceramic types were made and used, and domestic architecture was diversified. The people of the Mimbres region did not disappear, nor were they all drawn into developments to the south, at Casas Grandes. Some people remained in the region as farmers.

The settlement change within the Eastern Mimbres area was accomplished by expansion of the residential space on field-house sites. Isolated and ephemeral structures were remodeled and expanded to incorporate more people and more domestic activities. The shift in population from villages to hamlets was not necessarily a dramatic or rapid change. People may have gradually spent more time at their field camps because they depended more on their secondary fields for food or because of social stresses within the village, or both. As I have noted, I expect that not everyone in villages resettled within the region and continued to farm. They did not all have access to this option, and perhaps not everyone considered it the best choice. Assessing the extent of regional depopulation is made difficult by the possibility that Postclassic Mimbres farmers may have moved residence among several hamlets over the course of a year or several years. Further study of residential mobility is necessary before regional population dynamics can be evaluated.

Ceramic change in the Postclassic (and possibly in the Terminal Classic in the Mimbres Valley [Creel 1998]) initially involved the introduction of new types of painted and plainwares from other regions northwest, southeast, and northeast of the Mimbres region. Mimbres Black-on-white ceramics continued to be used, although use declined shortly after the mid-twelfth century. Changes in regional social relationships were responsible for the new ceramics; no longer were networks so internally focused. The people occupying the Eastern Mimbres area, and possibly the Mimbres Valley as well, expanded or changed the nature of their relationships with adjacent populations. The technology and style of Mimbres painted ware were mixed with that of Cibola Black-on-white ware in some of the ceramics from these sites (Hegmon, Nelson, and Ruth 1998), suggesting that some makers of the new ceramics were joining the local Mimbres population. New plainwares occur in rooms along with local Mimbres plainwares.

Architectural change was also toward greater diversity. No longer did each residence incorporate the same architectural styles. Within hamlets and between hamlets, residences had varied styles of hearth, mealing station, and wall construction. The standardization of Classic village domestic architecture was replaced with variation; the Classic hearth forms continued to be constructed in some rooms, but many new forms also were built. Styles of hearths and mealing stations were combined within rooms in ways that do not mirror domestic architecture within adjacent regions; thus, it does not seem reasonable that the new styles represent unit intrusions of households or larger groups (Hegmon, Nelson, and Ruth 1998). Instead, styles are combined in varied ways that simply indicate a lack of rules or traditions governing appropriate form. These architectural changes may have been part of a change in the way settlement integration was symbolized or in the way communities were integrated. Architectural standardization may no longer have been an important way to symbolize integration. Hamlet settlements were so small that face-to-face interaction sufficed, which would not have been true for some of the larger Classic period villages. Alternatively, hamlet settlements may not have been integrated communities, even though they were quite small. If households were residentially mobile and did not all occupy the hamlet at one time, they may have been integrated at a level outside or beyond the hamlet.

Expanded regional ties, as indicated by the diversity of ceramic and architectural styles, is interesting in light of the possible lack of local community integration. The absence of shared styles within the hamlet and within the Eastern Mimbres area begs the question of where shared identity resided. Thus far, survey and excavation have not revealed any communal structures on hamlet sites or in isolated locales between them. Some of the pit structures on hamlets may have served as communal structures during the Postclassic period, although all tested pit structures are filled with earlier Classic Mimbres period trash. Open areas may have served as gathering places, and it is possible that communal gathering places were not marked in ways that would be visible archaeologically. More attention must be paid to examining various kinds of evidence for the scale of community in the Postclassic Mimbres period. The Classic Mimbres room-block kivas and large ceremonial rooms are not currently evident on Postclassic sites. It is possible that households had their strongest ties to centers of population outside the Mimbres region. By a century after the end of the Classic Mimbres period and the depopulation of large villages, new villages were forming in the Mimbres region that incorporated the styles of Tularosa phase centers to the northwest and El Paso phase centers to the southeast.

Farming continued during the Postclassic Mimbres period. Hamlets were located adjacent to small patches of arable land along the floodplains and in alluvial fans. The farmers focused on local resources adjacent to hamlets, in some settings deriving more food from hunting artiodactyls than they had done during the earlier Classic period. Several aspects of the architecture and assemblages of artifacts, plant, and animal remains suggest the possibility of a residentially mobile approach to landscape use during the Postclassic. Hamlet dwellers may have farmed extensively, depending on the output from varied field areas within the region. This strategy would have reduced the risk of depending on a single plot for adequate yield. Further research is necessary to evaluate the residential pattern during the Postclassic Mimbres period.

Residentially mobile farming that incorporates varied plots may have had less impact on the natural environment than did focused, intensive farming of large field plots (Kohler 1992; Kohler and Matthews 1988; Minnis 1985a). For the people of the Mimbres region, however, it was not the ultimate solution. Dispersed settlements were burned at some time during the thirteenth century. Burning may either have signaled closure or the insistence by some that hamlet dwellers cease to live in this dispersed pattern. Burning may also have been the work of raiders. Whatever the cause, the hamlet dwellers left their settlements at the same time that new, large villages were forming in the region. The styles of ceramics in their abandonment assemblages on hamlet settlements are similar to those found in the new emerging centers of population, indicating their participation in a shift toward aggregation.

This book demonstrates that "what happened to the Mimbres people" was a reorganization by them of their use of the landscape. They had been adjusting by reorganizing throughout much of the time they had occupied the region. As pithouse dwellers, they had been fairly residentially mobile (Gilman 1987), with small dispersed villages, for the most part. As Classic period village dwellers, they employed a more logistical approach to movement, establishing camps at secondary fields and probably at other resource locales. Farming was extended even into the upland parks. During the Postclassic Mimbres, they were again dispersed. Each settlement change was accompanied by different changes in social relationships at all scales. One of those changes during the Postclassic period was an expansion of regional networks and a decline of the inward regional focus of the previous Classic period. Archaeologically, this is visible by replacement of the single Classic Mimbres Black-on-white type of pottery with an array of new painted ceramic types. Unfortunately, because we sometimes make the mistake of equating ceramics with people, we further extend the error by stating that the disappearance of a ceramic style implies the disappearance of a people. The people of the Mimbres region were flexible, arid-land cultivator-hunter-gatherers, who were able to maintain their place in their homeland by shifting their use of that homeland and their relationships with their neighbors. In the process, they redefined who they were, adopting new styles as appropriate.

Why Movement, Why Continuity?

Movement is an important strategy in arid landscapes (Horne 1993). Resources are less productive and may be more dispersed than in temperate regions. These conditions not only favor movement as a strategy for gaining access to resources, they also favor movement as a strategy for continuing to occupy a region. Long-term settlement or occupational stability is inconsistent with the conditions of arid landscapes. Periodically, repositioning settlements shifts the impact of people on their land.

If settlement patterns were solely determined by the conditions of landscape, then aggregation would be a rare occurrence in the Southwest as well as other arid places. But aggregation was not. Shortly after farming became an important aspect of subsistence (and in some cases before much cultivation was practiced), people formed large villages, for varied reasons, with relatively stable occupation. Reid et al. (1996) provide an interesting argument for aggregation in the late prehistory of the Mountain Mogollon. They argue that residentially mobile cultivator-hunter-gatherers aggregated into large settlements, such as Grasshopper Pueblo, because contestation over resources had become a significant issue with increases in population. Thus, aggregation was a response to need. Others have argued that it was a response to opportunity in the form of especially productive resources (Graves, Longacre, and Holbrook 1982; Fish, Fish, and Madsen 1990). A myriad of social reasons exist for aggregation, which may override any environmental limitations on long-term occupation by concentrated groups. But as many have noted, aggregation in the Southwest did not, in many cases, continue for long periods of time. Villages came apart. People moved.

The processes of movement are complicated, and the options for movement are varied. I discussed both regional reorganization and migration in chapter 1. I would like to emphasize that movement, whether within or away from a region, depends on a degree of household autonomy and flexibility in the structure of social relations. Throughout much of the prehistory of the Southwest, until very late—or perhaps into the protohistoric period—communities were fairly loosely organized. Regardless of the source of power of leaders (whether materially based, labor-based, or knowledge-based), their influence in controlling the movement of others was limited. Households, and perhaps individuals, moved within regions and between regions. The structure of many large settlements reflects this autonomy (see fig. 1.3).

Movement is not without cost, however. Leaving a place may have meant giving up immediate control over access to resources, breaking existing social ties, or walking away from ritual or civil obligations. Thus, the decision to move was not a simple one, and as a result household autonomy should not be seen simply as the freedom to decide. Household autonomy is the background against which to understand how communities came apart and why behavior within communities was variable. Those who stayed, even in depopulated villages, remained because the cost of leaving was too great, or because they did not perceive moving as an option for them.

People leave places because the advantage of being elsewhere is greater than the advantage of staying. This advantage is a combination of economic, social,

political, and religious considerations. Understanding the role of these considerations for a particular case helps researchers in examining why people moved
in a particular way. Why did some people migrate away from a region? Why did
they move to specific other regions? Why did people reposition themselves within
a region? Why those new places? Explaining abandonments becomes a challenge in understanding change rather than in explaining a mystery.

For the Eastern Mimbres, those with access to cultivable land (probably those
who claimed ownership to these lands) were able to resettle within the region
and continue their traditions of farming within their homeland. Accomplish-
ing this continuity carried with it many changes in land use and social relations.
Farming practices may have changed toward more extensive use of small fields
and higher residential mobility. Regional relations probably shifted to accommodate the needs of dispersed populations. Settlements may have become less
integrated and communities defined on a regional scale. The dispersed settlement of the late twelfth century was not the "optimal solution" for the people
of the Eastern Mimbres area. By the middle of the thirteenth century, large
villages had again formed. Hamlets burned for whatever reasons, and people
were again living in large groups. This cycle of movement is a fascinating element of the prehistory of arid landscape use.

Continuity has been defined archaeologically through the sustained residential use of places; in the Southwest for the periods after the Archaic, continuity
is assessed through continued use of architectural features. Continuity, however, may involve the continuation of an idea or tradition, a group, or a strategy.
People may emphasize one aspect over others under varied circumstances. The
continuation of the integrity of a group may require migration, which is a change
in settlement strategy. Continuation of the tradition of farming may require a
change in group composition and settlement strategy, as was the case for the
Eastern Mimbres.

The connection of people to landscapes is one form of continuity that has
been oversimplified. Our emphasis on residential continuity, our equation of
village-level abandonment with that of the regional level, and our equation of
residential abandonment with discontinuation of site use have led us to ignore
the varied ways in which people remained connected to land. We have given
too much attention to the "mystery" of leaving and not enough attention to the
many ways that connections to homeland were maintained. This book offers
one example of how prehistoric farmers maintained their presence within a
region.

NOTES

Chapter 3. Evidence for Mimbres Occupation

1. In an earlier paper (Nelson 1993a), I discuss forty-nine sites on Palomas and thirty-two on the Rio Grande. Changes have been made in these numbers based on revisitation of sites and reevaluation of ceramic assemblages. The largest site in the Postclassic sample was reclassified as Classic Mimbres, based on excavation data; one Classic Mimbres site was "downsized" from eleven-to-fourteen rooms to four-to-six rooms, and one new site was added to the Postclassic sample, also based on excavation data.

2. Most of the comparisons in this book use the chi-square statistic to identify significant associations between the temporal dimension and aspects of site form. In many cases the sample sizes and marginal totals are quite small, causing the expected cell values and some of the observed values to be small. While this has been perceived as a problem in chi-square analysis (Blalock 1960), recent evaluations of the distribution of the chi-square statistic in relation to sample size indicate that the problem is not as crucial as once thought (Feinberg 1981:172–76). Feinberg observes that "in the precomputer era, advice by . . . distinguished statisticians . . . was based on practical experience and intuition and led to standard adequacy rules such as 'the minimal expected cell size should exceed 5'" (1981:172). Feinberg summarizes a study by Larntz (1978) that examines the effect of small sample size and size of expected cell values on the distribution of chi-square. Two results are relevant to this analysis. First, minimum expected values of approximately 1 are adequate for chi-square tests conducted at a 0.05 level of significance. Second, values of N that are four to five times the number of cells are adequate for the application of chi-square used in this analysis. As Feinberg has noted, social science has many instances of "large sparse arrays, full of 0s and 1s, in need of careful analysis" (1981:175). Reducing those tables to a few values masks much interesting patterning. Thus, I have chosen to maintain small cell counts, following the two guidelines listed above, rather than collapse the tables to achieve higher observed and expected values. The chi-square value for table 3.2 was also

evaluated through a Monte Carlo analysis, which yielded p values of <.001. This analysis was conducted to check for the possible effect of the zero observed values.

3. Rio Vista or the Garfield Sites (LA 1082), located near Garfield on the east bank of the Rio Grande near the mouth of Tierra Blanca Creek, is a large village site. It was surface-collected by Yeo in the early 1900s, recorded by Hammack for the Laboratory of Anthropology of the New Mexico State Museum in the 1960s, rerecorded by Laumbach during Lekson's Rio Grande survey in 1985, and tested by Bussey with a New Mexico State University archaeological field school in 1973. Mills and Lekson (site data at Laboratory of Anthropology, New Mexico State Museum) identified in Yeo's collection, Mimbres Black-on-white styles I–III, Chupadero Black-on-white, Tularosa Black-on-white, El Paso Bichrome and Polychrome, and San Andres or Three Rivers Red-on-terracotta. In 1985, Laumbach described the excavation results in a set of site notes at the Laboratory of Anthropology as he remembered them from 1973, and Mayo (1994) reported on the results of the testing program as could be understood from excavation notes. While remains of pithouse and cobble surface architecture appear evident at the site, the testing program yielded little discernible information about the site occupational history. Laumbach, who worked on the testing program, believes that the site is a large Classic Mimbres village with little or no evidence of later occupation. Supporting his contention is the high frequency of Mimbres ceramics from the testing program and in Yeo's collection. Mayo's analysis of excavation materials and contexts (1994) led her to the same conclusion; this site is a large Classic Mimbres village.

4. Four sites were removed from the Postclassic category; all have fifteen or more rooms. Two of these were reclassified as Classic Mimbres: one was the excavated site identified as Classic by Mayo (1994), by far the largest in the area with at least one hundred rooms; the other had only one non-Mimbres ware, a nonspecific, carbon, painted form that could be contemporary with Classic. This second site has at least fifty rooms. The other two reclassified sites were dropped from the analysis because the majority of the architecture appears to be much later than Classic Mimbres. One site with at least fifteen rooms has adobe room blocks; the other, with at least twenty-five rooms, is oriented around a plaza, as are late village sites in the area. In addition, one site was dropped from the Classic category because it was originally misidentified as Classic Mimbres.

Chapter 4. Occupational Histories of Four Postclassic Hamlets

1. Not all postholes shown on floor maps are plotted. If the dimensions were not clear or completely recorded, the posthole was not plotted. Only a few postholes are not represented.

2. These shallow, wide depressions are removed from the plots of pit depth and diameter, which show only postholes from roof and furniture posts. Pits are shown on the floor-feature maps and discussed in the text.

3. These radiocarbon ages and their one-sigma ranges are uncalibrated because the procedure for combining probability distributions requires an assumption of normal distribution, which does not apply to calibrated ranges.

4. Obsidian hydration dates from roof and floor contexts vary wildly from a mean date of 1337 B.C. on one sample to a mean of A.D. 1533 on another. They are not useful for assigning an age range to the occupation of the site. This wide range may represent the true ages of the production of the obsidian flakes, with the early samples representing scavenged material and the late samples resulting from Apache use of this locale. Obsidian is a valued, nonlocal material that might have been reused many times and should have been used throughout the history of occupation in the area.

5. Chronometric dates have ranges too broad to distinguish the Classic Mimbres period from the Postclassic. The absence of later ceramics is a clear, commonly accepted index of occupation before A.D. 1150.

6. See table 3.1 for relevant painted ceramic types made before A.D. 1150.

7. A pithouse was excavated below Room 1 (Nelson 1993b), and two were found and tested beneath Rooms 2 and 4.

8. On Ronnie Pueblo, Rooms 1 and 2 are nearly identical architecturally. They differ in that Room 2 has a substantial floor assemblage, while Room 1 appears to have been disassembled with most whole artifacts and possibly all usable wood (posts and roof beams) removed.

9. In outward appearance this and the hearth in Room 1 are the same. However, the hearth in Room 1 has a cobble-lined rim beneath the adobe collar. Cobble lining is characteristic of the intact Classic Mimbres rooms excavated at a large village on Palomas drainage (Clark and Brady 1998). The hearth in Room 1 may initially have been cobble-lined, with the adobe collar added. This change would be consistent with a shift away from Mimbres styles during the Postclassic (Hegmon, Nelson, and Ruth 1998).

10. The depth and diameter of each possible posthole was plotted to determine which served as primary, secondary, and tertiary support, in the same way discussed for Buckaroo, Room 1. Data on the post dimensions are available from the author.

11. Two of these sites are among those currently being studied and are not fully reported here. They are temporally, architecturally, and ceramically similar to the four sites included in this study. Lee and Phelps Pueblos lack sufficient data for inclusion in this analysis.

12. I noted in a previous section that Ronnie Pueblo may have been abandoned before the others.

13. Also, the Postclassic period was the final phase of occupation at the four sites, with the exception possibly of Apache use centuries later, as indicated by some obsidian hydration dates (table 4.2).

14. Room 1 on Phelps Pueblo had a well-worn floor. The depression from walls to center was 19 cm.

Chapter 6. Social Contexts of the Postclassic

1. The Classic Mimbres and Tularosa villages temporally bracket the Postclassic period and represent a different, substantially larger kind of settlement. Sufficient excavation of

sites for these two periods has not been conducted in the Eastern Mimbres area, so samples are primarily from villages in the Mimbres Valley and Pine Lawn Valley, with the addition of data from the Eastern Mimbres. Selection of the sample is discussed in detail in Hegmon, Nelson, and Ruth 1998.

REFERENCES

Accola, Richard M.

1981   Mogollon Settlement Patterns in the Middle San Francisco River Drainage, West-Central New Mexico. *The Kiva* 46:155–68.

Accola, Richard M., and James Neely

1980   *Mogollon Settlement Patterns in the Middle San Francisco River Valley Drainage, West-Central New Mexico: A Report on the Reconnaissance of Selected Areas in 1979.* Report on file, Gila National Forest, Supervisors Office, Silver City, New Mexico.

Adams, E. Charles

1989   Change in Household and Community Patterning on the Hopi Reservation and Their Reflection of Changing Economic and Social Roles. In *From Chaco to Chaco: Papers in Honor of Robert H. Lister,* ed. Meliha S. Duran and David T. Kirkpatrick, pp. 171–87. The Archaeological Society of New Mexico, Albuquerque.

1991   *The Origin and Development of the Katsina Cult.* University of Arizona Press, Tucson.

Adams, E. Charles, and Jenny L. Adams

1993   Thirteenth-Century Abandonment of the Four Corners: A Reassessment. Paper presented at the Annual Meeting of the American Anthropological Association, Washington, D.C.

Adler, Michael A.

1990   Communities of Soil and Stone: An Archaeological Investigation of Population Aggregation among the Mesa Verde Region Anasazi, A.D. 900–1300. Ph.D. diss., University of Michigan, Ann Arbor.

1993   Perspectives on Northern Anasazi Abandonment: Collapsed Kivas and Resilient

Systems. Paper presented at the 58th Annual Meeting of the Society for American Archaeology, St. Louis.

Adler, Michael A., ed.

1996   *The Prehistoric Pueblo World*, A.D. 1150–1350. The University of Arizona Press, Tucson.

Ahlstrom, Richard V. N., Carla R. Van West, and Jeffrey S. Dean

1995   Environmental and Chronological Factors in the Mesa Verde–Northern Rio Grande Migration. *Journal of Anthropological Archaeology* 14:125–42.

Aiken, M. J.

1990   *Science-Based Dating in Archaeology*. Longman, New York.

Ames, Kenneth M.

1985   Hierarchies, Stress, and Logistical Strategies among Hunter-Gatherers in Northwestern North America. In *Prehistoric Hunter-Gatherers,* ed. T. Douglas Price and James A. Brown, pp. 271–98. Academic Press, New York.

Anyon, Roger, Patricia A. Gilman, and Steven A. LeBlanc

1981   A Reevaluation of the Mogollon-Mimbres Archaeological Sequence. *The Kiva* 46:209–25.

Anyon, Roger, and Steven A. LeBlanc

1980   The Architectural Evolution of Mogollon-Mimbres Communal Structures. *The Kiva* 45:253–77.

1984   *The Galaz Ruin: A Prehistoric Mimbres Village in Southwestern New Mexico.* Maxwell Museum of Anthropology and University of New Mexico Press, Albuquerque.

Bailey, V.

1932   Mammals of New Mexico. *North American Fauna* 53:1–412.

Bender, Barbara

1990   The Dynamics of Nonhierarchical Societies. In *The Evolution of Political Systems,* ed. Steadman Upham, pp. 247–63. Cambridge University Press, New York.

Bennett, Iven

1986a   Annual Precipitation. In *New Mexico in Maps,* 2d ed., ed. Jerry L. Williams, pp. 42–43. University of New Mexico Press, Albuquerque.

1986b   Frost. In *New Mexico in Maps,* 2d ed., ed. Jerry L. Williams, pp. 46–47. University of New Mexico Press, Albuquerque.

Berman, Mary Jane

1979   *Cultural Resources Overview of Socorro, New Mexico.* Prepared for the Cibola National Forest, Gila National Forest, and Socorro District Bureau of Land Management. GPO, Washington, D.C.

1989   *Prehistoric Abandonment of the Upper San Francisco River Valley, West Central New Mexico: An Economic Case Study.* Ph.D. diss., State University of New York,

Binghamton. University Microfilms, Ann Arbor.

Binford, Lewis R.

1980   Willow Smoke and Dogs' Tails: Hunter-Gatherer Settlement Systems and Archaeological Site Function. *American Antiquity* 45:4–20.

1990   Mobility, Housing and Environment: A Comparative Study. *Journal of Anthropological Research* 50:119–52.

Blake, T. Michael

1998   Some Social and Political Implications of Burial Mounds and Cairns in the Lower Fraser River Region, B.C. Paper presented at the 63rd Annual Meeting of the Society for American Archaeology, Seattle.

Blake, T. Michael, Steven A. LeBlanc, and Paul E. Minnis

1986   Changing Settlement and Population in the Mimbres Valley, sw New Mexico. *Journal of Field Archaeology* 13:439–64.

Blake, T. Michael, and Susan Narod

1977   Archaeological Survey and Analysis in the Deming Region, Southwestern New Mexico. Paper presented at the 42d Annual Meeting of the Society for American Archaeology, New Orleans.

Blalock, Hubert M., Jr.

1960   *Social Statistics*. McGraw-Hill, San Francisco.

Bluhm, Elaine A.

1957   The Sawmill Site: A Reserve Phase Village. *Fieldiana: Anthropology* 47 (1). Field Museum of Natural History, Chicago.

1960   Mogollon Settlement Patterns in Pine Lawn Valley, New Mexico. *American Antiquity* 25 (4): 538–46.

Bradfield, Wesley

1931   *Cameron Creek Village: A Site in the Mimbres Area in Grant County, New Mexico*. Reprint, El Palacio Press, Albuquerque. Originally published 1929, The School of American Research, Monograph 1, Santa Fe, New Mexico.

Brady, Jennifer

1997   Spatial Environmental Variation and Agricultural Productivity in the Eastern Mimbres Area. Manuscript in possession of author.

Brandt, Elizabeth

1994   Egalitarianism, Hierarchy, and Centralization in the Pueblos. In *The Ancient Southwestern Community*, ed. H. W. Wills and Robert Leonard, pp. 9–23. University of New Mexico Press, Albuquerque.

Brandt, Elizabeth, and Katherine A. Spielmann

1998   Sociopolitical Organization in the Pueblo IV Period. Prepared for *Migration and Reorganization: The Pueblo IV Period in the American Southwest*. Manuscript in possession of the author, Department of Anthropology, Arizona State University, Tempe.

Braun, David P., and Stephen Plog

1982   Evolution of "Tribal" Social Networks: Theory and Prehistoric Northern American Evidence. *American Antiquity* 47:504–25.

Breternitz, David A.

1966   *An Appraisal of Tree-Ring Dated Pottery in the Southwest.* Anthropological Papers of the University of Arizona, no. 10. The University of Arizona Press, Tucson.

Brethauer, Douglas Paul, and Margaret A. Hoyt

1977   *An Archaeological Survey of Two Proposed Powerlines, a Waterline, an Access Road, and Related Industrial Sites near Hillsboro, New Mexico.* Cultural Resources Management Division Report 159, New Mexico State University, Las Cruces.

Brody, J. J.

1977   *Mimbres Painted Pottery.* School of American Research, University of New Mexico Press, Albuquerque.

Brody, J. J., Catherine J. Scott, and Steven A. LeBlanc

1983   *Mimbres Pottery: Ancient Art of the American Southwest.* Hudson Hills Press, New York.

Brooks, Robert L.

1993   Household Abandonment among Sedentary Plains Societies: Behavioral Sequences and Consequences in Interpretation of the Archaeological Record. In *The Abandonment of Settlements and Regions: Ethnoarchaeological and Archaeological Approaches,* ed. Catherine M. Cameron and Steve A. Tomka, pp. 178–90. Cambridge University Press, New York.

Brown, David E., ed.

1994   *Biotic Communities: Southwestern United States and Northwestern Mexico.* University of Utah Press, Salt Lake City. ·

Bryan, Bruce

1931   Excavation of the Galaz Ruin, Mimbres Valley, New Mexico. *Art and Archaeology* 32 (1): 35–42.

Bussey, Stanley D., and Billy J. Naylor

1975   *An Archaeological Reconnaissance near Hillsboro, New Mexico.* Cultural Resources Management Division Report 24, New Mexico State University, Las Cruces.

Cameron, Catherine M.

1990   Pit Structure Abandonment in the Four Corners Region of the American Southwest: Late Basketmaker III and Pueblo I Periods. *Journal of Field Archaeology* 17:27–37.

1991   Architectural Change at a Southwestern Pueblo. Ph.D. diss., Department of Anthropology, University of Arizona, Tucson.

1992   An Analysis of Residential Patterns and the Oraibi Split. *Journal of Anthropological Archaeology* 11:173–86.

Cameron, Catherine M., guest ed.

1995   Migration and the Movement of Southwestern Peoples. *Journal of Anthropologi-*

cal Archaeology Special Issue 14(2).

Cameron, Catherine M., and Steve A. Tomka, eds.

1993   *The Abandonment of Settlements and Regions: Ethnoarchaeological and Archaeological Approaches.* Cambridge University Press, New York.

Carlson, Roy L.

1970   *White Mountain Redware: A Pottery Tradition of East-Central Arizona and Western New Mexico.* Anthropological Papers of the University of Arizona 19. The University of Arizona Press, Tucson.

1982   The Polychrome Complexes. In *Southwestern Ceramics: A Comparative Review,* ed. Albert H. Schroeder, pp. 201–34. The Arizona Archaeologist 15. Arizona Archaeological Society, Phoenix.

Carmichael, David L.

1981   Non-residential Occupation of the Prehistoric Southern Tularosa Basin, New Mexico. *Artifact* 19 (3 & 4): 59–68. Published by the El Paso Archaeological Society.

1983   Archaeological Settlement Patterns in the Southern Tularosa Basin, New Mexico: Alternative Models of Prehistoric Adaptations. Ph.D. diss., University of Illinois, Urbana–Champaign.

1986   *Archaeological Survey in the Southern Tularosa Basin of New Mexico.* Publications in Anthropology 10. El Paso Centennial Museum, The University of Texas, El Paso.

1990   Patterns of Residential Mobility and Sedentism in the Jornada Mogollon Area. In *Perspectives on Southwestern Prehistory,* ed. P. E. Minnis and C. L. Redman, pp. 122–34. Westview Press, Boulder.

Carneiro, Robert

1967   On the Relationship between Size of Population and Complexity of Social Organization. *Southwest Journal of Anthropology* 23:234–43.

Cashdan, Elizabeth

1983   Territoriality among Human Foragers: Ecological Models and an Application to Four Bushman Groups. *Current Anthropology* 24 (1): 47–66.

1984   G//ana Territorial Organization. *Human Ecology* 12 (4): 443–63.

Cashdan, Elizabeth, ed.

1990   *Risk and Uncertainty in Tribal and Peasant Economies.* Westview Press, Boulder.

Chapman, Richard C., Cye W. Gossett, and William J. Gossett

1985   *Class II Cultural Resources Survey, Upper Gila Water Supply Study, Central Arizona Project.* Bureau of Reclamation, Phoenix.

Clark, Tiffany C., and Jennifer Brady

1998   Report on the 1997 and 1998 Excavations of Avilas Canyon Village (LA 44997 and LA 45000). Manuscript in possession of author.

Cordell, Linda S.

1975   Predicting Site Abandonment at Wetherill Mesa. *The Kiva* 40:189–202.

1984   *Prehistory of the Southwest.* Academic Press, San Diego.

Cordell, Linda S., and George J. Gumerman

1989   Cultural Interaction in the Prehistoric Southwest. In *Dynamics of Southwestern Prehistory,* ed. Linda S. Cordell and George J. Gumerman, pp. 1–17. Smithsonian Institution Press, Washington, D.C.

Cordell, Linda S., and Fred Plog

1979   Escaping the Confines of Normative Thought: A Reevaluation of Puebloan Prehistory. *American Antiquity* 44:405–29.

Cosgrove, Harriet S., and Cornelius B. Cosgrove

1932   *The Swarts Ruin: A Typical Mimbres Site in Southwestern New Mexico.* Papers of the Peabody Museum of American Archaeology and Ethnography 15 (1). Harvard University Press, Cambridge, Massachusetts.

Cowgill, George L.

1996   Just Fuzzy Enough: Handling Random Errors in Archaeological Dating. Paper presented at the Annual Meeting of the American Anthropological Association, San Francisco.

Creel, Darrell G.

1995   *Status Report on Excavations at the Old Town Site (LA 1113), Luna County, New Mexico, summer 1994.* Report submitted to the U.S. Bureau of Land Management, New Mexico State Office by the Texas Archaeological Research Laboratory, The University of Texas at Austin.

1996   Environmental Variation and Prehistoric Culture in the Mimbres Area. Paper presented at the Sixty-first Annual Meeting of the Society for American Archaeology, New Orleans.

1998   The Black Mountain Phase in the Mimbres Area. In *The Casas Grandes World: A Diversity of Ideas,* ed. Curtis Schaafsma and Carroll Riley, in press.

Creel, Darrell G., and Charmion McKusick

1992   Prehistoric Macaws and Parrots in the Mimbres Area, New Mexico. Manuscript in possession of author.

Creel, Darrell G., Matthew Williams, Hector Neff, and Michael Glascock

1995   Neutron Activation Analysis of Black Mountain Phase Ceramics from Old Town and Other Sites in the Mimbres Area. Paper presented at the Sixtieth Annual Meeting of the Society for American Archaeology, Minneapolis.

Danson, Edward Bridge

1957   *An Archaeological Survey of West-Central New Mexico and East-Central Arizona.* Papers of the Peabody Museum of Archaeology and Ethnology, Harvard University 44 (1). Harvard University Press, Cambridge, Massachusetts.

Dean, Jeffrey S., William H. Doelle, and Janet D. Orcutt

1994   Adaptive Stress, Environment, and Demography. In *Themes in Southwest Prehistory,* ed. George J. Gumerman, pp. 53–86. School of American Research Press, Santa Fe.

Diehl, Michael W.

1992   Architecture as a Material Correlate of Mobility Strategies: Some Implications for Archaeological Interpretation. *Behavioral Science Research* 26 (1–4): 1–36.

1994   *Subsistence Economics and Emergent Social Differences: A Case Study from the Prehistoric North American Southwest.* Ph.D. diss., State University of New York, Buffalo. University Microfilms, Ann Arbor.

1996   The Intensity of Maize Processing and Production in Upland Mogollon Pithouse Villages A.D. 200–1000. *American Antiquity* 61:102–15.

DiPeso, Charles C., John B. Rinaldo, and Glorian Fenner

1974   *Casas Grandes,* vol. 6. Northland Press, Flagstaff, Arizona.

Douglas, John

1997   Loosening the Shackles of Cultures, Systems, and Boundaries: Lessons from the Prehistoric Ceramic-Period Occupants of the San Bernardino Valley, Arizona and Sonora. Paper presented at the Amerind Foundation Seminar in Archaeology, Dragoon, Arizona.

Earle, Timothy K.

1977   A Reappraisal of Distribution: Complex Hawaiian Chiefdoms. In *Exchange Systems in Prehistory,* ed. Timothy K. Earle and Jonathan E. Ericson, pp. 213–29. Academic Press, New York.

Eder, James F.

1984   The Impact of Subsistence Change on Mobility and Settlement Pattern in a Tropical Foraging Economy: Some Implications for Archaeology. *American Anthropologist* 86:837–53.

Enloe, James G., Paul McGuff, Dan Scurlock, Mark Stinger, and Joseph C. Winter

1981   *A Cultural Resources Overview and Preliminary Survey of the Cuchillo Negro, Mescal Arroyo, and Rio Grande Drainages near Truth or Consequences, New Mexico.* Proposal number 185–93. Prepared for U.S. Army Corps of Engineers, Albuquerque District.

Ensminger, Audrey H., M. E. Ensminger, James E. Konlande, and John R. K. Robson

1994   *Foods and Nutrition Encyclopedia,* 2d ed. CRC Press, Boca Raton, Florida.

Feinberg, Stephen E.

1981   *The Analysis of Cross-Classified Categorical Data.* The Massachusetts Institute of Technology Press, Cambridge, Massachusetts.

Feinman, Gary M.

1997   Corporate-Network: New Perspectives on Models of Political Action and the Puebloan Southwest. Paper presented at Social Theory in Archaeology: Setting the Agenda, Snowbird, Utah.

Feinman, Gary M., and Jill Neitzel

1984   Too Many Types: An Overview of Sedentary Prestate Societies in the Americas. In *Advances in Archaeological Method and Theory,* vol. 7, ed. Michael B. Schiffer, pp. 39–101. Academic Press, New York.

Ferguson, T. J.

1995   An Anthropological Perspective on Zuni Land Use. In *Zuni and the Courts: A Struggle for Sovereign Land Rights,* ed. E. Richard Hart, pp. 103–20. University Press of Kansas, Lawrence.

Ferguson, William M., and Arthur H. Rohn

1987   *Anasazi Ruins of the Southwest in Color.* The University of New Mexico, Albuquerque.

Fish, Paul R., Suzanne K. Fish, George J. Gumerman, and J. Jefferson Reid

1994   Toward an Explanation for Southwestern "Abandonments." In *Themes in Southwest Prehistory,* ed. George J. Gumerman, pp. 135–64. School of American Research Press, Santa Fe.

Fish, Suzanne K., and Paul R. Fish

1993   An Assessment of Abandonment Processes in the Hohokam Classic Period of the Tucson Basin. In *Abandonment of Settlements and Regions,* ed. Catherine M. Cameron and Steve A. Tomka, pp. 99–109. Cambridge University Press, New York.

Fish, Suzanne K., Paul R. Fish, and John Madsen

1990   Sedentism and Settlement Mobility in the Tucson Basin Prior to A.D. 1000. In *Perspectives on Southwestern Prehistory,* ed. Paul E. Minnis and Charles L. Redman, pp. 76–91. Westview Press, Boulder.

Fitting, James E.

1972a   Preliminary Notes on Cliff Valley Settlement Patterns. *The Artifact* 10 (4): 15–30.

1972b   Preliminary Report on the 1971 Intersession Excavations at the Sage-McFarland Site (MC146). Southwestern New Mexico Research Papers, no. 4. Department of Anthropology, Case Western Reserve, Cleveland.

Fowler, Andrew P.

1989   *Archaeological Studies Along the Arizona Interconnection Project Transmission Line Corridor.* Zuni Archaeology Program Report No. 292. Zuni Archaeology Program, Pueblo of Zuni.

Gero, Joan M.

1991   Genderlithics: Women's Roles in Stone Tool Production. In *Engendering Archaeology: Women and Prehistory,* ed. Joan M. Gero and Margaret W. Conkey, pp. 163–93. Basil Blackwell, Cambridge, Massachusetts.

Gilman, Patricia A.

1980   The Early Pueblo Period—Classic Mimbres. In *An Archaeological Synthesis of South-Central and Southwestern New Mexico,* ed. Steven A. LeBlanc and Michael E. Whalen, pp. 205–70. Office of Contract Archaeology, University of New Mexico, Albuquerque.

1987   Architecture as Artifact: Pit Structures and Pueblos in the American Southwest. *American Antiquity* 52:538–64.

1988   Ceramic Chronology. In *Charles C. DiPeso's Excavations at Wind Mountain Site: Pit Structures, Pueblos, and Ceramics in the Gila Valley, Southwestern New Mexico,* by Anne I. Woosley, Patricia A. Gilman, and Andrea R. Johnson, pp. 1–14. Manuscript on file at the Amerind Foundation, Dragoon, Arizona.

1989   Households, Communities, and Painted Pottery in the Mimbres Region of Southwestern New Mexico. In *Households and Communities: Proceedings of the Twenty-first Annual Chacmool Conference,* ed. Scott MacEachern, David J. W. Archer, and Richard D. Garvin, pp. 218–26. The Archaeological Association of the University of Calgary, Calgary.

1990   Social Organization and Classic Mimbres Period Burials in the sw United States. *Journal of Field Archaeology* 17:457–69.

1997   *Wandering Villagers: Pit Structures, Mobility, and Agriculture in Southeastern Arizona.* Arizona State University Anthropological Research Papers 49. Arizona State University, Tempe.

Gilman, Patricia A., and Steven A. LeBlanc

1998   Early Aggregation and Painted Pottery: The Mattocks Ruin in Southwestern New Mexico. Manuscript in possession of author.

Gilman, Patricia A., R. P. Mauldin, and V. S. Powell

1991   *The Mogollon Village Archaeological Project,* 1989. Manuscript on file at the Forest Service, U.S. Department of Agriculture, Silver City, New Mexico.

Graham, Martha

1993   Settlement Organization and Residential Variability among the Raramuri. In *Abandonment of Settlements and Regions: Ethnoarchaeological and Archaeological Approaches,* ed. Catherine M. Cameron and Steve A. Tomka, pp. 25–42. Cambridge University Press, New York.

Graves, Michael W., William A. Longacre, and Sally J. Holbrook

1982   Aggregation and Abandonment at Grasshopper Pueblo, Arizona. *Journal of Field Archaeology* 9:193–206.

Graybill, Donald

1973   *Prehistoric Settlement Pattern Analysis in the Mimbres Region, New Mexico.* Ph.D. diss., Department of Anthropology, University of Arizona, Tucson. University Microfilms, Ann Arbor.

1975   *Mimbres-Mogollon Adaptations in the Gila National Forest, Mimbres District, New Mexico.* Archaeological Report no. 9. U.S. Forest Service, Southwestern Region, Albuquerque.

Gumerman, George J., and Jeffrey S. Dean

1989   Prehistoric Cooperation and Competition in the Western Anasazi Area. In *Dynamics of Southwestern Prehistory,* ed. Linda S. Cordell and George J. Gumerman, pp. 99–148. Smithsonian Institution Press, Washington, D.C.

Hack, J. T.

1942   *The Changing Physical Environment of the Hopi Indians of Arizona.* Papers of the

Peabody Museum of American Archaeology and Ethnography 35 (1). Harvard University Press, Cambridge, Massachusetts.

Halstead, Paul, and John O'Shea, eds.

1989   *Bad Year Economics*. Cambridge University Press, New York.

Hammack, Laurens C.

1962   LA 5599, *A Pithouse Village near Rincon, New Mexico*. Laboratory of Anthropology, note no. 8. Museum of New Mexico, Santa Fe.

Hantman, Jeffrey L.

1989   Surplus Production and Complexity in the Upper Little Colorado Province, East-Central Arizona. In *Sociopolitical Structure of Prehistoric Southwestern Societies*, ed. Steadman Upham, Kent G. Lightfoot, and Roberta A. Jewett, pp. 419–45. Westview Press, Boulder, Colorado.

Hard, Robert J.

1983   A Model for Prehistoric Land Use, Fort Bliss, Texas. In *Proceedings 1983*, pp. 41–51. American Society for Conservation Archaeology, New York.

Hard, Robert J., Pamela Graeber, Jimmie Manasco, Cynthia Tennis, and Kevin Thuesen

1992   Dona Ana Phase Ceramics and Cultural Evolution in the Jornada Mogollon. Paper presented at the Mogollon Conference, Las Cruces, New Mexico.

Hard, Robert J., and William L. Merrill

1992   Mobile Agriculturists and the Emergence of Sedentism: Perspectives from Northern Mexico. *American Anthropologist* 94 (3): 601–20.

Harkey, Marylin

1981   *An Archaeological Clearance Survey of Nine Seismic Testing Transects in Dona Ana and Sierra Counties, New Mexico*. Cultural Resources Management Division Report 470, New Mexico State University, Las Cruces.

Haury, Emil

1936   The Mogollon Culture of Southwestern New Mexico. *Medallion Papers* 20. Gila Pueblo, Globe, Arizona.

Hawley, F. M.

1936   *Field Manual of Prehistoric Southwestern Pottery Types*. University of New Mexico Anthropological Series Bulletin, vol. 1, no. 4. University of New Mexico, Albuquerque.

Hayden, Brian D., and Aubry Cannon

1982   The Corporate Group as an Archaeological Unit. *Journal of Anthropological Archaeology* 1:132–58.

Hegmon, Michelle

1989   Risk Reduction and Variation in Agricultural Economics: A Computer Simulation of Hopi Agriculture. *Research in Economic Anthropology* 11:89–121.

1991   The Risks of Sharing and Sharing as Risk Reduction: Interhousehold Food Sharing in Egalitarian Societies. In *Between Bands and States*, ed. Susan A. Gregg, pp. 309–29. Center for Archaeological Investigations Occasional Paper 9, Southern Illinois University Press, Carbondale.

Hegmon, Michelle, ed.

1998   *The Archaeology of Regional Interaction in the American Southwest.* University of Colorado Press, Boulder, in press.

Hegmon, Michelle, Mark J. Ennes, and Margaret C. Nelson

1996   The Appearance of New Corrugated Pottery Traditions in the Eastern Mimbres Area, Southwestern New Mexico. Poster presented at the Southwest Symposium, Arizona State University, Tempe.

Hegmon, Michelle, and Margaret C. Nelson

1994   *Eastern Mimbres Archaeological Project: Archaeological Research on the Ladder Ranch.* Report submitted to the Turner Foundation.

Hegmon, Michelle, Margaret C. Nelson, and Susan Ruth

1998   Abandonment, Reorganization, and Social Change: Analysis of Pottery and Architecture from the Mimbres Region of the American Southwest. *American Anthropologist* 100:148–62.

Heidenreich, C. E.

1971   *Huronia: A History and Geography of the Huron Indians, 1600–1650.* McClelland and Stewart, Toronto.

Herr, Sarah A., Barbara J. Mills, and Joanne M. Newcomb

1996   Migration, Integration, and Community Reorganization in the Silver Creek Area, East-Central Arizona. Paper presented at the Sixty-first Annual Meeting of the Society for American Archaeology, New Orleans.

Herrington, La Verne

1979   *Settlement Patterns and Water Control Systems of the Mimbres Classic Phase, Grant County, New Mexico.* Ph.D. diss., University of Texas, Austin. University Microfilms, Ann Arbor.

1982   Water-Control Systems of the Mimbres Classic Phase. In *Mogollon Archaeology: Proceedings of the 1980 Mogollon Conference,* ed. Patrick H. Beckett and Kira Silverbird, pp. 75–90. Acoma Books, Ramona, California.

Hill, James N.

1970   *Broken K Pueblo: Prehistoric Social Organization in the American Southwest.* Anthropological Papers of the University of Arizona, no. 18. The University of Arizona Press, Tucson.

Horne, Lee

1993   Occupational and Locational Instability in Arid Land Settlement. In *The Abandonment of Settlements and Regions: Ethnoarchaeological and Archaeological Approaches,* ed. Catherine M. Cameron and Steve A. Tomka, pp. 43–53. Cambridge University Press, New York.

Hough, Walter

1907   *Antiquities of the Upper Gila and Salt Valleys in Arizona and New Mexico.* Bureau of American Ethnology Bulletin 35. U.S. Government Printing Office, Washington, D.C.

1914   *Culture of the Ancient Pueblos of the Upper Gila River Region, New Mexico and Arizona.* National Museum Bulletin 87. Washington, D.C.

Human Systems Research, Inc.

1973   *Technical Manual: 1973 Survey of the Tularosa Basin.* Human Systems Research, Tularosa, New Mexico.

Hunt, Nicola

1990   *Black Range Archaeological Survey* 1989. Report submitted to the U.S. Forest Service, Gila National Forest. On file at Forest Service Regional Office, Silver City, New Mexico.

Johnson, Gregory A.

1982   Organizational Structure and Scalar Stress. In *Theory and Explanation in Archaeology: The Southampton Conference,* ed. C. Renfrew, M. J. Rowlands, and B. A. Seagraves, pp. 389–421. Academic Press, New York.

1989   Dynamics of Southwestern Prehistory: Far Outside—Looking In. In *Dynamics of Southwestern Prehistory,* ed. Linda S. Cordell and George J. Gumerman, pp. 371–89. Smithsonian Institution Press, Washington D.C.

Joyce, Arthur A., and Sissel Johannessen

1993   Abandonment and the Production of Archaeological Variability at Domestic Sites. In *Abandonment of Settlements and Regions,* ed. Catherine M. Cameron and Steve A. Tomka, pp. 138–53. Cambridge University Press, New York.

Judge, W. James

1979   The Development of a Complex Cultural Ecosystem in the Chaco Basin, New Mexico. In *Proceedings of the First Conference on Scientific Research in the National Parks,* ed. Robert M. Linn, pp. 901–5. U.S. Government Printing Office, Washington, D.C.

Kardaman, Gretchen

1993   An Analysis of Vertebrate Faunal Remains from Three Sites in Southwestern New Mexico. Department of Anthropology, Honors thesis, State University of New York at Buffalo.

Kelley, Jane H.

1966   The Archaeology of the Sierra Blanca Region of Southeastern New Mexico. Ph.D. diss., Harvard University, Cambridge, Massachusetts.

1984   *The Archaeology of the Sierra Blanca Region of Southeastern New Mexico.* Anthropology Papers 74. University of Michigan Museum of Anthropology, Ann Arbor.

Kelley, Jane H., and Stewart L. Peckham

1962   *Two Fragmentary Pit House Sites near Mayhill, New Mexico.* University of New Mexico Anthropological Series Bulletin, vol. 3, no. 2. University of New Mexico, Albuquerque.

Kelly, R.

1983 Hunter-Gatherer Mobility Strategies. *Journal of Anthropological Research* 29 (3): 277–306.

Kent, Susan

1992 Studying Variability in the Archaeological Record: An Ethnoarchaeological Model for Distinguishing Mobility Patterns. *American Antiquity* 57:635–60.

Kidder, Alfred Vincent

1962 *An Introduction to the Study of Southwestern Archaeology.* Yale University Press, New Haven, Connecticut.

Kidder, Alfred V., H. S. Cosgrove, and C. B. Cosgrove

1949 The Pendleton Ruin, Hidalgo County, New Mexico. *Contributions to American Anthropology and History* 50:585, Carnegie Institute of Washington, Washington, D.C.

Kintigh, Keith W.

1994 An Archaeologist's Analytical Toolkit, C14 Program. K. W. Kintigh copyright, Tempe, Arizona.

Kirkpatrick, David T., and Meliha S. Duran

1982 *An Archaeological Clearance Survey of Eight Seismic Testing Transects in Sierra and Dona Ana County, New Mexico.* Cultural Resources Management Division Report 498, New Mexico State University, Las Cruces.

Klein, Pamela Y.

1992 Colorado State University Archaeomagnetic Laboratory Analysis. Manuscript report in possession of author.

Knight, Terry, and A. R. Gomolak

1981 *The Ceramics of* LA 1178, *Gallinas Springs, New Mexico.* Cibola National Forest, Albuquerque, New Mexico.

1987 Magdalena Ceramic Manufacturing Tradition. *Pottery Southwest* 14 (3): 1–3.

Kohler, Timothy A.

1992 Field Houses, Villages, and the Tragedy of the Commons in the Early Northern Anasazi Southwest. *American Antiquity* 57:617–35.

Kohler, Timothy A., and M. H. Matthews

1988 Long-Term Anasazi Land Use and Forest Reduction: A Case Study from Southwest Colorado. *American Antiquity* 53:537–64.

Kohler, Timothy A., and Carla R. Van West

1996 The Calculus of Self-Interest in the Development of Cooperation: Sociopolitical Development and Risk among the Northern Anasazi. In *Evolving Complexity and Environmental Risk in the Prehistoric Southwest,* ed. J. A. Tainter and B. B. Tainter, pp. 169–96. Santa Fe Institute Studies in Sciences of Complexity Proceedings, vol. 26. Addison-Wesley, Menlo Park, California.

Kralick, Kolleen M.

1990 Isolated Settlements and Economic Frontiers: Historical Archaeology in the

Black Range of New Mexico. Department of Anthropology, M.A. thesis, State University of New York at Buffalo.

Larntz, Kinley.

1978   Small Sample Comparisons of Exact Levels for Chi-Square Goodness-of-fit Statistics. *Journal of the American Statistical Association* 73:253–63.

Larsen, Clark Spencer, and Robert L. Kelly

1995   *Bioarchaeology of the Stillwater Marsh: Prehistoric Human Adaptation in the Western Great Basin.* Anthropological Papers of the American Museum of National History 77. American Museum of National History, New York.

Laumbach, Karl

1974   *An Archaeological Survey of Portions of the El Paso Electric Company's 13.8/24 KV Distribution Line in Sierra County, New Mexico.* Cultural Resources Management Division Report 5, New Mexico State University, Las Cruces.

1980   *Emergency Survey and Excavation in Southwestern New Mexico.* Cultural Resources Management Division Report 354, New Mexico State University, Las Cruces.

1981   *An Archaeological Survey of a Portion of a Petty-Ray Geophysical Seismic Testing Line in Sierra County, New Mexico.* Cultural Resources Management Division Report 484, New Mexico State University, Las Cruces.

1982   Perennial Use of Late Mimbres Small House Sites in the Black Range: A Reflection of Extended Economic Relationships or a Radical Shift in Settlement-Subsistence Patterning? In *Mogollon Archaeology: Proceedings of the 1980 Mogollon Conference,* ed. Patrick H. Beckett and Kira Silverbird, pp. 103–9. Acoma Press, Ramona, California.

1992   *Reconnaissance Survey of the National Park Service Ojo Caliente Study Area, Socorro County, New Mexico.* Human Services Research, Tularosa, New Mexico.

Laumbach, Karl W., and David T. Kirkpatrick

1983   *The Black Range Survey: A 2% Archaeological Sample of State Lands in Western Sierra County, New Mexico.* Cultural Resource Management Division, New Mexico State University, Las Cruces.

Laumbach, Toni, and Karl W. Laumbach

1989   Ceramic Descriptions of Southwestern New Mexico. Presented at the New Mexico Archaeological Council Ceramic Workshop, Albuquerque.

LeBlanc, Steven A.

1975   *Mimbres Archeological Center: Preliminary Report of the First Season of Excavation, 1974.* The Institute of Archaeology, University of California, Los Angeles.

1976   Mimbres Archeological Center: Preliminary Report of the Second Season of Excavation 1975. *Journal of New World Archaeology* 1 (6): 1–23.

1977   The 1976 Field Season of the Mimbres Foundation in Southwestern New Mexico. *Journal of New World Archaeology* 2 (2): 1–24.

1980   The Early Pit House Period. In *An Archaeological Synthesis of South-Central and*

Southwestern New Mexico, ed. Steven A. LeBlanc and Michael E. Whalen, pp. 142–204. Office of Contract Archaeology, University of New Mexico, Albuquerque.

1982   Temporal Change in Mogollon Ceramics. In *Southwestern Ceramics: A Comparative Review,* ed. Albert H. Schroeder, pp. 107–27. Vol. 15 of The Arizona Archaeologist series. Arizona Archaeological Society, Phoenix.

1983   *The Mimbres People, Ancient Pueblo Painters of the American Southwest.* Thames and Hudson, New York.

1989   Cultural Dynamics in the Southern Mogollon Area. In *Dynamics of Southwestern Prehistory,* ed. Linda S. Cordell and George J. Gumerman, pp. 179–208. Smithsonian Institution Press, Washington D.C.

LeBlanc, Steven A., and Michael E. Whalen

1980   *An Archaeological Synthesis of South-Central and Southwestern New Mexico.* Office of Contract Archaeology, University of New Mexico, Albuquerque.

Lehmer, Donald J.

1948   *The Jornada Branch of the Mogollon.* University of Arizona Bulletin, Social Science Bulletin No. 17. University of Arizona Press, Tucson.

Lekson, Stephen H.

1982   Architecture and Settlement Plan in the Redrock Valley of the Gila River, Southwestern New Mexico. In *Mogollon Archaeology: Proceedings of the 1980 Mogollon Conference,* ed. Patrick H. Beckett and Kira Silverbird, pp. 61–73. Acoma Press, Ramona, California.

1983   *1982 Site Survey Along Palomas Drainage, Southern New Mexico.* Report to the New Mexico State Historic Preservation Office, Santa Fe.

1984   Prehistoric Settlement in the Middle Palomas Creek Drainage, Southern New Mexico. In *Ladder Ranch Research Project: A Report on the First Season,* ed. Margaret C. Nelson, pp. 15–23. Technical Series of the Maxwell Museum of Anthropology, no. 1, University of New Mexico Press, Albuquerque.

1985   *Archaeological Reconnaissance of the Rio Grande Valley, Sierra County, New Mexico.* Report submitted to the Historic Preservation Division, Santa Fe, New Mexico.

1986a   The Mimbres Region. In *Mogollon Variability,* ed. Charlotte Benson and Steadman Upham, pp. 147–55. The University Museum Occasional Papers, no. 15. New Mexico State University, Las Cruces.

1986b   Mimbres Riverine Adaptations. In *Mogollon Variability,* ed. Charlotte Benson and Steadman Upham, pp. 181–89. The University Museum Occasional Papers, no. 15. New Mexico State University, Las Cruces.

1986c   Mesa Verde-like Ceramics near T-or-C, New Mexico. *Pottery Southwest* 13 (4): 1–3.

1988   Regional Systematics in the Later Prehistory of Southern New Mexico. In *Fourth Jornada Mogollon Conferences Collected Papers,* ed. Meliha Duran and Karl Laumbach, pp. 1–37. Human Systems Research, Las Cruces, New Mexico.

1989 An Archaeological Reconnaissance of the Rio Grande Valley in Sierra County, New Mexico. *The Artifact* 27 (2): 1–87.

1990a Sedentism and Aggregation in Anasazi Archaeology. In *Perspectives on Southwestern Prehistory,* ed. P. E. Minnis and C. L. Redman, pp. 333–40. Westview Press, Boulder.

1990b *Mimbres Archaeology on the Upper Gila, New Mexico.* Anthropological Papers of the University of Arizona, no. 53. The University of Arizona Press, Tucson.

1992a The Surface Archaeology of Southwestern New Mexico. *The Artifact* 30 (3).

1992b *Archaeology Overview of Southwestern New Mexico.* Report submitted to the New Mexico State Historic Preservation Division, Santa Fe. Human Systems Research, Las Cruces, New Mexico.

1993 Chaco, Hohokam, and Mimbres: The Southwest in the 11th and 12th Centuries. *Expedition* 35 (1): 44–52.

Lekson, Steven H., and Catherine M. Cameron

1995 The Abandonment of Chaco Canyon, the Mesa Verde Migrations, and the Reorganization of the Pueblo World. *Journal of Anthropological Archaeology* 14:184–202

Lekson, Steven H., and Margaret C. Nelson

1984 1983 *Site Survey Along Palomas Drainage, Southern New Mexico.* Report of the University of New Mexico Archaeological Field School/Ladder Ranch Research Project to the State Historic Preservation Bureau.

Lightfoot, Ricky R.

1993 Abandonment Processes in Prehistoric Pueblos. In *The Abandonment of Settlements and Regions: Ethnoarchaeological and Archaeological Approaches,* ed. Catherine M. Cameron and Steve A. Tomka, pp. 165–77. Cambridge University Press, New York.

1994 *The Duckfoot Site, Volume 2: Archaeology of the House and Household.* Occasional Papers 4. Crow Canyon Archaeological Center, Cortez, Colorado.

Lipe, William D.

1995 The Depopulation of the Northern San Juan: Conditions in the Turbulent 1200's. *Journal of Anthropological Archaeology* 14:143–69.

Lipe, William D., and Michelle Hegmon, eds.

1989 *The Architecture of Social Integration in Prehistoric Pueblos.* Occasional Papers 1. Crow Canyon Archaeological Center, Cortez, Colorado.

Longacre, William A., and J. Jefferson Reid

1974 The University of Arizona Archaeological Field School at Grasshopper: Eleven Years of Multidisciplinary Research and Testing. *The Kiva* 40:3–38.

Lowell, Julie C.

1991 *Prehistoric Households at Turkey Creek Pueblo, Arizona.* Anthropological Papers of the University of Arizona, no. 54. The University of Arizona Press, Tucson.

1995 Illuminating Fire-feature Variability in the Grasshopper Region of Arizona. *The*

Kiva 60:351–70.

Lucas, Jason

1996   Three Circle Phase Architecture at Old Town, A Prehistoric Mimbres Site in Luna County, Southwestern New Mexico. M.A. thesis, University of Texas, Austin.

Lynch, Thomas F., and Christopher M. Stevenson

1992   Obsidian Hydration Dating and Temperature Controls in the Punta Negra Region of Northern Chile. *Quaternary Research* 37:117–24.

Marshall, Michael P.

1973   Background Information on the Jornada Culture Area. In *Human Systems Research Technical Manual, 1973 Survey of the Tularosa Basin,* pp. 49–120. Human Systems Research, Tularosa, New Mexico.

Martin, Alexander C., and William D. Barkley

1961   *Seed Identification Manual.* University of California Press, Berkeley.

Martin, John H., Warren H. Leonard, and David L. Stamp

1976   *Principles of Field Crop Production.* Macmillan, New York.

Martin, Paul S.

1979   Prehistory: Mogollon. In *Handbook of North American Indians: Southwest,* vol. 9, ed. Alfonso Ortiz, pp. 61–74. Smithsonian Institution Press, Washington, D.C.

Martin, Paul S., and John B. Rinaldo

1950a   Sites of the Reserve Phase, Western New Mexico. *Fieldiana: Anthropology* 38. Field Museum of Natural History, Chicago.

1950b   Turkey Foot Ridge Site: A Mogollon Village, Pine Lawn Valley, Western New Mexico. *Fieldiana: Anthropology* 38. Field Museum of Natural History, Chicago.

Martin, Paul S., John B. Rinaldo, and Eloise R. Barter

1957   Late Mogollon Communities: Four Sites of the Tularosa Phase, Western New Mexico. *Fieldiana: Anthropology* 49. Field Museum of Natural History, Chicago.

Martin, Paul S., John B. Rinaldo, Elaine A. Bluhm, and Hugh C. Cutler

1956   Higgins Flat Pueblo, Western New Mexico. *Fieldiana: Anthropology* 45:9–218. Field Museum of Natural History, Chicago.

Mayo, Jill E.

1994   Garfield Revisited: Further Research on a Mimbres Site in the Southern Rio Grande Valley. M.A. thesis, Department of Sociology and Anthropology, New Mexico State University, Las Cruces.

Mayo, Jill E., Michelle Hegmon, and Margaret Nelson

1993   The Eastern Mimbres Archaeological Project: Survey Along Las Animas Creek. Preliminary Report of 1993 Field Season on the Ladder Ranch, Private Land. Manuscript in possession of author.

Mazer, J. J., C. M. Stevenson, W. L. Ebert, and J. K. Bates

1991   The Experimental Hydration of Obsidian as a Function of Relative Humidity and Temperature. *American Antiquity* 56:504–13.

McAllister, Shirley P., and Fred Plog

1978   Small Sites in the Chevlon Drainage. In *Limited Activity and Occupation Sites: A Collection of Conference Papers,* ed. Albert E. Ward, pp. 17–23. Contributions to Anthropological Studies, no. 1. Center for Anthropological Studies, Albuquerque.

McGregor, John. C.

1965   *Southwestern Archaeology.* University of Illinois Press, Urbana, Illinois.

McGuire, Randall H., and Michael B. Schiffer

1983   A Theory of Architectural Design. *Journal of Anthropological Archaeology* 2:227–303.

McKenna, Peter J., and Marcia L. Truell

1986   *Small Site Architecture of Chaco Canyon, New Mexico.* Publications in Archaeology 18D Chaco Canyon Studies. National Park Service, U.S. Department of the Interior, Santa Fe.

Miksicek, Charles H.

1987   Formation Processes of the Archaeobotanical Record. In *Advances in Archaeological Method and Theory,* no. 7, ed. Michael B. Schiffer, pp. 211–47. University of Arizona Press, Tucson.

Mills, Barbara J.

1983   *Black Range, Gila National Forest, Archaeological Survey.* Report to the U.S. Forest Service. On file at the Gila National Forest Supervisor's Office, Silver City, New Mexico.

1984   Functional Analysis of Ceramics from the Anderson Site. In *Ladder Ranch Research Project: A Report of the First Season,* ed. M. C. Nelson, pp. 33–50. Technical Series of the Maxwell Museum of Anthropology, no. 1, University of New Mexico Press, Albuquerque.

1986   Temporal Variability in the Ceramic Assemblages of the Eastern Slope of the Black Range, New Mexico. In *Mogollon Variability,* ed. Charlotte Benson and Steadman Upham, pp. 169–80. University Museum Occasional Papers, no. 15. New Mexico State University, Las Cruces.

Mills, Barbara J., and T. J. Ferguson

1980   Processes of Architectural Change: Examples from the Historic Zuni Farming Villages. Paper presented at the Forty-fifth Annual Meeting of the Society for American Archaeology, Philadelphia.

1993   The Social Consequences of Spatial Reorganization at Zuni during the Historic Period. Paper presented at the Annual Meeting of the American Anthropological Association, Washington, D.C.

Mills, Barbara J., and Stephen H. Lekson

1983   The Ladder Ranch Surveys: An Evaluation of Methods. Paper presented at the Society of Independent Anthropologists, Albuquerque.

Minc, Leah D., and Kevin Smith

1989   The Spirit of Survival: Cultural Responses to Resource Variability in North Alaska. In *Bad Year Economics,* ed. Paul Halstead and John O'Shea, pp. 8–39. Cambridge University Press, New York.

Mindeleff, Victor

1989   *A Study of Pueblo Architecture in Tusayan and Cibola.* Smithsonian Institution Press, Washington, D.C. Originally published in 1891.

Minnis, Paul E.

1980   Prehistoric Population and Settlement Configuration in Southwestern New Mexico: An Analysis of Systematic Archaeological Surveys. Appendix A in *An Archaeological Synthesis of South-Central and Southwestern New Mexico,* ed. Steven A. LeBlanc and Michael E. Whalen, pp. 460–505. Office of Contract Archaeology, University of New Mexico, Albuquerque.

1981   Seeds in Archaeological Sites: Sources and Some Interpretive Problems. *American Antiquity* 46:143–52.

1985a   *Social Adaptation to Food Stress: A Prehistoric Southwestern Example.* University of Chicago Press, Chicago.

1985b   Domesticating Plants and People in the Greater Southwest. In *Prehistoric Food Production in North America,* ed. Richard I. Ford, pp. 309–39. Anthropological Papers, no. 75. Museum of Anthropology, University of Michigan, Ann Arbor.

1987   Identification of Wood from Archaeological Sites in the American Southwest I: Keys for Gymnosperms. *Journal of Archaeological Science* 14:121–31.

1991   Famine Foods of the North American Desert Borderlands in Historic Context. *Journal of Ethnobiology* 11:231–57.

Mitchell, Donald

1971   *Archaeology of the Gulf of Georgia Area, a Natural Region and its Cultural Types,* syesis 4, supplement 1. British Columbia Provincial Museum, Victoria.

Mobley-Tanaka, Jeannette L.

1996   Endemic Conflict and Household Form: Assessing the Evidence for Intergroup Conflict in a Basketmaker III Population. Manuscript in possession of author.

Montgomery, Barbara Klie

1993   Ceramic Analysis as a Tool for Discovering Processes of Pueblo Abandonment. In *The Abandonment of Settlements and Regions: Ethnoarchaeological and Archaeological Approaches,* ed. Catherine M. Cameron and Steve A. Tomka, pp. 157–64. Cambridge University Press, New York.

Montgomery, F. H.

1977   *Seeds and Fruits of Plants of Eastern Canada and Northeastern United States.* University of Toronto Press, Toronto.

Naranjo, Tessie

1995   Thoughts on Migration by Santa Clara Pueblo. *Journal of Anthropological Archaeology* 14:247–50.

Neely, James A.

n.d.   Test Excavations at the WS Ranch (McKeen) Site, Gila National Forest, Catron County, New Mexico. In "Application for Permit to Conduct Archaeological or Paleontological Explorations of Excavations Upon Lands of the United States." Manuscript in possession of author.

Nelson, Ben A.

1981   Ethnoarchaeology and Paleodemography: A Test of Turner and Lofgren's Hypothesis. *Journal of Anthropological Research* 37 (2): 107–29.

Nelson, Ben A., and Roger Anyon

1996   Fallow Valleys: Asynchronous Occupations in Southwestern New Mexico. *Kiva* 61:275–94.

Nelson, Ben A., and Steven A. LeBlanc

1986   *Short-Term Sedentism in the American Southwest: The Mimbres Valley Salado.* Maxwell Museum of Anthropology and the University of New Mexico Press, Albuquerque.

Nelson, Ben A., and Margaret C. Nelson

1986   Spatial Distribution of Provisionally Discarded Artifacts in Highland Maya Households. Paper presented at the Fifty-first Annual Meeting of the Society for American Archaeology, New Orleans.

Nelson, Ben A., Margaret C. Rugge, and Steven A. LeBlanc

1978   LA 12109: A Small Classic Mimbres Ruin, Mimbres Valley. In *Limited Activity and Occupational Sites: A Collection of Conference Papers,* ed. Albert E. Ward. Contributions to Anthropological Studies, no. 1. Center for Anthropological Studies, Albuquerque.

Nelson, Margaret C.

1986   Occupational History of Palomas Drainage, Western Sierra County, New Mexico. In *Mogollon Variability,* ed. Charlotte Benson and Steadman Upham, pp. 157–68. New Mexico State University Museum Occasional Papers, no. 15. New Mexico State University, Las Cruces.

1989   The 1985 Survey on Lower Palomas Creek. An Appendix from An Archaeological Reconnaissance of the Rio Grande Valley in Sierra County, New Mexico. Republished in *The Artifact* 27 (2): 89–96.

1991   The Study of Technological Organization. In *Archaeological Method and Theory,* vol. 3, ed. Michael B. Schiffer, pp. 57–101. University of Arizona Press, Tucson.

1993a   Classic Mimbres Land Use in the Eastern Mimbres Region, Southwestern New Mexico. *The Kiva* 58:27–47.

1993b   Changing Occupational Pattern among Prehistoric Horticulturists in sw New Mexico. *Journal of Field Archaeology* 20 (1): 43–57.

Nelson, Margaret C., ed.

1984   *Ladder Ranch Research Project: A Report of the First Season.* Technical Series of the Maxwell Museum of Anthropology, vol. 1. University of New Mexico Press, Albuquerque.

Nelson, Margaret C., and Michelle Hegmon

1993   *Eastern Mimbres Archaeological Project: Archaeological Research on the Ladder Ranch.* Report submitted to the Turner Foundation.

1995   *Eastern Mimbres Archaeological Project: Archaeological Research on the Ladder Ranch,* 1995. Report submitted to the Turner Foundation.

1996   Regional Social and Economic Reorganization: The Mimbres. Project Report. Manuscript in possession of author.

1998   Mobility, Population, and Human Impacts on Environment: Mimbres in the Twelfth Century. Grant proposal submitted to the National Geographic Society.

Nelson, Margaret C., and Heidi Lippmeier

1993   Grinding-Tool Design as Conditioned by Land-Use Pattern. *American Antiquity* 58:286–305.

Nelson, Margaret C., and Ben A. Nelson

1986   Spatial Distribution of Provisionally Discarded Artifacts in Highland Maya Households. Paper presented at the Fifty-first Annual Meeting of the Society for American Archaeology, New Orleans.

Nesbitt, Paul H.

1931   *The Ancient Mimbrenos, Based on the Investigations at the Mattocks Ruin, Mimbres Valley, New Mexico.* Logan Museum Bulletin, no. 4. Beloit College, Beloit, Wisconsin.

Netting, Robert Mc.C.

1993   *Small Holders, Householders: Farm Families and the Ecology of Intensive, Sustainable Agriculture.* Stanford University Press, Palo Alto.

Netting, Robert McC., Richard R. Wilk, and Eric J. Arnould, eds.

1984   *Households: Comparative and Historical Studies of the Domestic Group.* University of California Press, Berkeley, California.

Newcomer, M. H., and G. deG. Sieveking

1980   Experimental Flake Scatter-Patterns: A New Interpretative Technique. *Journal of Field Archaeology* 7 (3): 345–52.

O'Laughlin, Thomas C.

1981   The Roth Site. *The Artifact* 19 (3–4): 133–49.

1985   Jornada Mogollon Occupation in the Rincon Valley, Southern New Mexico. In *Proceedings of the Third Jornada Mogollon Conference,* ed. Michael S. Foster and Thomas C. O'Laughlin, pp. 41–57. Republished in *The Artifact* 23 (1–2).

O'Shea, John

1989   The Role of Wild Resources in Small-Scale Agricultural Systems: Tales From the Lakes and the Plains. In *Bad Year Economics,* ed. Paul Halstead and John O'Shea, pp. 57-67. Cambridge University Press, New York.

Parker, Kittie F.

1990   *An Illustrated Guide to Arizona Weeds.* University of Arizona Press, Tucson.

Parsons, Elsie C.

1939   *Pueblo Indian Religion.* University of Chicago Press, Chicago.

Pearsall, Deborah M.

1989   *Paleoethnobotany: A Handbook of Procedures.* Academic Press, New York.

Peckham, Stuart, Fred Wendorf, and E. N. Ferdon

1956   Excavations near Apache Creek, New Mexico. *Highway Salvage Archaeology* 4 (17): 41–55.

Peterson, John A.

1988   Settlement and Subsistence Patterns in the Reserve Phase and Mountain Mogollon: A Test Case in Devil's Park, New Mexico. *The Kiva* 53:113–27.

Plog, Fred

1983   Political and Economic Alliances on the Colorado Plateaus, A.D. 400–1450. In *Advances in World Archaeology,* vol. 2, ed. Fred Wendorf and Angela E. Close, pp. 289–330. Academic Press, New York.

Plog, Stephen E.

1969   Prehistoric Population Movements: Measurements and Explanation. Manuscript on file at Field Museum of Natural History, Chicago.

Popper, Virginia S.

1988   Selecting Quantitative Measurements in Paleoethnobotany. In *Current Paleoethnobotany,* ed. C. A. Hastorf and V. S. Popper, pp. 53–71. University of Chicago Press, Chicago.

Potter, James M.

1997   Communal Ritual, Feasting, and Social Differentiation in Late Prehistoric Zuni Communities. Ph.D. diss., Department of Anthropology, Arizona State University, Tempe.

Powell, Shirley

1983   *Mobility and Adaptation: The Anasazi of Black Mesa, Arizona.* Southern Illinois University Press, Carbondale.

1990   Sedentism and Mobility: What Do the Data Say? What Did the Anasazi Do? In *Perspectives on Southwestern Prehistory,* ed. Paul E. Minnis and Charles L. Redman, pp. 92–102. Westview Press, Boulder, Colorado.

Powell, Valli S.

1996   Regional Diversity in Mogollon Red-on-brown Pottery. *Kiva* 62:185–204.

Preucel, R. W.

1988   Seasonal Agricultural Circulation and Residential Mobility: A Prehistoric Example from the Pajarito Plateau, New Mexico. Ph.D. diss., Department of Anthropology, University of California, Los Angeles.

Rautman, Alison E.

1993   Resource Variability, Risk, and the Structure of Social Networks: An Example from the Prehistoric Southwest. *American Antiquity* 58:403–24.

1995   *Final Report on the Excavation of Pueblo de la Mesa: Economic Organization and Social Networks among Prehistoric Agriculturists in Central New Mexico.* Final Report submitted to the USDA Forest Service, Cibola National Forest.

Reid, J. Jefferson

1982   *Cholla Project Archaeology, Volumes 1 and 2.* Cultural Resource Management Division Archaeological Series 161, Arizona State Museum, University of Arizona, Tucson.

1989   A Grasshopper Perspective on the Mogollon of the Arizona Mountains. In *Dynamics of Southwestern Prehistory,* ed. Linda S. Cordell and George J. Gumerman, pp. 65–98. Smithsonian Institution Press, Washington, D.C.

Reid, J. Jefferson, Michael B. Schiffer, Stephanie M. Whittlesey, Madeleine J. Hinkes, Alan P. Sullivan III, Chris Downum, William A. Longacre, and H. David Tuggle

1989   Perception and Interpretation in Contemporary Southwestern Archaeology: Comments on Cordell, Upham, and Brock. *American Antiquity* 54:802–14.

Reid, J. Jefferson, John R. Welsh, Barbara K. Montgomery, and María Nieves Zedeño

1996   A Demographic Overview of the Late Pueblo III Period in the Mountains of East-Central Arizona. In *The Prehistoric Pueblo World,* A.D. 1150–1350, ed. Michael A. Adler, pp. 73–85. The University of Arizona Press, Tucson.

Renouf, M.A.P.

1991   Sedentary Hunter-Gatherers: A Case for Northern Coasts. In *Between Bands and States,* ed. Susan A. Gregg, pp. 89–107. Center for Archaeological Investigations Occasional Papers, no. 9. Southern Illinois University Press, Carbondale.

Rinaldo, John B., and Elaine A. Bluhm

1956   Late Mogollon Pottery Types in the Reserve Area. *Fieldiana: Anthropology* 36 (7).

Rocek, Thomas R.

1991   Research at LA 51344, The Dunlap-Salazar Pithouse Site, near Lincoln, New Mexico. In *Mogollon V,* ed. Patrick Beckett, pp. 106–18. COAS Publishing and Research, Las Cruces, New Mexico.

1995   *Navajo Multi-Household Social Units: Archaeology on Black Mesa, Arizona.* University of Arizona Press, Tucson.

1996   Sedentism and Mobility in the Southwest. In *Interpreting Southwestern Diversity: Underlying Principles and Overarching Patterns,* ed. P. Fish and J. G. Reid, pp. 17–22. Arizona State University Anthropological Papers, no. 48, Arizona State University, Tempe.

Sahlins, Marshall D.

1968   *Tribesmen.* Prentice-Hall, Englewood Cliffs, New Jersey.

Sanchez, Julia L. J.

1996   A Re-evaluation of Mimbres Faunal Subsistence. *Kiva* 61: 295–307.

Sauer, Carl, and Donald Brand

1930   Pueblo Sites in Southeastern Arizona. *University of California Publications in Geography* 3:451–58.

Saul, William Emmett

1955   A Descriptive Catalogue of the Trees and Larger Woody Shrubs of Utah Based on the Anatomy of Wood. Ph.D. diss., Department of Botany, University of Utah.

Scheetz, Barry E., and Christopher M. Stevenson

1988   The Role of Resolution and Sample Preparation in Hydration Rim Measurement: Implications for Experimentally Determined Hydration Rates. *American Antiquity* 53:110–17.

Schiffer, Michael B.

1972   Archaeological Context and Systemic Context. *American Antiquity* 37:156–65.

1982   Hohokam Chronology: An Essay on History and Methods. In *Hohokam and Patayan Prehistory of Southwestern Arizona,* ed. Randall H. McGuire and Michael B. Schiffer, pp. 299–344. Academic Press, New York.

1985   Is There a "Pompeii Premise" in Archaeology? *Journal of Anthropological Research* 41:18–41.

Schlanger, Sarah H.

1988   Patterns of Population Movement and Long-Term Population Growth in Southwestern Colorado. *American Antiquity* 53:773–93.

Schlanger, Sarah H., and Richard H. Wilshusen

1993   Local Abandonments and Regional Conditions in the North American Southwest. In *Abandonment of Settlements and Regions: Ethnoarchaeological and Archaeological Approaches,* ed. Catherine M. Cameron and Steve A. Tomka, pp. 85–98. Cambridge University Press, New York.

Schlegel, Alice

1992   African Political Models in the American Southwest: Hopi as an Internal Frontier Society. *American Anthropologist* 94 (2): 376–97.

Schutt, Jeanne A., Richard C. Chapman, and June-el Piper, eds.

1991   *The Cuchillo Negro Archaeological Project: On the Periphery of the Mimbres-Mogollon.* Office of Contract Archaeology Report 185-403D, University of New Mexico, Albuquerque.

Scott, Catherine J.

1983   The Evolution of Mimbres Pottery. In *Mimbres Pottery: Ancient Art of the American Southwest,* ed. J. J. Brody, Catherine J. Scott, and Steven A. LeBlanc, pp. 39–67. Hudson Hills Press, New York.

Seaman, Timothy J., and Barbara J. Mills

1988   What Are We Measuring? Rim Thickness Indices and Their Implications for Changes in Vessel Ise. In *Fourth Jornada Mogollon Conference Collected Papers,* ed. Meliha S. Duran and Karl W. Laumbach, pp. 163–94. Human Systems Research, Tularosa, New Mexico.

Shafer, Harry J.

1982   Classic Mimbres Phase Households and Room Use Patterns. *The Kiva* 48 (1–2): 17–37.

1987   *The Nan Ranch Archaeology Project, 1986 Interim Report.* Report submitted to Earthwatch by the Anthropology Laboratory, Texas A & M University, College Station.

1988   *Archaeology at the Nan Ranch Ruin: 1987 Season.* Anthropology Laboratory, Texas A & M University Special Series, Texas A & M University, College Station.

1990   Archaeology at the NAN Ruin, 1984 Interim Report. *The Artifact* 28 (4): 1–27.

1991a   Archaeology at the NAN Ruin: 1986 Interim Report. *The Artifact* 29 (2): 1–42.

1991b   Archaeology at the NAN Ruin: The 1987 Season. *The Artifact* 29 (3): 1–44.

1991c   Archaeology at the NAN Ruin: The 1989 Season. *The Artifact* 29 (4): 1–44.

1995   Architecture and Symbolism in Transitional Pueblo Development in the Mimbres Valley, sw New Mexico. *Journal of Field Archaeology* 22:23–47.

1996   The Classic Mimbres Phenomenon and Some New Interpretations. Paper presented at the Ninth Mogollon Conference, Silver City, New Mexico.

Shafer, Harry J., and Anna J. Taylor

1986   Mimbres Mogollon Architectural Dynamics and Ceramic Style Change. *Journal of Field Archaeology* 13 (1): 43–68.

Shaffer, Brian S.

1991   The Economic Importance of Vertebrate Faunal Remains from the NAN Ruin (LA 15049), A Classic Mimbres Site, Grant County, New Mexico. M.A. thesis, Department of Anthropology, Texas A & M University, College Station.

Shaw, Robert H.

1977   Water Use and Requirements of Maize: A Review. In *Agrometeorology of the Maize (Corn) Crop,* pp. 119–34. World Meteorological Organization, no. 481. Geneva.

Smiley, Terah L., Stanley A. Stubbs, and Bryant Bannister

1953   *A Foundation for the Dating of Some Late Archaeological Sites in the Rio Grande Area, New Mexico.* University of Arizona Bulletin, vol. 24, no. 3, and Laboratory of Tree-Ring Research Bulletin, no. 6. University of Arizona, Tucson.

Smith, Marian F., Jr.

1983   The Study of Ceramic Function from Artifact Size and Shape. Ph.D. diss., Department of Anthropology, University of Oregon, Eugene.

Smith, Pamela

1985   An Area Survey of 1,435.91 Acres in the Vicinity of Hillsboro, New Mexico. Manuscript on file at the Bureau of Land Management, Las Cruces, New Mexico.

Speth, John D., and Katherine A. Spielmann

1983   Energy Source, Protein Metabolism, and Hunter-Gatherer Subsistence Strategies. *Journal of Anthropological Archaeology* 2:1–31.

Stallings, W. S.

1931   *El Paso Polychrome.* Laboratory of Anthropology Technical Series, Bulletin no. 3. Museum of New Mexico, Santa Fe.

Stevenson, Christopher M.

1993   Hydration Analysis of Obsidian Artifacts from the 86NM612 and 86NM613, New Mexico. Manuscript in possession of author.

Stevenson, Christopher M., and Maria Klimkiewicz

1990   X-Ray Fluorescence Analysis of Obsidian Sources in Arizona and New Mexico. *The Kiva* 55:235–43.

Steward, Julian H.

1938   *Basin-Plateau Aboriginal Sociopolitical Groups.* Bureau of Ethnology Bulletin, no. 120. Washington, D.C.

Stone, Glenn Davis

1993   Agricultural Abandonment: A Comparative Study in Historical Ecology. In *The Abandonment of Settlements and Regions: Ethnoarchaeological and Archaeological Approaches,* ed. Catherine M. Cameron and Steve A. Tomka, pp. 74–84. Cambridge University Press, New York.

1996   *Settlement Ecology: The Social and Spatial Organization of Kofyar Agriculture.* Arizona Studies in Human Ecology. The University of Arizona Press, Tucson.

Stuart, David E., and Rory P. Gauthier

1984   *Prehistoric New Mexico: Background for Survey,* 2d ed. New Mexico Archaeological Council, Albuquerque.

Stuiver, M., and B. Becker

1986   High Precision Calibration of the Radiocarbon Time Scale, A.D. 1950–2500 B.C.. *Radiocarbon* 28:805–38.

Stuiver, M., and G. W. Pearson

1986   High Precision Calibration of the Radiocarbon Time Scale, A.D. 1950–500 B.C.. *Radiocarbon* 28:990–1021.

Sudar-Laumbach, Toni

1982   Observations on Mimbres Whiteware. In *Mogollon Archaeology: Proceedings of the 1980 Mogollon Conference,* ed. P. Beckett and K. Silverbird, pp. 137–46. Acoma Books, Ramona, California.

Szuter, Christine R.

1991   Hunting by Hohokam Desert Farmers. *The Kiva* 56:277–92.

Tainter, Joseph A.

1985   Perspectives on the Abandonment of the Northern Tularosa Basin. In *Views of the Jornada Mogollon,* ed. Collen M. Beck, pp. 143–47. Eastern New Mexico University Contributions in Anthropology, no. 12. Eastern New Mexico University, Portales.

1988   *The Collapse of Complex Societies.* Cambridge University Press, New York.

Tainter, Joseph A., and Frances Levine

1987   *Cultural Resources Overview, Central New Mexico.* USDA Forest Service Southwestern Region, Albuquerque.

Taylor, Anna J.

1984   An Analysis of Form and Function of Mimbres Mogollon Bowls. M.A. thesis, Department of Anthropology, Texas A & M University, College Station.

Taylor, R. E.

1987   *Radiocarbon Dating: An Archaeological Perspective.* Academic Press, Orlando.

Titiev, Mischa

1944   *Old Oraibi: A Study of the Hopi Indians of Third Mesa.* Papers of the Peabody Museum of American Archaeology and Ethnology, vol. 22, no. 1. Harvard University, Cambridge, Massachusetts.

Tomka, Steve A.

1993   Site Abandonment Behavior among Transhumant Agro-Pastoralists: The Effects of Delayed Curation on Assemblage Composition. In *The Abandonment of Settlements and Regions: Ethnoarchaeological and Archaeological Approaches,* ed. Catherine M. Cameron and Steve A. Tomka, pp. 11–24. Cambridge University Press, New York.

Torrence, Robin

1989   Tools as Optimal Solutions. In *Time, Energy, and Stone Tools,* ed. Robin Torrence, pp. 1–6. Cambridge University Press, New York.

Tuggle, H. David, and J. Jefferson Reid

1982   Cross-Dating Cibola White Wares. In *Cholla Project Archaeology: Ceramic Studies,* ed. J. J. Reid, pp. 8–17. Arizona State Museum Archaeological Series, vol. 161, no. 5. Arizona State Museum, Tucson.

United States Department of Agriculture, Forest Service

1974   *Seeds of Woody Plants in the United States.* GPO, Washington, D.C.

Upham, Steadman

1982   *Politics and Power: An Economic and Political History of the Western Pueblo.* Academic Press, New York.

1984   Adaptive Diversity and Southwestern Abandonment. *Journal of Anthropological Research* 40 (2): 235–56.

Upham, Steadman, Kent G. Lightfoot, and Gary Feinman

1981   Explaining Socially Determined Ceramic Distributions in the Prehistoric Plateau Southwest. *American Antiquity* 46:822–33.

Upham, Steadman, Kent G. Lightfoot, and Roberta Jewett, eds.

1989   *Sociopolitical Structure of Prehistoric Southwestern Societies.* Westview Press, Boulder.

Varien, Mark

1997   New Perspectives on Settlement Patterns: Sedentism and Mobility in a Social Landscape. Ph.D. diss., Department of Anthropology, Arizona State University, Tempe.

Vivian, R. Gwinn

1970   Aspects of Prehistoric Society in Chaco Canyon, New Mexico. Ph.D. diss., Department of Anthropology, University of Arizona, Tucson.

Ward, Albert E., ed.

1978   *Limited Activity and Occupation Sites: A Collection of Conference Papers.* Contributions to Anthropological Studies, no. 1. Center for Anthropological Studies, Albuquerque.

Watkins, Trevor, ed.

1975   *Radiocarbon: Calibration and Prehistory.* Edinburgh University Press, Edinburgh.

Watson, James B.

1970   Society as Organized Flow: The Tairora Case. *Southwestern Journal of Anthropology* 26 (2): 107–24.

Way, Karen L.

1979   Early Pueblo Occupation in the Southern Tularosa Basin, New Mexico. In *Jornada Mogollon Archaeology,* ed. P. H. Beckett and R. N. Wiseman, pp. 41–51. New Mexico State University, Las Cruces.

Wendorf, Fred

1956   Excavations near Apache Creek, New Mexico. *Highway Salvage Archaeology* 2:17–86. New Mexico State Highway Department and Museum of New Mexico, Santa Fe.

Weyer, Jonathan K., and Mark Strong

1976   *An Archaeological Survey of Six Seismograph Test Lines for Exxon Company in Sierra, Luna, and Dona Ana Counties, New Mexico.* Cultural Resources Management Division Report, no. 200, New Mexico State University, Las Cruces.

Whalen, Michael E.

1980   The Pueblo Periods of South-central New Mexico. In *Archaeological Synthesis of South-central and Southwestern New Mexico,* ed. Steven A. LeBlanc and Michael E. Whalen, pp. 387–448. Office of Contract Archaeology, University of New Mexico, Albuquerque.

1981   Origin and Evolution of Ceramics in Western Texas. *Bulletin of the Texas Archaeological Society* 52:215–29.

1994   *Turquoise Ridge and Late Prehistoric Residential Mobility in the Desert Mogollon Region.* University of Utah Anthropological Papers, no. 118. University of Utah Press, Salt Lake City.

Whalen, Michael E., and Patricia A. Gilman

1990   Transitions to Sedentism. In *Perspectives on Southwestern Prehistory*, ed. P. E. Minnis and C. L. Redman, pp. 71–75. Westview Press, Boulder.

Whiteley, Peter

1987   *Deliberate Acts*. University of Arizona Press, Tucson.

1988   *Bacavi: Journey to Reed Springs*. Northland Press, Flagstaff, Arizona.

Whittlesey, Stephanie M.

1978   Status and Death at Grasshopper Pueblo: Experiments Toward an Archaeological Theory of Correlates. Ph.D. diss., Department of Anthropology, University of Arizona, Tucson.

1984   The Uses and Abuses of Mogollon Mortuary Data. In *Recent Research in Mogollon Archaeology*, ed. S. Upham, F. Plog, D. G. Batcho, and B. E. Kauffman, pp. 276–84. The University Museum Occasional Papers, no. 10. New Mexico State University, Las Cruces.

1989   The Individual, the Community and Social Organization: Issues of Evidence and Inference Justification. In *Households and Communities: Proceedings of the 21st Annual Chacmool Conference*, ed. Scott MacEachern, David J. W. Archer, and Richard D. Garvin, pp. 227–36. The University of Calgary Archaeological Association, Calgary.

Whittlesey, Stephanie M., and J. Jefferson Reid

1982   Cholla Project Settlement Summary. In *Cholla Project Archaeology, Volume 1: Introduction and Special Studies*, ed. J. Jefferson Reid, pp. 205–16. Cultural Resource Management Division Archaeological Series, no. 161, Arizona State Museum, University of Arizona, Tucson.

Wilk, Richard R.

1983   Little House in the Jungle: The Causes of Variation in House Size among Modern Kekchi Maya. *Journal of Anthropological Archaeology* 2:99–116.

1991   *Household Ecology: Economic Change and Domestic Life among the Kekchi Maya in Belize*. The University of Arizona Press, Tucson.

Wilk, Richard R., and William L. Rathje

1982   Household Archaeology. In *Archaeology of the Household: Building a Prehistory of Domestic Life*, ed. Richard R. Wilk and William L. Rathje, pp. 617–39. *American Behavioral Scientist* 25 (6).

Williams, Jerry L., ed.

1986   *New Mexico in Maps*, 2d ed. University of New Mexico Press, Albuquerque.

Wills, Wirt. H.

1985   *Early Agriculture in the Mogollon Highlands of New Mexico*. Ph.D. diss., University of Michigan, Ann Arbor. University Microfilms, Ann Arbor.

1988   Early Agriculture and Sedentism in the American Southwest: Evidence and Interpretations. *Journal of World Prehistory* 2 (4): 445–88.

Wills, Wirt H., and Bruce B. Huckell

1994 Economic Implications of Changing Land-use Patterns in the Late Archaic. In *Themes in Southwest Prehistory*, ed. George J. Gumerman, pp. 33–52. School of American Research Press, Santa Fe.

Wilshusen, Richard H.

1986 The Relationship between Abandonment Mode and Ritual Use in the Pueblo I Anasazi Protokivas. *Journal of Field Archaeology* 13:245–54.

Wilson, C. Dean, James M. Skibo, and Michael B. Schiffer

1996 Designing of Southwestern Pottery: A Technological and Experimental Approach. In *Interpreting Southwestern Diversity: Underlying Principles and Overarching Patterns*, ed. Paul R. Fish and J. Jefferson Reid, pp. 249–62. Arizona State University Anthropological Research Papers, no. 48. Arizona State University, Tempe.

Wimberly, M., and P. Eidenbach

1980 *Reconnaissance Study of the Archaeological and Related Resources of the Lower Puerco and Salado Drainages, Central New Mexico*. Human Systems Research, Tularosa, New Mexico.

Winterhalder, Bruce

1990 Open Field, Common Pot: Harvest Variability and Risk Avoidance in Agricultural and Foraging Societies. In *Risk and Uncertainty in Tribal and Peasant Economies*, ed. Elizabeth Cashdan, pp. 67–88. Westview Press, Boulder.

Wiseman, Regge N.

1982 The Intervening Years—New Information on Chupadero Black-on-White and Corona Corrugated. *Pottery Southwest* 9 (4): 5–7.

1986 *An Initial Study of the Origins of Chupadero Black-on-White*. Albuquerque Archaeological Society Technical Note. no. 2, Albuquerque.

Wobst, H. Martin

1977 Stylistic Behavior and Information Exchange. In *For the Director: Research Essays in Honor of James B. Griffin*, ed. C. E. Cleland, pp. 317–42. Museum of Anthropology Anthropological Papers, no. 61. University of Michigan, Ann Arbor.

Woosley, Anne I., and Allan J. McIntyre

1996 *Mimbres Mogollon Archaeology, Charles C. DiPeso's Excavations at Wind Mountain*. University of New Mexico Press, Albuquerque.

Yellen, John, and Henry Harpending

1972 Hunter-Gatherer Populations and Archaeological Inference. *World Archaeology* 4:244–52.

Yoffee, Norman, and George Cowgill, eds.

1988 *The Collapse of Ancient States and Civilizations*. University of Arizona Press, Tucson.

Zedeño, María Nieves

1994   *Sourcing Prehistoric Ceramics at Chodistaas Pueblo, Arizona: The Circulation of People and Pots in the Grasshopper Region.* Anthropological Papers of the University of Arizona, no. 58. The University of Arizona Press, Tucson.

INDEX

activities, 85–88, 99, 116, 119, 121–22, 129, 132, 134–36, 150, 152, 162, 165; activity areas, 85, 90, 103, 136–37; activity surfaces, 84, 129–30; ceremonial, 9, 45; domestic, 22, 117, 119, 122–23, 126, 128, 188; maintenance, 86, 135–36; subsistence, 31, 162

activity areas. *See* activities: activity areas

aggregations, 7, 19, 21, 180, 184, 191; and abandonment, 11, 18, 43; advantages and consequences of, 10; arid landscape, relation to, 187, 192; and control of land ownership, 14, 20; and dispersion, 10–11, 18, 43, 182–83, 187; and population growth, 35, 40, 45, 192; and social organization or structure, 15, 17, 18, 192

agricultural domesticates, 146. *See also* agricultural plants; cultigens

agricultural plants, 146, 164. *See also* cultigens

agriculture, 31, 33; fields, 149, 150, 152, 158; intensification of, 152, 187; land and, 14, 24, 39, 151, 181; as land use,

12, 152; productivity of, 14, 166; as resource base, 9, 11

Alamosa Creek, 48, 58–59, 61–64, 181, 184

alluvial fans, 4, 31, 162, 173, 175, 190

Anderson site, 55

animal bone. *See* bone, animal

archaeomagnetic dating, 74, 81, 97–98, 125

arid land use. *See* land use: arid

artiodactyls: deer, 154–55, 160, 164; mountain sheep, 154, 160–61

assemblages, 57, 122–23, 132–33, 137–38, 140, 162, 190; abandonment, 96, 98, 113, 122–23, 129, 132, 135, 137, 191; artifact, 22, 25, 73, 84, 87, 132–33, 136–37, 139–40; ceramic, 33, 51, 56, 59–60, 65, 84, 88, 97–98, 106, 111, 128, 141, 174, 176–83, 185; composition, 113, 127, 135; domestic, 123, 127, 129, 132, 135, 137–38; faunal, 155, 158–59, 162, 164; floor, 88, 93, 96–97, 109, 117, 119, 124, 127, 135, 136–37; household, 117, 135, 137; in situ, 81,

ABOUT THE AUTHORS

Margaret Nelson, Associate Professor of Anthropology at Arizona State University, has conducted research in the Mimbres region for more than two decades, with particular interest in how subsistence farmers adjusted to the aridity and unpredictability of the Southwestern landscape. She views movement and flexible social relations as integral to prehistoric adaptations in this context. Her research has addressed resource selection, the organization of technology, the organization of mobility, and processes of abandonment and reorganization. She currently collaborates with Michelle Hegmon on the Eastern Mimbres Archaeological Program (EMAP), a long-term archaeological study and education program. Nelson also has a strong professional interest in the public dissemination of archaeological information and was co-curator with Michelle Hegmon and Margaret Lindauer of the exhibit "Mimbres Lives and Landscapes." Nelson has published her work in *American Anthropologist, American Antiquity*, the *Journal of Field Archaeology*, and *The Kiva*, and she has collaborated on the writing and presentation of pre-collegiate study materials using research data from EMAP to teach critical thinking and research skills.

Michelle Hegmon, Associate Professor of Anthropology, Arizona State University, has extensive experience in Southwestern archaeology in both the Four Corners and Mogollon regions. She is the author of *The Social Dynamics of Pottery Style in the Early Puebloan Southwest* and has collaborated with Nelson on the Eastern Mimbres Archaeological Project since 1993.

Michael W. Diehl, Research Archaeologist, Center for Desert Archaeology, Tucson, has conducted research in the Mogollon region of the Southwest for ten years, working with Nelson as one of her doctoral students during the late 1980s and early 1990s. His forthcoming book is entitled *Hierarchies in Action: Cui Bono?*